Mark How

AHEAD ON THE FLAT

The Top Flat Horses
To follow For **2016**

www.mhpublications.co.uk

THE AUTHOR

Mark Howard is 41 and graduated from Manchester University with a BA Honours Degree in History. This is the 19th year of *Ahead On The Flat* and, for the last 23 years, he has written the National Hunt horses to follow book *One Jump Ahead*. In addition, he has previously worked for *Racing & Football Outlook* as well as contributing to *The Irish Field* and trainer Tom Tate's website (www.tomtate.co.uk). He also appears as a regular guest on *Racing UK* (Sky Channel 432) and, prior to that, *Attheraces*.

FRONT COVER: INTILAAQ, featured in last year's *Top 40 Prospects*, wins the Group 3 Rose of Lancaster Stakes at Haydock under Paul Hanagan on Saturday 8th August 2015.

Cover photograph supplied by GROSSICK RACING PHOTOGRAPHY. The Steadings, Rockhallhead, Collin, Dumfries. DG1 4JW. Telephone: 01387 750 512.

Published by MARK HOWARD Publications Ltd. 69, Fairgarth Drive,
Kirkby Lonsdale, Carnforth, Lancashire. LA6 2FB.
Telephone: 015242 71826 Fax: 015242 79010
Email Address: mark.howard@mhpublications.co.uk
Website: www.mhpublications.co.uk

Please Note: If you are currently NOT on the *Mark Howard Publications Ltd* mailing list and you would like to be, and therefore receive all information about future publications, then please send / phone / email your name and address to the above.

Printed by H & H REEDS PRINTERS. Southend Road, Penrith, Cumbria. CA11 8JH. Telephone: 01768 864214.

All information correct at the time of going to press. Every care is taken with compilation of *Ahead On The Flat*, but no responsibility is accepted by the publishers, for error or omissions or their consequences.

ISBN 978-0-9929224-1-2

CONTENTS

INTRODUCTION

There was rarely a dull moment during the 2015 Flat season. Just when John Gosden was wondering where his next superstar was coming from as he watched the brilliant Kingman head off to stallion duties, along came Golden Horn, Jack Hobbs and Shalaa. The trio won seven Group 1 races between them and the head of Clarehaven Stables regained the trainers' crown by over £1.5m. The Frankie Dettori ridden Epsom Derby winner lit up the summer and beyond with some stunning displays. The now retired son of Cape Cross won the Feilden, Dante, Derby, Eclipse, Irish Champion and Prix de L'Arc de Triomphe during an aggressive campaign with his only defeats coming at York and Keeneland on unsuitably slow ground. Despite already having an Irish Derby on his CV, Jack Hobbs promises to be even better at four and Shalaa may have finished last of eight on his racecourse debut but never looked back thereafter. Five straight wins followed, including twice at the highest level, and he will be bidding to follow in the hoofprints of former stablemate Oasis Dream and become champion sprinter as a three year old.

On the jockey front, Silvestre De Sousa was crowned champion for the first time with 132 winners, which was thoroughly deserved. Conversely, three times champion jockey Richard Hughes hung up his boots on the 1st August at Glorious Goodwood. The Irishman rode his first winner on the 2nd August 1988 at Roscommon and, during a glittering career, partnered two British Classic winners, namely on Sky Lantern (1000 Guineas) and Talent (Oaks) in 2013. One of the most gifted riders of his generation, he is now concentrating on a training career.

Ryan Moore rode 15 Group/Grade 1 winners during 2015, including the 1000 and 2000 Guineas at Newmarket, 9 Royal Ascot successes and two victories at the Breeders' Cup at Keeneland. Then, to round off the year, he added the Hong Kong Vase and Mile to his collection. It was a phenomenal season for the dual champion. At a slightly lesser level, the likeable Phil Makin enjoyed an excellent season booting home 92 domestic winners, including a 4,799/1 four timer at York in July.

One of the saddest pieces of news which broke last year was the announcement in November that eleven times champion jockey Pat Eddery had passed away at the age of 63. One of the best of all-time, Pat rode 4,633 winners, including 14 British Classics (3 Epsom Derbys) and 4 Prix de L'Arc de Triomphe. The Irishman rode some outstanding horses including Dancing Brave, El Gran Senor, Warning and Zafonic amongst many others. One of my favourite moments of his career was when he partnered Rainbow Quest to success in the Coronation Cup at Epsom in 1985 – it is well worth watching again on *Youtube*.

Another legend of the sport, Clive Brittain, called time on his training career at the age of 81. Responsible for winning six British Classics, he, too, was associated with some magnificent horses including Jupiter Island, Katies, Pebbles, Sayyedati and User Friendly. He trained 18 Royal Ascot winners with Rizeena his final one in the Coronation Stakes in 2014. Fellow Newmarket trainer James Toller also called it a day last year and Hayley Turner followed in the footsteps of Richard Hughes by hanging up her boots.

I am delighted to say *Sky Sports* Football frontman Ed Chamberlin has kindly written this year's *Foreword*. Rather like his favourite football team Southampton, Ed has come a long way in a short space of time in recent years and has rapidly developed into one of the best sports presenters around. Ed is fresh from a successful Cheltenham Festival and is now looking forward to the summer ahead.

As in previous years, there are full details towards the back of the book regarding the *Ahead On The Flat Updates*. Last year's Royal Ascot preview proved particularly successful with no less than 11 winners. The highlights included Amazing Maria (advised @ 33/1) winning the Duke of Cambridge Stakes and tipping the first three home in the Royal Hunt Cup. Fingers crossed for more of the same in June.

Many thanks to all those who have contributed to *Ahead On The Flat*, and thank you to subscribers for purchasing a copy. I hope you find it informative and, most importantly, value for money. Best wishes for an enjoyable and profitable summer.

Mark Howard

FOREWORD
By
ED CHAMBERLIN
Sky Sports presenter
Super Sunday & MNF

No sooner has the dust settled on the Cheltenham Festival and thoughts immediately turn to the new turf Flat season - and I wouldn't dream of going into it without a copy of *Ahead On The Flat*.

I've known Mark Howard for many years, from the dim and distant past when I was editor of *Sports Advisor* and Mark one of the journalists who contributed to the publication. It was clear then he had an incredibly deep knowledge of horse racing and an instinctive gift to latch onto the right horses at the right time. It's no surprise to see his career develop as it has.

What Mark has added since is an incredible contact book, people who want to talk to him and share their thoughts throughout the campaign.

Just look at the stable interviews in this year's edition. Where else can you get the inside track from Henry Candy, Roger Charlton, Luca Cumani, James Fanshawe, William Haggas, Mark Johnston, David O'Meara, Hugo Palmer and Roger Varian all in one place? They all make for fascinating reading and there are countless winners to be gleaned.

Then there's the *Ahead Of The Flat Top 40*, which last year pointed readers towards Golden Horn, Twilight Son, Mahsoob and Intilaaq, all Pattern winners.

The Royal Ascot *Update* was another goldmine for punters - no fewer than 11 winners were selected over the five days of the great meeting, including Amazing Maria at 33/1 in the Duke Of Cambridge Stakes. Impressive stuff - although even that was eclipsed with the 1-2-3 in the Royal Hunt Cup!

If you had Gm Hopkins (8/1), Temptress (9/1) and Chil The Kite (16/1) in a tricast or trifecta it's a fair bet you're rattling through this *Foreword* to get to the content inside! That's the beauty of Mark's work - it points punters in the right direction.

As I write this copy, Leicester City are odds-on to spring one of THE great sporting surprises by winning the Barclays Premier League. It would be a stunning achievement, the like of which many of us had thought impossible in modern football.

But in between working on *Super Sunday* and *Monday Night Football* and watching this incredible story unfold I'm preparing myself for the year ahead on the turf.

The thing I love about the Flat season is the momentum it gathers - from the early spring clues at the Craven and Greenham meetings, through Chester and York in May, Epsom in June, Royal Ascot, Glorious Goodwood, York Ebor Meeting, Doncaster St Leger, Champions Day. It's relentless, it's breathless and it's wonderful.

There are far more questions than answers at this stage of the campaign but at least with *Ahead On Flat* we have a chance to get ahead of the curve. Enjoy the book, the winners it finds you and the season ahead. We're in very good company with Mark Howard for what promises to be a wonderful campaign.

TYPE OF TRACK

ASCOT	Right Handed	Galloping
AYR	Left Handed	Galloping
BATH	Left Handed	Tight
BEVERLEY	Right Handed	Stiff / Undulating
BRIGHTON	Left Handed	Tight / Undulating
CARLISLE	Right Handed	Stiff / Undulating
CATTERICK BRIDGE	Left Handed	Tight / Undulating
CHELMSFORD CITY (AW)	Left Handed	Tight
CHEPSTOW	Left Handed	Stiff / Undulating
CHESTER	Left Handed	Tight
DONCASTER	Left Handed	Galloping
EPSOM	Left Handed	Tight / Undulating
FFOS LAS	Left Handed	Galloping
GOODWOOD	Right Handed	Tight / Undulating
HAMILTON PARK	Right Handed	Stiff / Undulating
HAYDOCK PARK	Left Handed	Galloping
KEMPTON PARK (AW)	Right Handed	Tight
LEICESTER	Right Handed	Stiff / Undulating
LINGFIELD PARK	Left Handed	Tight / Undulating
All Weather	Left Handed	Tight
MUSSELBURGH	Right Handed	Tight
NEWBURY	Left Handed	Galloping
NEWCASTLE	Left Handed	Galloping
NEWMARKET (Rowley)	Right Handed	Galloping
(July)	Right Handed	Galloping
NOTTINGHAM	Left Handed	Galloping
PONTEFRACT	Left Handed	Stiff / Undulating
REDCAR	Left Handed	Galloping
RIPON	Right Handed	Galloping
SALISBURY	Right Handed	Galloping
SANDOWN PARK	Right Handed	Galloping
SOUTHWELL (AW)	Left Handed	Tight
THIRSK	Left Handed	Galloping
WINDSOR	Right Handed	Tight
WOLVERHAMPTON (AW)	Left Handed	Tight
YARMOUTH	Left Handed	Galloping
YORK	Left Handed	Galloping

IRELAND

BALLINROBE	Right-Handed, Tight
BELLEWSTOWN	Left-Handed, Tight / Undulating
CLONMEL	Right-Handed, Tight / Undulating
CORK	Right-Handed, Galloping
CURRAGH	Right-Handed, Galloping
DOWNPATRICK	Right-Handed, Tight / Undulating
DOWN ROYAL	Right-Handed, Tight / Undulating
DUNDALK (AW)	Left-Handed, Tight
FAIRYHOUSE	Right-Handed, Galloping
GALWAY	Right-Handed, Tight / Undulating
GOWRAN PARK	Right-Handed, Tight / Undulating
KILLARNEY	Left-Handed, Tight
LEOPARDSTOWN	Left-Handed, Galloping
LIMERICK	Right-Handed, Galloping
LISTOWEL	Left-Handed, Tight
NAAS	Left-Handed, Galloping
NAVAN	Left-Handed, Galloping
ROSCOMMON	Right-Handed, Tight
SLIGO	Right-Handed, Tight / Undulating
THURLES	Right-Handed, Tight / Undulating
TIPPERARY	Left-Handed, Tight
TRAMORE	Right-Handed, Tight
WEXFORD	Right-Handed, Tight

ACKNOWLEDGEMENTS

I would like to take this opportunity to express my thanks to the following trainers who have given up their time, during a busy period of the year, to discuss their horses' plans for the season:

Henry Candy, Roger Charlton, Luca Cumani, James Fanshawe, William Haggas, Mark Johnston, David O'Meara, Hugo Palmer and Roger Varian.

Also, many thanks to the following secretaries for arranging the interviews and faxing/emailing lists of horses in training: Bronwyn (Henry Candy), Tor Sturgis & Harry Charlton (Roger Charlton), Cat Elliott (Luca Cumani), Janet (James Fanshawe), Jack Nicol (William Haggas), Emma & Nicky McGrath (Mark Johnston), Jason Kelly (David O'Meara), Sarah Minifie (Hugo Palmer) and Jim (Roger Varian).

Thanks to Ed Chamberlin (Sky Sports) for his *Foreword*, Harry Herbert (Managing Director of Highclere Thoroughbred Racing), Tom O'Ryan (*Racing UK*), Michael Shinners, Ruairi Stirling & David Hutchinson (Skybet), Jon Hughes (Owners For Owners) and Hannah Parlett (*Racing UK*).

ALSVINDER

3 b c Footstepsinthesand - Notting Hill (BRZ) (Jules (USA))
OWNER: F.GILLESPIE
TRAINER: D.O'MEARA. Upper Helmsley, York, North Yorkshire.

Owner Frank Gillespie enjoyed his best season in 2014 when The Grey Gatsby won the Dante, Prix du Jockey Club and Irish Champion Stakes for Kevin Ryan, Louis The Pious won the Buckingham Palace Stakes at Royal Ascot and the Ayr Gold Cup for David O'Meara, and stablemate That Is The Spirit won the first three races of his career, including a Listed race at Epsom on Oaks day. It was a magnificent season for the two shades of green colours.

Gillespie, who hails from Donegal in Ireland, is believed to have a potentially exciting unraced three year old with David O'Meara in Alsvinder. The son of Footstepsinthesand was purchased for 185,000gns at the Doncaster Breeze-Up Sale last April (a May foal). His dam was a four times winner in Brazil and the US, and was placed at Grade 1 level, too, over nine and ten furlongs. A half-brother to Aldermoor, who won seven times for Stuart Williams over trips ranging from five to seven furlongs, Alsvinder has been pleasing his connections in his homework and is expected to make his racecourse bow early in the spring. He is one to watch out for.

Even though he isn't covered in David's interview, I also suggest readers make a note of the name **SUNNYSIDE BOB**. A new arrival to the stable, he is a three year old gelding by Big Bad Bob who was placed in four of his seven races as a juvenile for Geoff Oldroyd. Runner-up at Beverley, Musselburgh and Wolverhampton over the minimum trip, he is a half-brother to five times winner Toccata Blue and is officially rated 77. Don't be surprised if he leaves his previous form behind for his new handler.

POINTS TO NOTE:

Probable Best Distance	-	**6f - 1 mile**
Preferred Going	-	**Good**

AMANAAT (IRE)

3 b c Exceed And Excel (AUS) – Pietra Dura (Cadeaux Genereux)
OWNER: Sheikh HAMDAN AL MAKTOUM
TRAINER: J.H.M.GOSDEN. Newmarket, Suffolk.
CAREER FORM FIGURES: 1
CAREER WINS: 2015: Nov KEMPTON Standard Mdn 7f

Sheikh Hamdan Al Maktoum was responsible for some high quality three year olds last season, most notably champion sprinter Muhaarar, who won four Group 1 races, Group 2 winner Adaay and the hugely promising Intilaaq. The seven times winning champion owner had some very exciting juveniles last year, too, and retained rider Paul Hanagan was suitably impressed with the once raced Amanaat when he made a winning debut at Kempton in November.

Purchased for 280,000gns as a yearling, the son of Exceed And Excel is out of a Cadeaux Genereux mare (Listed placed over seven furlongs) and he arrived at the Sunbury track with a lofty reputation. Sent off a shade of odds on, Amanaat was slowly away and green throughout the first half of the race. However, the penny dropped inside the final quarter of a mile and he swept clear to win by a length and a half from Enreaching (runner-up again since) and Broadway Icon (beaten another four times since and rated 77). The form may not be the strongest but John Gosden's colt's finishing effort was most taking and he is clearly above average.

Last year's champion trainer has introduced some top notch performers on the all-weather, namely Jack Hobbs, Mahsoob and Western Hymn, in recent seasons and Amanaat could be another. Despite the fact he is by a sprinter and there is plenty of speed in his pedigree, it is worth noting one of his half-brothers (by Pivotal) won a Grade 3 over ten furlongs in the US for Simon Callaghan. Paul Hanagan is a very good judge of his mounts and the fact he liked the once raced colt a lot speaks for itself.

Along the same lines, watch out for another Gosden trained three year old **TATHQEEF**, who justified short odds at Wolverhampton in late October. Bought for $1,100,000, he looked a big, raw individual who can only improve with age and experience. Very slowly away, he came wide turning for home before powering home to win by two and a quarter lengths from the 79 rated Templier. Entered in the Derby, he impressed Paul Hanagan and is another Sheikh Hamdan Al Maktoum three year old to look forward to.

POINTS TO NOTE:
Probable Best Distance - 1 mile
Preferred Going - Good/Firm
Connection's Comments: "Amanaat was very green, as expected, and was slowly away. I didn't want to rush him, so I sat and suffered, but he got the job done well. He's got quite a reputation, but he's got a lovely temperament to go with it." Paul HANAGAN at Kempton (18/11/15)

GOING:	R	W	P	TRACK:	R	W	P
Standard	1	1	0	Right	1	1	0
				Tight	1	1	0

TRIP:	R	W	P	JOCKEY:	R	W	P
7f	1	1	0	P.Hanagan	1	1	0

ARISTOCRATIC

3 b f Exceed And Excel (AUS) – Peeress (Pivotal)
OWNER: CHEVELEY PARK STUD
TRAINER: Sir M.R.STOUTE. Newmarket, Suffolk.
CAREER FORM FIGURES: 33

The Sandringham Handicap (15th June), or formerly known as the Fern Hill Stakes until 2001, is one of the few races at Royal Ascot to have evaded ten times Champion trainer Sir Michael Stoute. However, the head of Freemason Lodge may have a live contender for the 2016 renewal in Aristocratic.

Owned and bred by Cheveley Park Stud, she is a daughter of Exceed And Excel out of their dual Group 1 winning mare Peeress. Third in both her races last year over seven furlongs at Newmarket, she ought to appreciate a step up to a mile as a three year old. Beaten around four lengths by subsequent Group 2 Rockfel Stakes winner Promising Run on her debut on the July course in August, she then chased home another Godolphin owned filly a month later on the Rowley Mile when two lengths in arrears of First Victory, who went on to win the Group 3 Oh So Sharp Stakes over the same course and distance next time.

Aristocratic's form therefore looks strong and it will be interesting to see if she reappears in the seven furlongs fillies' maiden at Newmarket's Craven meeting (14th April). She needs to have one more run before qualifying for the aforementioned Sandringham Handicap. A mile on fast ground ought to bring out the best in this impeccably bred filly.

POINTS TO NOTE:
Probable Best Distance - 1m
Preferred Going - Good/Firm
Connection's Comments: "Aristocratic a lovely, scopey filly. The dam (Peeress) took a little time to come to herself, but this filly is a bit leggy and a bit weak at the moment, but we like her. It´s too early to tell what she´ll turn into, but she´s nice." Sir Michael STOUTE at Newmarket (26/9/15)

GOING:	R	W	P
7f	2	0	2

TRACK:	R	W	P
Right	2	0	2
Galloping	2	0	2

TRIP:	R	W	P
7f	2	0	2

JOCKEY:	R	W	P
Ryan Moore	1	0	1
Ted Durcan	1	0	1

BESS OF HARDWICK

4 b f Dansili – Request (Rainbow Quest (USA))
OWNER: DUKE OF DEVONSHIRE
TRAINER: L.M.CUMANI. Newmarket, Suffolk.
CAREER FORM FIGURES: 31
CAREER WINS: 2015: Oct WOLVERHAMPTON Standard Mdn 1m 4f

Bedford House Stables may not be housing any more horses owned by Sheikh Mohammed Obaid Al Maktoum but Luca Cumani has plenty to look forward to, especially as far as his fillies are concerned. The likes of Beautiful Morning, Farandine, Koora, Materialistic, Pamona, Tiptree and Very Dashing are all held in high regard and expected to make an impact in 2016.

Arguably the most interesting filly in the stable though is the unexposed Bess of Hardwick. A beautifully bred daughter of Dansili, she is a half-sister to dual Group 1 winner Ask. Owned and bred by the Duke of Devonshire, she made her debut in a twelve furlongs maiden on the Rowley Mile at her local track in mid May. Having been outpaced and showing signs of inexperience, Luke Morris' mount ran on strongly to finish a most encouraging third behind fellow debutant Gretchen (subsequently won a Listed and Group 2 and rated 106). Only beaten two lengths, the runner-up Forever Popular is well thought of by her trainer William Haggas. Unfortunately, Bess of Hardwick wasn't seen again until early October, due to a splint problem. When she did return on the Tapeta at Wolverhampton, she justified strong market support to win a similar event by nearly three lengths. Leading on the bridle with a furlong to run, she barely broke sweat to beat David Simcock's Red Cardinal. As a result of those performances, Luca Cumani's filly has been granted an official mark of 87, which appears generous considering her close proximity to John Gosden's subsequent dual Pattern winner on her debut at Headquarters.

Another splint issue, this time on a different leg, prevented Bess of Hardwick from having a third run but she is reportedly back to full fitness and is a filly with immense potential. It is hoped she takes advantage of her handicap mark before dipping her toe in black type races. It is not inconceivable she could develop into a Lancashire Oaks filly (2nd July), a race her trainer has won twice in the past (Pongee (2004), Emirates Queen (2013)). A race such as the Group 3 Pinnacle Stakes (28th May) over the same course and distance could also come under consideration (Pongee also won this for the yard in 2004).

POINTS TO NOTE:

Probable Best Distance	-	**1m 4f**
Preferred Going	-	**Good**

GOING:	**R**	**W**	**P**
Standard	**1**	**1**	**0**
Good	**1**	**0**	**1**

TRACK:	**R**	**W**	**P**
Left Handed	**1**	**1**	**0**
Right	**1**	**0**	**1**
Galloping	**1**	**0**	**1**
Tight	**1**	**1**	**0**

TRIP:	**R**	**W**	**P**
1m 4f	**2**	**1**	**1**

JOCKEY:	**R**	**W**	**P**
A.Kirby	**1**	**1**	**0**
Luke Morris	**1**	**0**	**1**

BOUNCE

3 b f Bahamian Bounty – Black Belt Shopper (IRE) (Desert Prince (IRE))
OWNER: LANDMARK RACING LIMITED
TRAINER: H.CANDY. Wantage, Oxon.
CAREER FORM FIGURES: 51
CAREER WINS: 2015: Sept KEMPTON Standard Mdn 6f

Despite the fact Group 2 winner Limato is expected to step up to a mile for the first time this season, Henry Candy is still responsible for some tremendous sprinters this year. Twilight Son leads the challenge following a superb three year old campaign, which saw the Kyllachy colt progress through the handicap ranks before capturing the Group 1 Betfred Sprint at Haydock in September. La Rioja is already a Group 3 winner and looked one of the best juvenile fillies in training in 2015, while the twice raced Bounce is another who holds realistic black type aspirations.

In terms of prize-money, the Wantage based trainer had his best ever season with his 33 winners accumulating £902,022 (previous best was in 2014 with £537,538). This lightly raced daughter of Bahamian Bounty contributed £3,235 to that tally when winning her maiden at the second attempt on the polytrack at Kempton in September. Prior to that, Bounce had reportedly impressed James Doyle when a running on fifth on her debut at Newbury in mid August. Three and a quarter lengths behind Czabo, the third and fourth have won since, and she confirmed the promise at the Sunbury venue next time. Dane O'Neill took over in the saddle and, having been slowly away and then racing keenly early on, she soon got her act together and bounded four and a half lengths clear (runner-up and fifth won since). Yet to be allocated an official rating, Henry Candy feels Bounce possesses the ability to develop into a black type filly and, on the evidence of her Kempton success, it is difficult to argue. She looks another fine sprinter residing at Kingston Warren.

POINTS TO NOTE:

Probable Best Distance	-	**6 furlongs**
Preferred Going	-	**Good/Soft**

GOING:	**R**	**W**	**P**
Standard	**1**	**1**	**0**
Good/Soft	**1**	**0**	**0**

TRACK:	**R**	**W**	**P**
Left Handed	**1**	**0**	**0**
Right	**1**	**1**	**0**
Galloping	**1**	**0**	**0**
Tight	**1**	**1**	**0**

TRIP:	**R**	**W**	**P**
6f	**2**	**1**	**0**

JOCKEY:	**R**	**W**	**P**
Dane O'Neill	**1**	**1**	**0**
James Doyle	**1**	**0**	**0**

CARPE VITA (IRE)

4 b f Montjeu (IRE) – Dance Parade (USA) (Gone West (USA))
OWNER: Sir ROBERT OGDEN
TRAINER: D.O'MEARA. Little Helmsley, York, North Yorkshire.
CAREER FORM FIGURES: 06812
CAREER WINS: 2015: Aug REDCAR Good/Firm Hcap 1m 6f

Having been transferred to David O'Meara at the start of last year, the former jump jockey did a superb job with the Sir Robert Ogden owned Amazing Maria in 2015. The daughter of Mastercraftsman was rated 98 when she arrived at Arthington Barn on the outskirts of Helmsley and, twelve months later, she has two Group 1 wins and a Royal Ascot success on her CV, plus an official mark of 117. A two lengths winner of the Group 2 Duke of Cambridge Stakes at the Royal meeting was swiftly followed by victories in the Falmouth Stakes on the July course at HQ and the Prix Rothschild at Deauville when beating triple Group 1 winner Ervedya.

The same owner also sent O'Meara the well bred Carpe Vita in August last year and, in two races, the full-sister to Ascot Gold Cup winner Leading Light has improved twelve pounds according to the handicapper. The Montjeu filly beat five horses in three races for Charlie Hills (wore a hood twice) before being relocated in North Yorkshire. Stepped up in trip on her first run for her new trainer at Redcar in late August, she was given a confident ride by Danny Tudhope as she cut through the field and came from last to first to win going away by a length and a half off a mark of 60. Raised nine pounds, Carpe Vita was sent off 5/2 favourite for a 0-70 staying handicap at Ayr's Western meeting and, once again, was held up in the early stages. Beaten nearly two lengths by Jim Goldie's Sir Chauvelin, she may not have been suited by the drop back in trip but still ran well in second. Despite another three pounds rise in the weights, the four year old remains unexposed and favourably handicapped off 72.

Given her brother stayed two and a half miles to win the Gold Cup in 2014, Carpe Vita looks open to significant improvement when tackling at least two miles for the first time. I was working for *Racing UK* when she won at Redcar and she is a fine, big scopey filly. David O'Meara is already eyeing those marathon handicaps over two and a quarter miles at Pontefract this summer, plus expect this beautifully bred daughter of Montjeu to ply her trade on the Knavesmire at some stage in 2016. O'Meara has been the dominant force at York in recent seasons (22 winners in the last two seasons) and the track stages a good programme of two mile handicaps throughout the course of the year. Indeed, there is a 71-90 two miles handicap on Thursday 12th May, which is sure to come under consideration.

POINTS TO NOTE:

Probable Best Distance	-	**1m 6f +**
Preferred Going	-	**Good/Firm**

GOING:	**R**	**W**	**P**
Standard	1	0	0
Good	2	0	1
Good/Firm	2	1	0

TRACK:	**R**	**W**	**P**
Left Handed	4	1	1
Right	1	0	0
Galloping	3	1	1
Tight	1	0	0
Tight/Undul.	1	0	0

TRIP:	**R**	**W**	**P**
1m 2f	1	0	0
1m 3f	1	0	0
1m 4f	1	0	0
1m 5f	1	0	1
1m 6f	1	1	0

JOCKEY:	**R**	**W**	**P**
D.Tudhope	2	1	1
S.Drowne	1	0	0
D.O'Neill	1	0	0
W.T-Davies	1	0	0

CENTRAL SQUARE (IRE)

4 b g Azamour (IRE) – Lucky Clio (IRE) (Key of Luck (USA))
OWNER: CLIPPER LOGISTICS
TRAINER: R.VARIAN. Newmarket, Suffolk.
CAREER FORM FIGURES: 24

Despite the fact he is a four year old, Central Square has only raced twice but he looks a promising individual nevertheless and the gelded son of Azamour is expected to develop into a smart handicapper at least this season.

Bought for €50,000 as a yearling, Roger Varian's charge is a half-brother to four times winning sprinter Lucky Beggar, but Central Square takes more after another of his siblings, Kingsdesire, who won over ten furlongs for Marco Botti in 2012. Making his belated racecourse debut at Doncaster in August in a mile and a quarter maiden, he was well touted beforehand (11/4) and ran an excellent race to finish a length second behind Koora, who subsequently won the Group 3 St Simon Stakes at Newbury and is rated 107. Over seven lengths back in fourth on Town Moor was Star Storm, who won his next three races, including the Group 3 Cumberland Lodge Stakes, and has an official mark of 107. In other words, the form looks outstanding. It was therefore disappointing to see Central Square only finish fourth next time when a short price favourite in a similar event at Chester. The fact the Andrew Balding trained Mr Quicksilver reversed form with him strongly suggests he didn't run his race and the performance is best forgotten.

Speaking to Roger Varian in February, the twice raced gelding is clearly held in high esteem and there is no arguing with the strength of the form of his run at Doncaster. Winning a maiden ought to prove a formality before hopefully making a big impression in better company.

POINTS TO NOTE:

Probable Best Distance	-	**1m 2f**
Preferred Going	-	**Good**

GOING:	**R**	**W**	**P**	**TRACK:**	**R**	**W**	**P**
Good/Soft	**1**	**0**	**0**	**Left Handed**	**2**	**0**	**1**
Good	**1**	**0**	**1**	**Galloping**	**1**	**0**	**1**
				Tight	**1**	**0**	**0**

TRIP:	**R**	**W**	**P**	**JOCKEY:**	**R**	**W**	**P**
1m 2f	**2**	**0**	**1**	**N.Callan**	**1**	**0**	**1**
				T.Eaves	**1**	**0**	**0**

COSMIC STORM

3 b f Sea The Stars (IRE) – Riotous Applause (Royal Applause)
OWNER: The ECLIPSE Partnership
TRAINER: D.SIMCOCK. Newmarket, Suffolk.
CAREER FORM FIGURES: 8

Dream Ahead provided David Simcock with his first Group 1 winner in 2010 when landing the Prix Morny at Deauville. Last summer, Balios gave Luca Cumani's former assistant his first Royal Ascot winner in the King Edward VII Stakes. Responsible for 84, 78 and 63 winners during the last three seasons, Simcock has a lot to look forward to in 2016.

Cosmic Storm has only raced once catching the eye on her debut at Newmarket in a seven furlongs fillies' maiden in October. A filly by Sea The Stars, she is out of Riotous Applause, who was Listed placed over six furlongs for James Fanshawe in 2007. Her dam is a half-sister to *Racing Post* Trophy winner Crowded House. Sent off 20/1 on the Rowley Mile, she stayed on nicely under tender handling to finish less than five lengths behind the winner Materialistic in eighth (the sixth has won since). Jamie Spencer was reportedly impressed and considers her a promising type for this year.

Even though Cosmic Storm is out of a sprinter, she should stay at least a mile this year and is most likely to come into her own over ten furlongs. It will be disappointing if she can't win a maiden before developing into a useful three year old. Black type looks a realistic aim.

POINTS TO NOTE:
Probable Best Distance - 1m – 1m 2f
Preferred Going - Good/Firm

GOING:	R	W	P	TRACK:	R	W	P
7f	1	0	0	Right	1	0	0
				Galloping	1	0	0

TRIP:	R	W	P	JOCKEY:	R	W	P
7f	1	0	0	J.P.Spencer	1	0	0

DIRECT TIMES (IRE)

5 b g Acclamation – Elegant Times (IRE) (Dansili)
OWNER: ALLAN BELSHAW
TRAINER: P.CHAPPLE-HYAM. Newmarket, Suffolk.
CAREER FORM FIGURES: 3 – 1 - 1215
CAREER WINS: 2014: Oct NEWCASTLE Good/Firm Mdn 6f: 2015: May NEWMARKET Good Hcap 6f; June NEWMARKET Good Hcap 6f

Dual Epsom Derby winning trainer Peter Chapple-Hyam tasted Group 1 glory once again last Autumn with Marcel capturing the *Racing Post* Trophy at odds of 33/1. The Newmarket based trainer has sent out 7 Royal Ascot winners during his illustrious career but hasn't had a Royal victor since Winker Watson won the Norfolk Stakes in 2007. That may change this summer though because the lightly raced Direct Times looks an ideal candidate for the Wokingham Stakes on the final day of the fixture (18th June).

Officially rated 93, a mark of 97 was required to get in the 2015 version of the six furlongs cavalry charge, so Direct Times may need a rise in the weights in the interim. With that in mind, there is a six furlongs handicap at Newmarket's Guineas meeting (1st May), which could fit the bill, especially as he is already a course and distance winner on the Rowley Mile. Having only raced twice during his first two seasons, the gelded son of Acclamation has clearly had his problems but he enjoyed a much smoother run last year winning two of his four races. Successful twice at HQ (Rowley Mile & July course) off marks of 73 and 85, he reportedly found the ground too slow when runner-up behind Claim The Roses in between. His final run last term came in the Stewards' Cup consolation, for which Direct Times was sent off 13/2 favourite. Considering his lack of experience, he acquitted himself well finishing two and a half lengths fifth behind Golden Steps.

Peter Chapple-Hyam's charge is eight pounds higher than his latest win but remains open to further improvement, especially when encountering his favoured quick ground. There is a big sprint handicap to be won with him this year with the Wokingham and Stewards' Cup springing to mind.

POINTS TO NOTE:
Probable Best Distance - 6 furlongs
Preferred Going - Good/Firm
Connection's Comments: "The ground beat Direct Times at Haydock last time as he must have fast ground." Peter CHAPPLE-HYAM at Newmarket (20/6/15)

GOING:	R	W	P
Soft	1	0	1
Good	3	2	1
Good/Firm	2	1	0

TRACK:	R	W	P
Left Handed	3	1	2
Right	3	2	0
Galloping	5	3	2
Tight	1	0	0

TRIP:	R	W	P
6f	6	3	2

JOCKEY:	R	W	P
W.Buick	2	1	1
T.Marquand	2	1	0
K.Lundie	1	1	0
L.Dettori	1	0	1

EYESHINE

3 b f Dubawi (IRE) - Casual Look (USA) (Red Ransom (USA))
OWNER: FLAXMAN STABLES IRELAND & W.S.FARISH
TRAINER: J.H.M.GOSDEN. Newmarket, Suffolk.

A beautifully bred unraced daughter of Dubawi, Eyeshine didn't see a racecourse last year but she is reportedly a talented filly who is expected to start making up for lost time this spring. Bought for $1,450,000 as a yearling, she is out of Andrew Balding's 2003 Epsom Oaks winner Casual Look and a half-sister to the same stable's Grade 3 winner Casual Smile.

Interestingly, John Gosden's filly held an entry in the same seven furlongs fillies' maiden at Newmarket last September former stablemate Taghrooda won in 2013. Ironically, Casual Smile chased home the subsequent Oaks and King George winner that day. Even though Eyeshine didn't race as a juvenile, she has wintered well, by all accounts, and the champion trainer has given her an entry in the Prix De Diane at Chantilly (19th June), a race Gosden won last year with Star of Seville. She is expected to make her debut during the spring and is very much one to follow.

POINTS TO NOTE:

Probable Best Distance	-	**1m 2f - 1m 4f**
Preferred Going	-	**Good**

FARANDINE

3 ch f Rock of Gibraltar (IRE) - Rivara (Red Ransom (USA))
OWNER: FITTOCKS STUD
TRAINER: L.M.CUMANI. Newmarket, Suffolk.
CAREER FORM FIGURES: 231
CAREER WINS: 2015: Oct NEWMARKET Good/Soft Mdn 7f

Unfortunately, we will no longer see the well known brown and beige silks of the late Gerald Leigh on British racecourses. They were associated with some tremendous horses over the years, including dual Group 1 winner Act One, Fillies Mile and Irish 1000 Guineas winner Gossamer and QEII Stakes winner Markofdistinction. The last two named were, of course, trained in Newmarket by Luca Cumani and they were carried to victory for the final time last Autumn when Farandine won a seven furlongs fillies' maiden at Newmarket.

The daughter of Rock of Gibraltar subsequently went through the sales ring at Tattersalls in early December and was bought back by the trainer's operation, Fittocks Stud, for 190,000gns. While black type is ultimately the goal for Farandine, she looks to be on an exploitable mark at present with an official rating of 83. Yet to race beyond seven furlongs, she should have no trouble staying a mile and possibly ten furlongs in time. Therefore she looks one to follow in fillies' handicaps before hopefully progressing to a higher level. Runner-up on her debut on the July course at one of her local tracks, she was beaten a length and a quarter by Gypsy Eyes with Thesis (won next time before finishing second in the Group 2 Rockfel Stakes and now rated 102) a head back in third. Reportedly unsuited by the polytrack at Kempton when only third behind Barleysugar and Dutch Destiny (won since) from a wide draw (stall 13) next time, she lost her maiden tag at the third time of asking on the Rowley Mile. Making all under Adam Kirby, she easily saw off the challenge of Ejayteekay to win by nearly three lengths. The third, Izmir, has won since.

Given her level of form, Farandine doesn't look overburdened off her mark and the fact she is now owned by Fittocks Stud means she won't be thrust straight into Pattern company, which is often the case if a filly is owned by a patron who doesn't like handicaps.

POINTS TO NOTE:
Probable Best Distance - 1m – 1m 2f
Preferred Going - Good
Connection's Comments: "I think she is a very nice filly." Luca CUMANI at Newmarket (21/10/15)

GOING:	R	W	P	TRACK:	R	W	P
Standard	1	0	1	Right	3	1	2
Good/Soft	1	1	0	Galloping	2	1	1
Good/Firm	1	0	1	Tight	1	0	1

TRIP:	R	W	P	JOCKEY:	R	W	P
7f	3	1	2	A.Kirby	2	1	1
				L. De Souza	1	0	1

FOREVER POPULAR (USA)

4 b or br f Dynaformer (USA) – Pussycat Doll (USA) (Real Quiet (USA))
OWNER: LAEL STABLE
TRAINER: W.J.HAGGAS. Newmarket, Suffolk.
CAREER FORM FIGURES: 2215
CAREER WINS: 2015: June CHEPSTOW Good/Firm Mdn 1m 4f

The **ten furlongs fillies' maiden at Newbury** (15th April) is invariably won or contested by at least one high quality three year old. The race's roll of honour includes Islington (2002), Eswarah (2005), Folk Opera (2007) and Dancing Rain (2011). It is a race William Haggas invariably targets and, in addition to his subsequent Oaks winner five years ago, Vow won the same event twelve months later en route to a Lingfield Oaks Trial victory before finishing fourth at Epsom.

The well bred Forever Popular was his representative last year and she was sent off 9/4 favourite under Richard Hughes. While failing to make a winning start to her career, the Dynaformer filly ran well in second behind Paul Cole's Jasmine Blue. Once again, she was market leader for her next outing over an extra couple of furlongs at Newmarket. However, it was the same outcome with another sound performance, but she found John Gosden's subsequent Listed and Group 2 Park Hill Stakes winner Gretchen a length and three quarters too strong with the aforementioned Bess of Hardwick in third. Entered in the English and Irish Oaks last year, she managed to get off the mark at the third time of asking at Chepstow. Momentarily held in on the far rail, she quickened up well once in the clear to win by a length and a quarter. Given a mark of 83 for her handicap debut at Ascot in July, she didn't run up to her best behind Asyad (Group 2 placed since) or Dreamlike but she was found to have suffered a fracture shortly afterwards.

Forever Popular is back to full fitness and has progressed physically during the winter. Considering she was beaten less than two lengths by the 106 rated Gretchen on the Rowley Mile in May, there is a strong belief the daughter of Dynaformer is well handicapped off a mark of 82. Her connections have black type hopes for her – if that's the case, then she really ought to be mopping up off her current rating. **Don't forget William Haggas doesn't run average fillies in the ten furlongs maiden at Newbury in April, so watch out for his runner in the 2016 renewal – Rasmiya perhaps?**

POINTS TO NOTE:
Probable Best Distance - 1m 4f
Preferred Going - Good/Firm

GOING:	R	W	P
Good	1	0	1
Good/Firm	3	1	1

TRACK:	R	W	P
Left Handed	2	1	1
Right	2	0	1
Galloping	3	0	2
Stiff/Undul.	1	1	0

TRIP:	R	W	P
1m 2f	1	0	1
1m 4f	3	1	1

JOCKEY:	R	W	P
P.Cosgrave	2	1	1
R.Hughes	1	0	1
Shane Kelly	1	0	0

HIGHER POWER

4 b g Rip Van Winkle (IRE) – Lady Stardust (Spinning World (USA))
OWNER: Mrs MARTIN ARMSTRONG
TRAINER: J.R.FANSHAWE. Newmarket, Suffolk.
CAREER FORM FIGURES: 4 - 62

With 44 winners, James Fanshawe had his best season numerically in 2015 for nine years and ended the campaign particularly strongly. The head of Pegasus Stables sent out 7 winners in August (21% strike-rate), 11 in September (24%) and another 11 in October (33%). With the likes of Arthenus (rated 100), Fly (80), High Jinx (112), Return Ace (87), Speedy Boarding (104), Star Storm (107) and The Tin Man (112), the stable is blessed with a formidable team of older horses.

Higher Power featured in last year's *Top 40 Prospects* and, while he failed to win either of his two races, he retains his place because we almost certainly haven't seen the best of him. Fourth on his sole outing as a juvenile in 2014, he wasn't given an aggressive ride when finishing sixth behind potential Group 1 horse Intilaaq in a mile maiden at Newbury's spring meeting. Ridden by Tom Queally, he was beaten by fifteen lengths but his jockey accepted the situation once it became apparent he wasn't going to trouble Roger Varian's runaway winner. Stepping up to ten furlongs at Nottingham in late June, he only failed by three parts of a length to reel in the more experienced Barreesh (won again next time) with the subsequent Listed placed Twitch in third. Had Higher Power started his run sooner, the result may have been different. Found to be jarred up soon afterwards, the son of Rip Van Winkle hasn't been seen since. Gelded in the meantime, he has reportedly returned to his work looking much more the finished article and an official rating of 80 looks exploitable.

There is every chance Higher Power will stay twelve furlongs and he looks more than capable of winning a good middle distance handicap for James Fanshawe this summer. He couldn't be in better hands and is one to follow from a stable who have a lot of depth amongst their established performers.

POINTS TO NOTE:

Probable Best Distance	-	**1m 2f – 1m 4f**
Preferred Going	-	**Good**

GOING:	R	W	P
Good/Soft	1	0	0
Good	1	0	1
Good/Firm	1	0	0

TRACK:	R	W	P
Left Handed	3	0	1
Galloping	3	0	1

TRIP:	R	W	P
1m	2	0	0
1m 2f	1	0	1

JOCKEY:	R	W	P
T.Queally	2	0	1
Shane Kelly	1	0	0

INTILAAQ (USA)

4 b c Dynaformer (USA) – Torrestrella (IRE) (Orpen (USA))
OWNER: Sheikh HAMDAN AL MAKTOUM
TRAINER: R.VARIAN. Newmarket, Suffolk.
CAREER FORM FIGURES: 3 – 1011 - 8
CAREER WINS: 2015: Apr NEWBURY Good/Firm Mdn 1m; July NEWBURY Good/Firm Listed 1m 2f; Aug HAYDOCK Good/Firm Group 3 1m 2f

Despite only finishing eighth in the Dubai Turf at Meydan over an inadequate nine furlongs in late March, Intilaaq remains a top-class prospect for this summer. Featured in the *Top 40 Prospects* last year, the Sheikh Hamdan Al Maktoum owned colt won Listed and Group 3 races in scintillating fashion which marked him down as a potential Group 1 winner in the making.

An eight lengths winner of his maiden at Newbury in the spring, he was supplemented at a cost of £30,000 for the 2000 Guineas as a result. Unfortunately, the colts' first Classic came too soon in his career and he finished a well beaten fifteenth behind Gleneagles. Roger Varian then gave Intilaaq a break and he didn't return until mid July. However, the son of Dynaformer was back to his best when beating St James's Palace third Consort by two and a half lengths in the Listed Steventon Stakes at Newbury. Having chased down pacemaker Mustadeem, Paul Hanagan's mount went for home over a furlong out before staying on strongly to beat Sir Michael Stoute's runner decisively with high-class handicapper Fire Fighting seven lengths further back in third. He was even more impressive next time when landing the Group 3 Rose of Lancaster Stakes at Haydock by five lengths. Given a positive ride by the former dual champion jockey, Intilaaq hit the front with seven furlongs to run and dominated from thereafter. Very strong at the line, his finishing effort suggested twelve furlongs will be within his reach, if necessary, in time. Richard Hills, representing the owner said afterwards: **"He's a very similar horse to Nayef. He was tough and had a good cruising speed and he quickened and lengthened and kept building on it. We are really excited."** Roger Varian entered him in the English and Irish Champion Stakes but a minor issue with a joint, plus the prospect of softening ground ruled him out of the former event in October.

Returning in Dubai in March, he was forced to race wide and was unable to find the necessary change of gear in the latter stages and was beaten around four lengths by Real Steel. Intilaaq will be a different proposition back on home soil over a longer trip. There are undoubtedly more Group races to be won with him and it will be no surprise if he bags one at the highest level this summer, possibly over a mile and a half.

POINTS TO NOTE:
Probable Best Distance - 1m 2f – 1m 4f
Preferred Going - Good/Firm
Connection's Comments: "Next year he will be very exciting and we ought to have our eye on all the top middle distance races." Roger VARIAN at Haydock (8/8/15)

GOING:	R	W	P
Good	1	0	0
Good/Firm	5	3	1

TRACK:	R	W	P
Left Handed	4	3	0
Right	2	0	1
Galloping	6	3	1

TRIP:	R	W	P
7f	1	0	1
1m	2	1	0
1m 1f	1	0	0
1m 2f	2	2	0

JOCKEY:	R	W	P
P.Hanagan	5	3	1
D.O'Neill	1	0	0

INTIMATION

4 b f Dubawi (IRE) – Infallible (Pivotal)
OWNER: CHEVELEY PARK STUD
TRAINER: Sir M.R.STOUTE. Newmarket, Suffolk.
CAREER FORM FIGURES: 9 - 11
CAREER WINS: 2015: May NOTTINGHAM Good/Soft Mdn 1m; July LEICESTER Good/Soft Hcap 1m 2f

Cheveley Park Stud and Sir Michael Stoute have enjoyed a tremendous amount of success with older fillies over the years. Allegretto (Prix Royal Oak), Echelon (Matron Stakes), Integral (Falmouth & Sun Chariot), Peeress (Sun Chariot & Lockinge) and Russian Rhythm (Lockinge) were all Group 1 winners as older horses for the partnership.

The lightly raced Intimation has a long way to go before she can be considered Group 1 class but she looks a black type filly in the making, if her performances last season are anything to go by. A daughter of Dubawi out of John Gosden's 2008 Nell Gwyn Stakes winner Infallible (runner-up in the Group 1 Coronation & Falmouth Stakes), she is a half-sister to the smart pair Intrinsic and Mutakayyef. Only ninth of eleven at Leicester (the race contained the subsequent Fred Darling and French Oaks winners) on her sole outing as a juvenile in 2014, she improved markedly last term winning both her starts and leaving her on a favourable looking rating of 90.

A half length winner at Nottingham in late May from Bella Nouf (won twice since), she came with a strong late run under Ted Durcan and appreciated the underfoot conditions in the process. Given an official mark of 80, the Dubawi filly seemingly relished the step up to ten furlongs for her handicap debut at Leicester in early July and destroyed a handful of rivals by upwards of four and a half lengths. Leading with a furlong to run, Intimation readily pulled clear in the manner of a fast improving filly who may stay further in time. While it was disappointing we didn't see her again, presumably due to a setback, I received news in March that Sir Michael Stoute's four year old is back in work and going very well. There is a feeling at Freemason Lodge that she is at least Listed class and may be better. If that is the case, Intimation will have no problem winning another handicap before her attentions are turned to Pattern events. She promises to make a lovely four year old.

POINTS TO NOTE:
Probable Best Distance - 1m 2f – 1m 4f
Preferred Going - Good/Soft
Connection's Comments: "She's a gorgeous filly who could get a mile and a half in time." Cam HARDIE at Leicester (4/7/15)

GOING:	R	W	P
Good/Soft	2	2	0
Good	1	0	0

TRACK:	R	W	P
Left Handed	1	1	0
Right	2	1	0
Stiff/Undul.	2	1	0
Galloping	1	1	0

TRIP:	R	W	P
7f	1	0	0
1m	1	1	0
1m 2f	1	1	0

JOCKEY:	R	W	P
T.Durcan	1	1	0
C.Hardie	1	1	0
Ryan Moore	1	0	0

JUST POUR NOUS

3 b c Pour Moi (IRE) – Steam Cuisine (Mark of Esteem (IRE))
OWNER: HOLLEYHEAD, ROSS, WHITE & JOHNSTON
TRAINER: M.JOHNSTON. Middleham, North Yorkshire.
CAREER FORM FIGURES: 41
CAREER WINS: 2015: Sept HAMILTON Good/Soft Mdn 1m

Epsom Derby winner and first season stallion Pour Moi produced some promising juveniles last year. The likes of Diamonds Pour Moi (Ralph Beckett), Mr Khalid (Marco Botti) and Vincent's Forever (John Gosden) all looked above average when winning their maidens last Autumn and it will be interesting to see how far they can progress as three year olds.

Just Pour Nous is another son of Andre Fabre's Classic winner and looks the type to develop into a high-class middle distance handicapper, at least. Purchased for 27,000gns and from the family of Epsom Oaks runner-up Slightly Dangerous, Mark Johnston's charge was green on his debut in a mile maiden Chelmsford in August. Despite that, he stayed on nicely to finish fourth behind Danehill Kodiac (won again since and rated 87). Beaten around six lengths, the third Rockley has also won subsequently. Reappearing ten days later, Just Pour Nous had clearly learned plenty from his debut and was much more streetwise at Hamilton in early September. Making all, he hung late on but still withstood the challenge of Karl Burke's Colour Me Happy (won at Newmarket next time) to win by half a length with the pair eight lengths clear of the third.

Kingsley House Stables has assembled a fine team of three year olds and it is not hard to envisage Just Pour Nous developing into a Royal Ascot candidate. The King George V Stakes (16th June) looks an obvious target and is a race the yard have already won a handful of times (Diaghilef (1995), Systematic (2002), Fantastic Love (2003), Linas Selection (2006) and Fennell Bay (2012)). Officially rated 81, the handicapper has given the son of Pour Moi every chance and it will be a surprise if his mark doesn't escalate once tackling longer trips.

POINTS TO NOTE:
Probable Best Distance - 1m 4f
Preferred Going - Good
Connection's Comments: "We've always thought he was more of a three year old and I can't believe how much he's growing. He's shown a fantastic attitude and Joe (Fanning) said he kept finding and finding." Deirdre JOHNSTON at Hamilton (1/9/15)

GOING:	R	W	P
Standard	1	0	0
Good/Soft	1	1	0

TRACK:	R	W	P
Left Handed	1	0	0
Right	1	1	0
Stiff/Undul.	1	1	0
Tight	1	0	0

TRIP:	R	W	P
1m	2	1	0

JOCKEY:	R	W	P
J.Fanning	1	1	0
J.Crowley	1	0	0

LA RIOJA

3 b f Hellvelyn – Talampaya (USA) (Elusive Quality (USA))
OWNER: QATAR RACING Limited
TRAINER: H.CANDY. Wantage, Oxon.
CAREER FORM FIGURES: 211
CAREER WINS: 2015: July NEWBURY Good/Firm Mdn 6f; Sept SALISBURY Soft Group 3 6f

It is widely acknowledged within the sport that when it comes to training sprinters, Henry Candy has few, if any peers. Airwave, Kyllachy, Markab and Twilight Son have all won at the highest level for the Wantage trainer. The last named stays in training as a four year old and threatens to take the sprinting scene by storm this summer having won the Betfred Sprint at Haydock in September.

Anothing exciting speedster currently residing at Kingston Warren is the dual winner La Rioja. Officially rated 110, the daughter of Hellvelyn was purchased for 50,000gns as a yearling and is a half-sister to Listed placed Lilbourne Lass. Half a length runner-up on her debut at Lingfield in June, the Qatar Racing Limited owned filly made amends in no uncertain terms next time at Newbury when destroying thirteen rivals by upwards of five lengths in a six furlongs fillies' maiden (subsequent Cheveley Park and Coronation Stakes winner Indian Ink won the same race in 2006). Following her victory, Henry Candy commented: **"La Rioja is very able. She's scopey and has got a great temperament. She wouldn't cope with proper firm ground. I think she is a black type filly."** That proved a very accurate assessment because she was even more impressive next time in the Group 3 Dick Poole Stakes at Salisbury on much slower ground. Indeed, La Rioja relished the conditions sluicing to a four and a half lengths win from the 104 rated Whatdoiwantthatfor. Once in the clear, she quickened in the manner of a top-class filly and bounded clear.

The Commonwealth Cup at Royal Ascot (17th June) is an obvious target but the six furlongs event is also the chief aim for one of last year's outstanding juveniles Shalaa. Firm ground may rule La Rioja out in any case. However, she looks ideal for something like the Group 2 Sandy Lane Stakes at Haydock (28th May), a race stablemate Limato finished runner-up in last year before filling the same position in the inaugural running of the Commonwealth Cup. Henry Candy also has the option of dropping his filly back to five furlongs for the first time because she certainly isn't short of speed. She is a tremendous prospect.

POINTS TO NOTE:
Probable Best Distance - 6 furlongs
Preferred Going - Good/Soft
Connection's Comments: "Andrea (Atzeni) has come back and said she is only going to get quicker and I doubt she'll be getting a yard over six furlongs as she's going to be all about speed, and lots of it. She loved the soft ground and, once she got a run, she settled things very quickly." Henry CANDY at Salisbury (3/9/15)

GOING:	R	W	P
Soft	1	1	0
Good/Firm	2	1	1

TRACK:	R	W	P
Left Handed	2	1	1
Right	1	1	0
Galloping	2	2	0
Tight/Undul.	1	0	1

TRIP:	R	W	P
6f	3	2	1

JOCKEY:	R	W	P
A.Atzeni	2	1	1
O.Murphy	1	1	0

LAST TANGO INPARIS

3 ch f Aqlaam – Strictly Lambada (Red Ransom (USA))
OWNER: HELENA SPRINGFIELD LTD
TRAINER: H.MORRISON. East Ilsley, Berkshire.
CAREER FORM FIGURES: 31
CAREER WINS: 2015: Oct NEWBURY Good/Soft Mdn 1m

Helena Springfield Ltd and Hughie Morrison came within a neck of winning the Investec Oaks in 2012 when Shirocco Star was narrowly denied by the Ballydoyle trained Was. To add insult to injury for her trainer, stablemate Coquet was repeatedly denied a run before finishing a desperately unlucky sixth in the same race. Indeed, Morrison has also run the likes of Banoffee (7th in 2013 having won the Cheshire Oaks) and Marsh Daisy (won the Listed Height of Fashion Stakes at Goodwood but could only finish 13th at Epsom in 2014) in the fillies' Classic in recent years.

He will therefore be hoping for better fortune for the promising Last Tango Inparis. A homebred, her dam is a half-sister to the aforementioned Marsh Daisy and the Aqlaam filly is a half-sister to former stablemate Sleep Easy (won three times over 1m 4f & 1m 6f). She is therefore bred to relish middle distances this year and could easily develop into a live contender for the 2016 Epsom Oaks. She made her debut in a nine furlongs maiden at Goodwood in early October and caught the eye with her relentless late progress. Held up and showing signs of greenness during the first half of the race, she stayed on with real purpose to finish third behind two more experienced rivals. Back in fourth was subsequent winner Algometer. Ironically, Last Tango Inparis reappeared thirteen days later in the same one mile fillies' maiden at Newbury which Shirocco Star had won four years earlier. Despite the quick turnaround, she had evidently learned a lot from her debut because she was to the fore from the outset and seemingly appreciated the easy underfoot conditions. Leading with a couple of furlongs to run, the Aqlaam filly ran on well and was a cosy one and three quarters of a length winner from David Simcock's debutant High Hopes (the fifth has won since). It was a pleasing performance and one which suggested she could develop into a smart middle distance filly this year. She most definitely looks Pattern race material but may want some cut in the ground.

It is possible Last Tango Inparis will follow a similar route to Epsom as Shirocco Star and contest the ten furlongs Listed Oaks Trial at Newbury (14th May). However, Hughie Morrison has also used the Cheshire Oaks (4th May - Banoffee won it three years ago) and, as discussed, the Listed Height of Fashion Stakes at Goodwood (19th May – both Coquet (2012) & Marsh Daisy (2014) won it en route to Epsom) as stepping stones. Whichever route she takes, hopefully she will be lining up in the Investec Oaks on Friday 3rd June and providing Hughie Morrison with realistic claims of winning his first British Classic.

POINTS TO NOTE:
Probable Best Distance - 1m 4f
Preferred Going - Good/Soft
Connection's Comments: "Last Tango Inparis loves that ground (Good/Soft) and will stay a mile and a half next year. She's got a great attitude." Liam KENIRY at Newbury (24/10/15)

GOING:	R	W	P
Good/Soft	2	1	1

TRACK:	R	W	P
Left Handed	1	1	0
Right	1	0	1
Galloping	1	1	0
Tight/Undul.	1	0	1

TRIP:	R	W	P
1m	1	1	0
1m 1f	1	0	1

JOCKEY:	R	W	P
Liam Keniry	2	1	1

LORD GEORGE (IRE)

3 gr c Sir Percy – Mahima (FR) (Linamix (FR))
OWNER: FRED ARCHER RACING – BEND OR
TRAINER: J.R.FANSHAWE. Newmarket, Suffolk.
CAREER FORM FIGURES: 31
CAREER WINS: 2015: Oct WOLVERHAMPTON Standard Mdn 1m

A €25,000 purchase as a yearling at the Arqana Sale in October 2014, Lord George looks a good investment if his two runs last year are anything to go by. Indeed, he looks the type who James Fanshawe excels with and it will be a major surprise if he doesn't win more races off his current mark of 81.

The son of Sir Percy was a running on third on his debut at Salisbury in the second division of a median auction maiden stakes in September. Only beaten a length and three quarters by Richard Hannon's In The Red (won again next time and now rated 87), who was having his fourth run, the runner-up Dream of Summer won two months later at Lingfield. Lord George confirmed the promise three weeks later at Wolverhampton when scoring a shade cleverly in an extended one mile maiden. Pushed out under hands and heels by Tom Queally, the winning margin of a neck flattered the runner-up Hepplewhite (finished runner-up twice more since and rated 83). Nearly five lengths back in fourth was James Tate's Cape of Glory, who has won twice since and is officially rated 87. Therefore James Fanshawe's colt could have been let in lightly for his second season off a mark in the low 80s.

It will be interesting to see how far Lord George stays as a three year old but ten furlongs should be within his stamina range. He looks the sort to win a nice prize this year and is one of a number of promising youngsters at Pegasus Stables on the Snailwell Road in Newmarket.

POINTS TO NOTE:

Probable Best Distance	-	**1m 2f**
Preferred Going	-	**Good**

GOING:	**R**	**W**	**P**	**TRACK:**	**R**	**W**	**P**
Standard	**1**	**1**	**0**	**Left Handed**	**1**	**1**	**0**
Good	**1**	**0**	**1**	**Right**	**1**	**0**	**1**
				Galloping	**1**	**0**	**1**
				Tight	**1**	**1**	**0**

TRIP:	**R**	**W**	**P**	**JOCKEY:**	**R**	**W**	**P**
1m	**2**	**1**	**1**	**Tom Queally**	**2**	**1**	**1**

LUMIERE

3 gr f Shamardal (USA) – Screen Star (IRE) (Tobougg (IRE))
OWNER: Sheikh HAMDAN BIN MOHAMMED AL MAKTOUM
TRAINER: M.JOHNSTON. Middleham, North Yorkshire.
CAREER FORM FIGURES: 121
CAREER WINS: 2015: July NEWMARKET Good/Firm Mdn 6f; Sept NEWMARKET Good Group 1 6f

Mark Johnston believes last year's Group 1 Cheveley Park Stakes winner Lumiere is the best horse he has trained since previous stable stars Attraction and Shamardal. The former won 10 of her 15 races between 2003 and 2005, including five Group 1 races, and earned £899,597 in prize-money. The latter was unbeaten as a juvenile winning three times, including the Group 1 Dewhurst Stakes at Newmarket by two and a half lengths in 2004. The son of Giant's Causeway subsequently won the French 2000 Guineas, Prix du Jockey Club and St James's Palace Stakes for Saeed Bin Suroor and Godolphin the following year. He accumulated £1,099,290 in career prize-money. It was a golden era for Kingsley House Stables.

It is therefore fitting that one of last season's outstanding juveniles is by Shamardal as she bids to follow in the hoofprints of Attraction by winning the 1000 Guineas (1st May) on the Rowley Mile twelve years after her former stablemate. Out of another ex-Johnston trained horse Screen Star, who was an eleven lengths winner of her only start at Redcar in 2007, she was all the rage on her racecourse debut at Newmarket's July meeting having reportedly worked exceptionally well beforehand. Contesting a six furlongs fillies' maiden, she trounced subsequent winners Sharja Queen and Shadow Hunter (Listed winner) and five other rivals by upwards of six lengths. Immediately elevated in class, Lumiere took her chance in the Group 2 Lowther Stakes at York the following month. A combination of rain softened ground, a far from smooth preparation and racing keenly contributed to her downfall as she chased home William Haggas' battle hardened filly Besharah. Beaten two and a half lengths, the daughter of Shamardal was back to her best on the Rowley Mile five weeks later as she turned the tables on her York conqueror and won the Group 1 Cheveley Park Stakes by half a length. Making all, once again, she raced enthusiastically before showing a determined attitude to fend off all comers.

Lumiere's attacking style of racing is very similar to Attraction and one would expect a similar approach in the Guineas ie. race prominently, even though there is a doubt about the trip in some quarters. Her pedigree suggests she will stay a mile because she is a half-sister to a twelve furlongs winner and her dam over easily over seven furlongs as a juvenile. The fact Mark Johnston is even mentioning Lumiere in the same breath as superstars Attraction and Shamardal is good enough for me. I think she will be a very tough nut to crack in the fillies' first Classic on Sunday 1st May.

POINTS TO NOTE:
Probable Best Distance - 1 mile
Preferred Going - Good/Firm
Connection's Comments: "I haven't been as nervous about a race for a long time because I thought she's the best horse I've had for a long, long time. We always thought there was no shortage of stamina but we also know she's very fast and has a tremendous cruising speed. William Buick had said after York she's a proper six furlongs filly, but I said I was sure she'd stay. I'm very hopefuly she can stay a mile." Mark JOHNSTON at Newmarket (26/9/15)

GOING:	R	W	P	TRACK:	R	W	P
Good/Soft	1	0	1	Left Handed	1	0	1
Good	1	1	0	Right	2	2	0
Good/Firm	1	1	0	Galloping	3	2	1

TRIP:	R	W	P	JOCKEY:	R	W	P
6f	3	2	1	W.Buick	3	2	1

MAZZINI

3 ch c Exceed And Excel (AUS) – Firenze (Efisio)
OWNER: Mr & Mrs P.HOPPER, Mr & Mrs M.MORRIS
TRAINER: J.R.FANSHAWE. Newmarket, Suffolk.
CAREER FORM FIGURES: 2

The once raced Mazzini is bred to be a smart sprinter being out of dual Listed winner and Group 2 placed Firenze. He is therefore from the family of the 2004 July Cup winner Frizzante and Stewards' Cup winner Zidane. All three were trained by James Fanshawe and it is therefore no surprise to learn the Newmarket based handler is excited about the prospects of this son of Exceed And Excel.

Mazzini was only beaten a neck on his sole racecourse appearance at Kempton in a six furlongs maiden in early December. The highly regarded winner Tailwind used his experience and made all the running, while the runner-up was very slowly away forfeiting considerably more ground than the winning margin. Tom Queally's mount made good late headway though and was bearing down on Roger Varian's winner. Narrowly denied, he pulled three lengths clear of the third and going one better should prove a formality this spring.

Described as a strong powerful colt, Mazzini is set to follow the family tradition and compete in three year old sprints this term. Expected to improve with age, he could even be competing at Pattern level later in the campaign. He is a very promising individual.

POINTS TO NOTE:

Probable Best Distance	-	**6 furlongs**
Preferred Going	-	**Good/Firm**

GOING:	R	W	P	TRACK:	R	W	P
Standard	1	0	1	Right	1	0	1
				Tight	1	0	1

TRIP:	R	W	P	JOCKEY:	R	W	P
6f	1	0	1	Tom Queally	1	0	1

MONOTYPE (IRE)

4 b g Makfi – Mill Guineas (USA) (Salse (USA))
OWNER: Sheikh MOHAMMED OBAID AL MAKTOUM
TRAINER: R.VARIAN. Newmarket, Suffolk.
CAREER FORM FIGURES: 315
CAREER WINS: 2015: June DONCASTER Soft Mdn 1m 4f

Despite Postponed winning the King George VI and Queen Elizabeth Stakes at Ascot in July and Connecticut a Group 2 in Turkey less than two months later, high profile owner Sheikh Mohammed Obaid Al Maktoum decided to remove his 35 horses (23 three year olds + & 12 juveniles) from Bedford House Stables in Newmarket and transfer them the short journey to Kremlin House Stables in September. Luca Cumani's loss is very much Roger Varian's gain as Postponed has already proved this spring by winning twice at Meydan in March, including the Group 1 Sheema Classic.

One of those horses, Monotype, is a lightly raced son of Makfi who could have a lot more to offer for his new handler. A 300,000gns yearling, he is officially rated 89 and may develop into a live contender for the Ebor, although his owner is always keener to pursue the Pattern route rather than valuable handicaps. Three lengths third on his debut at Nottingham in May over ten furlongs, he appreciated the step up to a mile and a half next time at Doncaster over a month later. Ridden by William Buick, he seemingly relished the easy conditions before staying on strongly to beat subsequent dual winner She Is No Lady (rated 87) by half a length. Five lengths further back in third was Sands of Fortune, who won the marathon Goodwood Stakes at their summer Festival. Elevated in class next time, Monotype contested the Group 3 Bahrain Trophy at Newmarket's July meeting. Encountering much faster ground, he failed to make an impact and finished last of five behind Mr Singh.

Absent since, Monotype has been gelded during the Autumn/Winter and, despite the fact he has already tackled Pattern company, he remains a well treated four year old off a rating of 89. Unexposed, ease in the ground may be imperative for him but it will be disappointing if he can't win a big handicap, at least, given the opportunity.

POINTS TO NOTE:

Probable Best Distance	-	**1m 4f – 1m 6f**
Preferred Going	-	**Good/Soft**

GOING:	**R**	**W**	**P**
Soft	**2**	**1**	**1**
Good/Firm	**1**	**0**	**0**

TRACK:	**R**	**W**	**P**
Left Handed	**2**	**1**	**1**
Right	**1**	**0**	**0**
Galloping	**3**	**1**	**1**

TRIP:	**R**	**W**	**P**
1m 2f	**1**	**0**	**1**
1m 4f	**1**	**1**	**0**
1m 5f	**1**	**0**	**0**

JOCKEY:	**R**	**W**	**P**
W.Buick	**1**	**1**	**0**
A.Kirby	**2**	**0**	**1**

MUTAWAALY (IRE)

3 b c Cape Cross (IRE) – Sana Abel (IRE) (Alhaarth (IRE))
OWNER: Sheikh HAMDAN AL MAKTOUM
TRAINER: R.VARIAN. Newmarket, Suffolk.
CAREER FORM FIGURES: 1
CAREER WINS: 2015: Dec WOLVERHAMPTON Standard Mdn 1m

Mutawaaly is bred to be a smart colt hailing from the family of Classic winners Midway Lady (1000 Guineas and Oaks) and Eswarah (Oaks). Owned and bred by Sheikh Hamdan Al Maktoum, the son of Cape Cross will be hoping to emulate another subsequent Classic winner, Jack Hobbs, by winning an extended one mile maiden at Wolverhampton in December on his sole outing as a juvenile.

Well drawn in stall 3, Mutawaaly was always to the fore and once asked for his effort approaching the final furlong, Jack Mitchell's mount found plenty and quickly settled the issue with an impressive change of gear. A three and three quarters of a length winner from the 68 rated Canford Crossing (9 race maiden), the form is nothing to get excited about but at least the third, Mayasa, won by six lengths next time and is rated 75. Bred to come into his own over middle distances, Roger Varian's colt is also a half-brother to former stablemate Reesha, who won over ten furlongs and was placed twice over a mile and a half. At the time of writing, Mutawaaly hasn't been granted an official rating and, while he is likely to go down the handicap route initially, his connections harbour hopes the Cape Cross colt will be competing at a higher level at some stage in 2016.

POINTS TO NOTE:

Probable Best Distance	-	**1m 2f – 1m 4f**
Preferred Going	-	**Good/Firm**

GOING:	**R**	**W**	**P**	**TRACK:**	**R**	**W**	**P**
Standard	**1**	**1**	**0**	**Left Handed**	**1**	**1**	**0**
				Tight	**1**	**1**	**0**

TRIP:	**R**	**W**	**P**	**JOCKEY:**	**R**	**W**	**P**
1m	**1**	**1**	**0**	**Jack Mitchell**	**1**	**1**	**0**

MYTIMEHASCOME

3 b f Montjeu (IRE) – Vital Statistics (Indian Ridge)
OWNER: MITAAB ABDULLAH
TRAINER: R.VARIAN. Newmarket, Suffolk.
CAREER FORM FIGURES: 52

Roger Varian trained Ashaadd to win three times during his career in the UK in 2012 and 2013, earning an official rating of 100 in the process, before continuing as a four year old in Dubai. The Newmarket handler is particularly enthusiastic about the prospect of training his half-sister Mytimehascome, a daughter of Montjeu.

While she failed to win either of her two races as a juvenile, Varian believes Mytimehascome is good enough to be steered towards an Oaks trial in the spring. Hopefully, she will have won her maiden in the meantime. A promising two lengths fifth on her debut in a seven furlongs fillies' maiden at Newmarket in October behind Materialistic, her trainer felt the trip was too sharp for her. Stepped up to a mile at Kempton in late November, the Montjeu filly was sent off 11/10 favourite. She held every chance inside the final couple of furlongs but was unable to reel in winning debutant Diamonds Pour Moi and was beaten a length. The steady early gallop may not have helped her cause.

Mytimehascome reportedly works well at home and going one better should prove a formality. Roger Varian **"will be disappointed if she isn't a stakes filly."** Held in the highest regard, it will be interesting to see how far she can progress as a middle distance three year old.

POINTS TO NOTE:

Probable Best Distance	-	**1m 2f – 1m 4f**
Preferred Going	-	**Good**

GOING:	**R**	**W**	**P**	**TRACK:**	**R**	**W**	**P**
Standard	**1**	**0**	**1**	**Right**	**2**	**0**	**1**
Good/Soft	**1**	**0**	**0**	**Galloping**	**1**	**0**	**0**
				Tight	**1**	**0**	**1**

TRIP:	**R**	**W**	**P**	**JOCKEY:**	**R**	**W**	**P**
7f	**1**	**0**	**0**	**A.Atzeni**	**1**	**0**	**0**
1m	**1**	**0**	**1**	**Jack Mitchell**	**1**	**0**	**1**

NESSITA

3 ch f Shamardal (USA) – Neshla (Singspiel (IRE))
OWNER: SAEED MANANA
TRAINER: H.PALMER. Newmarket, Suffolk.
CAREER FORM FIGURES: 31
CAREER WINS: 2015: Oct KEMPTON Standard Mdn 1m

Classic winning trainer Hugo Palmer has made giant strides in a short space of time. Responsible for 24 winners in 2014, the head of Kremlin Cottage Stables sent out 34 winners last year with his domestic prize-money totalling £1,042,340. Galileo Gold (Group 2 Vintage Stakes), Gifted Master (Group 3 Autumn Stakes) and Hawksmoor (Group 3 Prestige Stakes) were all Pattern winning juveniles.

Amongst the three year olds, Home of The Brave won the Free Handicap and New Providence won the Group 3 Summer Stakes but the star of the show was undoubtedly Covert Love. The Azamour filly won her maiden at Chelmsford in early May and never looked back thereafter winning a handicap at York off 83. The Listed Hoppings Stakes at Newcastle followed before she was supplemented for the Irish Oaks at a cost of €40,000. The rest, as they say, is history as she won at the Curragh under a brilliant ride from Pat Smullen and added another Group 1 for good measure in the Prix de L'Opera at Longchamp on Arc day. Between the 6th May and 17th October, Covert Love won five of her seven races and earned £500,668. It was a superb piece of training by one of the rising stars of his profession.

Speaking to Hugo in February, he is hoping Kempton maiden winner Nessita can develop into a high-class filly this year, too. Reported to have thrived during the winter, she is only rated 77 but her trainer has his eye on an Oaks trial rather than a handicap in the spring. Beaten less than two lengths on her debut at Leicester in September, she built on that performance at the Sunbury track the following month. Martin Harley made use of her low draw and had the Shamardal filly in a good position throughout. Shaken up inside the final quarter of a mile, she was kept up to her work to deny Sir Michael Stoute's Percy's Romance by a length. Strictly on form, Nessita has a mountain to climb between now and early June, if she is to develop into a realistic Oaks contender. However, she has already achieved more than Covert Love had at the same stage.

POINTS TO NOTE:

Probable Best Distance	-	**1m 2f – 1m 4f**
Preferred Going	-	**Good/Firm**

GOING:	**R**	**W**	**P**
Standard	**1**	**1**	**0**
Good	**1**	**0**	**1**

TRACK:	**R**	**W**	**P**
Right	**2**	**1**	**1**
Stiff/Undul.	**1**	**0**	**1**
Tight	**1**	**1**	**0**

TRIP:	**R**	**W**	**P**
1m	**2**	**1**	**1**

JOCKEY:	**R**	**W**	**P**
M.Harley	**2**	**1**	**1**

OUT AND ABOUT (IRE)

3 b g Fastnet Rock (AUS) – Starship (IRE) (Galileo (IRE))
OWNER: The STARSHIP PARTNERSHIP
TRAINER: W.J.HAGGAS. Newmarket, Suffolk.
CAREER FORM FIGURES: 41
CAREER WINS: 2015: Oct REDCAR Good Mdn 7f

Fast Or Free provided William Haggas with success in the Britannia Stakes at Royal Ascot (16th June) four years ago and the Somerville Lodge operation believe they may have a live contender for the 2016 renewal in the form of twice raced Out And About.

From a family William Haggas knows well, the gelded son of Fastnet Rock is a half-brother to former stablemates Bilimbi (2 wins), Martian (2 wins) and Pickled Pelican (2 wins). Out And About made an encouraging start to his career in the second division of a seven furlongs maiden at Newbury in mid August. Having been slowly into stride, Pat Cosgrave's mount made good headway with a quarter of a mile to run before keeping on well in the closing stages. Beaten around seven lengths in fourth, the race was won by Justice Law (now rated 96) with the places being filled by subsequent winners Tashweeq (rated 110) and Nice Future. The form looks solid and the winning time was 1.25 seconds quicker than the first division of the same maiden. He confirmed the promise next time when winning a similar event at Redcar in early October by a length and a quarter. Sent off 11/10 favourite, Out And About was driven out by Liam Jones to beat Karl Burke's Colour Me Happy, who won next time at Newmarket and is rated 81.

Bearing in mind the strength of the form of his two races, William Haggas' lightly raced gelding looks a well handicapped three year old off a mark of 84. Interestingly, one of Out And About's siblings, namely Bilimbi, finished fourth in the Britannia Stakes in 2014 and William feels this horse is better than him. Expect him to have one or possibly two races before the Royal meeting. The Silver Bowl at Haydock (21st May) could be used as a stepping stone. Either way, he is very much a three year old to follow in 2016.

POINTS TO NOTE:

Probable Best Distance	-	**1m – 1m 2f**
Preferred Going	-	**Good**

GOING:	R	W	P	TRACK:	R	W	P
Soft	1	0	0	Left Handed	2	1	0
Good	1	1	0	Galloping	2	1	0

TRIP:	R	W	P	JOCKEY:	R	W	P
7f	2	1	0	Liam Jones	1	1	0
				P.Cosgrave	1	0	0

POINT OF VIEW (IRE)

3 b c New Approach (IRE) – Artisti (Cape Cross (IRE))
OWNER: Sheikh MOHAMMED OBAID AL MAKTOUM
TRAINER: R.VARIAN. Newmarket, Suffolk.

New patron Sheikh Mohammed Obaid Al Maktoum has a number of potentially exciting three year olds with Roger Varian which have yet to see a racecourse. UAE Prince, a colt by Sea The Stars who cost 650,000gns, holds an entry in the Derby and has already been well touted.

His stablemate Point of View is another who is considered a nice prospect. Bought for 400,000gns at the Tattersalls October Sales as a yearling, he, too, is entered in the Epsom Derby, plus the French equivalent (5th June) and Grand Prix de Paris at Saint-Cloud (14th July). Roger Varian intends starting him off in a ten furlongs maiden during the spring. A well bred colt, he is a half-brother to dual Group 3 winner and Group 1 placed Magic Artist and comes from the family of 2009 St Leger winner Mastery. His racecourse debut will be monitored with plenty of interest.

POINTS TO NOTE:

Probable Best Distance	-	**1m 2f – 1m 4f**
Preferred Going	-	**Good/Firm**

PREDILECTION (USA)

3 b c First Defence (USA) – Summer Shower (Sadler's Wells (USA))
OWNER: PRINCE KHALID ABDULLAH
TRAINER: J.H.GOSDEN. Newmarket, Suffolk.
CAREER FORM FIGURES: 21
CAREER WINS: 2015: Nov KEMPTON Standard Mdn 1m

Despite holding an entry in the 2000 Guineas at Newmarket, it is likely impressive Kempton maiden winner Predilection will come into his own over ten furlongs as a three year old. Indeed, John Gosden's First Defence colt is a half-brother to former stablemate Starboard, who won a Group 3 at Longchamp over a mile and a quarter in 2012.

Making his debut at Newbury's Lockinge meeting in mid May, the Khalid Abdulla owned colt had the misfortune to bump into King of Rocks, who went on to win the Listed National Stakes before being placed at Royal Ascot and Glorious Goodwood. Partnered by Frankie Dettori, he stayed on well but was still half a dozen lengths adrift of Richard Hannon's winner. Absent until the second half of November, Predilection returned at Kempton and appreciated the step up to a mile. Always prominent, Robert Havlin's mount made his move inside the final quarter of a mile and, once taking over, he powered clear to register a most decisive five lengths win from Hughie Morrison's Van Dyke in the manner of a smart colt.

Predilection is also from the family of Doctor Fremantle, who finished fourth in the Epsom Derby behind New Approach in 2008. Interestingly, Sir Michael Stoute's colt started his three year old career in the traditionally very strong ten furlongs handicap (81 – 95) at Newmarket's Craven meeting (12th April) and I wonder if this son of First Defence may do likewise. The race has also been contested by the likes of subsequent Pattern performers Papal Bull (2006), Bronze Cannon (2008), Wigmore Hall (2010), Main Sequence (2012), Hillstar (2013) and Windshear & Volume (2014). Regardless of whether he reappears on the Rowley Mile in April, he looks a very useful colt in the making. The fact he doesn't hold an entry in the Epsom Derby suggests his connections feel twelve furlongs may be beyond him. Mind you, Golden Horn wasn't entered in Flat racing's Blue Riband at this stage last year either.

POINTS TO NOTE:
Probable Best Distance - **1m 2f**
Preferred Going - **Good/Firm**
Connection's Comments: "Predilection travelled nicely and hit top gear a furlong and a half out before galloping out well. He´s pretty straightforward and I think he just wanted time." Robert Havlin at Kempton (18/11/15)

GOING:	R	W	P	TRACK:	R	W	P
Standard	1	1	0	Left Handed	1	0	1
Good	1	0	1	Right	1	1	0
				Galloping	1	0	1
				Tight	1	1	0

TRIP:	R	W	P	JOCKEY:	R	W	P
6f	1	0	1	R.Havlin	1	1	0
1m	1	1	0	L.Dettori	1	0	1

RICHIE McCAW

3 b c Zamindar (USA) – Cochin (USA) (Swain (IRE))
OWNER: MICHAEL H. WATT
TRAINER: M.JOHNSTON. Middleham, North Yorkshire.
CAREER FORM FIGURES: 51
CAREER WINS: 2015: Oct CHELMSFORD Standard Mdn 1m

Richie McCaw is named after the New Zealand Rugby Union player, who captained his country in 110 of his 148 test match appearances. His equine namesake isn't bad either, if his two appearances last year are anything to go by. Officially rated 77, the Zamindar colt is a half-brother to Australian Grade 2 and 3 winner Permit (won over 1m 6f) and therefore ought to come into his own over middle distances as a three year old.

A relatively cheap purchase at €12,000, the Mark Johnston trained colt was beaten less than two lengths on his debut in a seven and a half furlongs maiden at Beverley in mid September, only weakening late on. Stepped up to a mile a month later at Chelmsford City, he made all the running and wasn't hard pressed to beat the 81 rated Gold Trade by a couple of lengths. The third Cape of Glory has won twice since and is now rated 87. Unfortunately, Richie McCaw was found to have been struck into afterwards and split his hoof hence he didn't run again.

The good news is that he is back in work and considered a well handicapped three year old off a rating of 77. Joe Fanning, who rode his 2000th winner aboard Fireglow in the Listed Montrose Stakes at Newmarket at the end of October, was reportedly impressed and Richie McCaw is the type his trainer excels with.

POINTS TO NOTE:
Probable Best Distance - **1m 4f +**
Preferred Going - **Good**
Connection's Comments: "I wanted to keep Richie McCaw out of the kickback so I had him up there from the off. He did it well and will make a nice horse next year." Joe FANNING at Chelmsford (15/10/15)

GOING:	R	W	P
Standard	1	1	0
Good	1	0	0

TRACK:	R	W	P
Left Handed	1	1	0
Right	1	0	0
Stiff/Undul.	1	0	0
Tight	1	1	0

TRIP:	R	W	P
7.5f	1	0	0
1m	1	1	0

JOCKEY:	R	W	P
J.Fanning	2	1	0

ROYAL ARTILLERY (USA)

3 b or br c War Front (USA) – Masseuse (USA) (Dynaformer (USA))
OWNER: Mrs JOHN MAGNIER & MICHAEL TABOR & DERRICK SMITH
TRAINER: J.H.GOSDEN. Newmarket, Suffolk.
CAREER FORM FIGURES: 1
CAREER WINS: 2015: Oct DONCASTER Good/Soft Mdn 7f

War Front was responsible for one of last year's outstanding juveniles and triple Group 1 winner Air Force Blue and stablemate and Grade 1 Breeders' Cup Juvenile Turf winner Hit It A Bomb. The son of Danzig also sired the once raced Royal Artillery, who is the one three year old I am most looking forward to seeing in 2016.

Champion trainer John Gosden invariably runs some very smart juveniles at Doncaster's *Racing Post* Trophy meeting in late October. Lancashire Oaks winner Gertrude Bell finished second in 2009, dual Group 1 winner Izzi Top did likewise twelve months later and Star of Seville scored by six lengths in 2014 before capturing the Prix de Diane at Chantilly last year. Therefore it could be significant that the Newmarket trainer introduced this €450,000 purchase in the seven furlongs maiden at the fixture last Autumn. The subject of a strong word beforehand, Frankie Dettori's mount was sent off Evens favourite and the son of War Front didn't disappoint. Despite racing on a surface which may have been easier than ideal, he readily saw off a dozen rivals to win going away by two and a half lengths. The runner-up, third and fourth have all been beaten again since but the fifth and seventh have won subsequently.

Entered in the 2000 Guineas at Newmarket, it is possible Royal Artillery will be at his best over ten or twelve furlongs (not entered in the Epsom Derby) even though his sire isn't renowned for producing middle distance horses. However, he is out of Dynaformer mare and is related to a mile and three winner. The French Derby over ten furlongs could be an option but he is more likely to encounter faster ground in the UK.

Owned by the Coolmore team, it is worth pointing out they are strong as far as the 2000 Guineas is concerned with the aforementioned Air Force Blue spearheading their challenge. However, Ballydoyle don't appear to have a stand out Epsom Derby contender, at this stage. Therefore don't be surprised if the potentially exciting Royal Artillery emerges a major contender. He certainly looked very good at Town Moor last Autumn.

POINTS TO NOTE:
Probable Best Distance - 1m – 1m 4f
Preferred Going - Good/Firm
Connection's Comments: "Royal Artillery is very big and he has taken time to come to himself. I was a bit concerned about the ground as those by his sire are not known for going on it, but he did it nicely. If he is training well in the spring, there is no reason not to go for a Classic trial." John GOSDEN at Doncaster (23/10/15)

GOING:	R	W	P	TRACK:	R	W	P
Good/Soft	1	1	0	Left Handed	1	1	0
				Galloping	1	1	0

TRIP:	R	W	P	JOCKEY:	R	W	P
7f	1	1	0	F.Dettori	1	1	0

SATISH

3 b c Dansili – Maycocks Bay (Muhtarram (USA))
OWNER: Lady BAMFORD
TRAINER: J.H.M.GOSDEN. Newmarket, Suffolk.
CAREER FORM FIGURES: 4

Dual Classic winner Sariska may have blotted her copybook towards the end of her successful career by refusing to race in the Yorkshire Oaks and Prix Vermeille in 2010, but she was a hugely talented daughter of Pivotal, especially when encountering her favoured soft ground. A head winner of the Investec Oaks at Epsom in 2009, her best performance came in the Irish equivalent at the Curragh five weeks later when barely coming off the bridle on heavy ground under a motionless Jamie Spencer. It would have taken an exceptional filly to have beaten her that day in such conditions. The Michael Bell trained filly won 5 of her 11 races in total and earned £728,724 in prize-money. She also won the Group 3 Musidora Stakes en route to Epsom and the Group 2 Middleton Stakes, both at York, the following season.

Her half-brother Satish has only made one public appearance thus far and it came in a seven furlongs maiden at Ascot in early September (Telescope finished a close second in the 2012 renewal). Slowly away, the early gallop was sedate and Robert Havlin's mount was not ideally positioned at the rear when the tempo eventually lifted. A running on fourth behind Culturati (won a nursery next time and is now rated 94), John Gosden's colt was only beaten two and three quarters of a length. The form looks extremely strong with the first, second, third, sixth and seventh all winning since.

The son of Dansili hasn't been seen since but he still holds an entry in the Derby at Epsom. Owner Lady Bamford has enjoyed a lot of success in the three year old maidens at Newbury's April fixture (15th – 16th) with Feels Like Dancing winning there on her racecourse debut in 2013, Eagle Top did likewise twelve months later and Mr Singh made it a three timer in 2015. Therefore it will be no surprise if Satish reappears at the Berkshire venue in the spring. Provided he builds on his promising introduction, the well bred colt looks very much one to follow. Given his family, it is possible he, too, will prefer some ease in the ground.

POINTS TO NOTE:
Probable Best Distance - 1m 4f
Preferred Going - Good/Soft

GOING:	R	W	P	TRACK:	R	W	P
Good/Soft	1	0	0	Right	1	0	0
				Galloping	1	0	0

TRIP:	R	W	P	JOCKEY:	R	W	P
7f	1	0	0	R.Havlin	1	0	0

SHABEEB (USA)

3 b c Smart Strike (CAN) – Sortita (GER) (Monsun (GER))
OWNER: Sheikh HAMDAN AL MAKTOUM
TRAINER: R.VARIAN. Newmarket, Suffolk.
CAREER FORM FIGURES: 6

The Roger Varian trained Mutashaded won a ten furlongs handicap at Sandown in May 2013 off a mark of 79 before being thrust in at the deep end at Royal Ascot less than a month later. Rated 88, the son of Raven's Pass was a running on third in the Group 2 King Edward VII Stakes behind subsequent Grade 1 Canadian International winner Hillstar. Unfortunately, due to injury, he only raced once more and never got the opportunity to fulfil his potential. From a very good middle distance German family, his half-brother Shabeeb is also now residing at Kremlin House Stables.

A colt by Smart Strike, he made his debut in what appeared a strong maiden over a mile at Newbury during the Autumn. The race was won by Sir Michael Stoute's impeccably bred Midterm (out of Midday) with Shabeeb running on to grab sixth. Only beaten three and a half lengths, he was still unfurnished last year but has developed and matured during the winter, according to his trainer. Bred to come into his own over ten and twelve furlongs, he should have little trouble winning a maiden before emerging as a very useful handicapper at least. Still entered in the Epsom Derby, he could be one for the King George V Handicap at Royal Ascot or, perhaps he will follow in the hoofprints of his older brother and contest a Pattern event at the Royal meeting.

POINTS TO NOTE:

Probable Best Distance	-	**1m 2f – 1m 4f**
Preferred Going	-	**Good**

GOING:	R	W	P	TRACK:	R	W	P
Good/Soft	1	0	0	Left Handed	1	0	0
				Galloping	1	0	0

TRIP:	R	W	P	JOCKEY:	R	W	P
1m	1	0	0	P.Hanagan	1	0	0

SO MI DAR

3 b f Dubawi (IRE) – Dar Re Mi (Singspiel (IRE))
OWNER: LORD LLOYD-WEBBER
TRAINER: J.H.M.GOSDEN. Newmarket, Suffolk.
CAREER FORM FIGURES: 1
CAREER WINS: 2015: Oct WINDSOR Good Mdn 1m

Dar Re Mi was a top-class filly/mare who won 6 of her 17 races for John Gosden and Lady and Lord Lloyd Webber between 2007 and 2010. A three times Group 1 winner, including the Sheema Classic at Meydan six years ago, the daughter of Singspiel earned £2,698,880 in prize-money. She was also a half-sister to another Sheema Classic winner, namely the ill-fated Rewilding, who lost his life in the 2011 King George at Ascot.

Switched to the breeding sheds, Dar Re Mi has already produced De Treville, who won twice for Andre Fabre in France and Group placed on four occasions. She is also the dam of Windsor maiden winner So Mi Dar. Contesting an extended one mile maiden, which is usually run at Yarmouth, in October, she was described as **"next year's filly"** by John Gosden beforehand. However, that didn't prevent her from making a winning start to her career as she gained a narrow advantage over Golden Stunner (third since and rated 80) close home. A neck winner, her trainer added that she was **"still quite petite but has grown and strengthened in recent weeks."**

The Lloyd Webbers will obviously have black type in mind for So Mi Dar but it will be interesting to see if John Gosden aims the Dubawi filly at a handicap during the spring. Don't forget the stable's Epsom Oaks winner Taghrooda was due to contest a ten furlongs handicap at Sandown's Bet365 meeting in late April 2014 until soft ground ruled her out. Long-term, she appears to have Pattern race potential.

POINTS TO NOTE:
Probable Best Distance - 1m 2f – 1m 4f
Preferred Going - Good
Connection's Comments: "You couldn´t ask for any more from a two-year-old filly first time. So Mi Dar was a little bit green, suddenly got the message and found the extra gear which is what you want to see." Lady LLOYD WEBBER at Windsor (20/10/15)

GOING:	R	W	P	TRACK:	R	W	P
Good	1	1	0	Right	1	1	0
				Tight	1	1	0

TRIP:	R	W	P	JOCKEY:	R	W	P
1m	1	1	0	R.Havlin	1	1	0

STATUS QUO (IRE)

3 br g Thewayyouare (USA) – Again Royale (IRE) (Royal Academy (USA))
OWNER: G.MOORE – OSBORNE HOUSE II
TRAINER: Sir M.R.PRESCOTT. Newmarket, Suffolk.
CAREER FORM FIGURES: 641
CAREER WINS: 2015: Sept WOLVERHAMPTON Standard Mdn 7f

In traditional manner for a Sir Mark Prescott trained juvenile, Status Quo had three relatively quick races (21 days) in September last year before being put away for the winter. However, unlike the vast majority of his stablemates, the son of Thewayyouare was a winner on his final run at Wolverhampton. While the handicapper hasn't taken too many chances granting him an official mark of 77, there is every possibility he will improve appreciably as a three year old.

Acquired for €28,000 at Goffs as a yearling, he caught the eye in no uncertain terms on his debut at Leicester. An unconsidered outsider at 100/1, Status Quo was slowly away and green throughout. However, he made encouraging late progress and was only beaten seven and a half lengths by Muntazah (subsequently third in the Group 2 Royal Lodge Stakes and rated 103). Despite finishing fourth at Beverley eight days later, the big strapping colt looked ill at ease on the track and was well held. His juvenile education was completed thirteen days later on the Tapeta at Wolverhampton when he gained his first win in a seven furlongs maiden. Overcoming a wide draw (stall 12), he responded to pressure before collaring the 77 rated Theos Lolly close home to prevail by half a length.

Gelded soon afterwards, Status Quo did well to win as a two year old and should come into his own when tackling trips in excess of a mile this year. There will doubtless be better handicapped three year olds at Heath House Stables, but it will be disappointing if Status Quo can't win more races.

POINTS TO NOTE:

Probable Best Distance	-	**1m 2f - 1m 4f**
Preferred Going	-	**Good**

Connection's Comments: "Status Quo is a lovely big horse and we hope, as he gets stronger, he will develop into a nice horse. I had to drop him in from that draw but things worked out nicely for him." Luke MORRIS at Wolverhampton (29/9/15)

GOING:	R	W	P
Standard	1	1	0
Good	2	0	0

TRACK:	R	W	P
Left Handed	1	1	0
Right	2	0	0
Stiff/Undul.	2	0	0
Tight	1	1	0

TRIP:	R	W	P
7f	2	1	0
7.5f	1	0	0

JOCKEY:	R	W	P
Luke Morris	3	1	0

STONEY BROKE

3 b f Dansili – Alvee (IRE) (Key of Luck (USA)
OWNER: MERRY FOX STUD Limited
TRAINER: J.R.FANSHAWE. Newmarket, Suffolk.
CAREER FORM FIGURES: 1
CAREER WINS: 2015: Sept NOTTINGHAM Good Mdn 1m

Craig Bennett and his Merry Fox Stud tasted Group 1 glory in Germany last summer when Second Step won the 125th Grosser Preis Von Berlin at Hoppegarten in August. His familiar orange and yellow silks are set to be carried with distinction this year, too, by the potentially very well handicapped filly Stoney Broke.

A homebred daughter of Dansili, she is related to Group 1 winning filly Allegretto (Prix Royal Oak). Her pedigree therefore suggests she will come into her own over middle distances as a three year old. Making her debut in the second division of an eight furlongs fillies' maiden at Nottingham in late September, she emerged on top in a blanket finish which involved the first four home. A head scorer from James Eustace's Shadow Spirit, the form looks ordinary but the winning rider Freddy Tylicki was impressed and James Fanshawe believes she will develop into a useful filly when stepped up in distance this term.

Given a mark of 75, she hails from a family who improve with age and distance and it will be disappointing, to say the least, if she can't win a ten or twelve furlongs 0-80 fillies' handicap before climbing the ladder.

POINTS TO NOTE:

Probable Best Distance	-	**1m 2f – 1m 4f**
Preferred Going	-	**Good**

Connection's Comments: "It was a great introduction and Stoney Broke will make a lovely filly next year." Freddy TYLICKI at Nottingham (30/9/15)

GOING:	R	W	P	TRACK:	R	W	P
Good	1	1	0	Left Handed	1	1	0
				Galloping	1	1	0

TRIP:	R	W	P	JOCKEY:	R	W	P
1m	1	1	0	F.Tylicki	1	1	0

TANEEN (USA)

3 b or br c Speightstown (USA) – Moon And Sun (USA) (Malibu Moon (USA))
OWNER: Sheikh HAMDAN AL MAKTOUM
TRAINER: R.VARIAN. Newmarket, Suffolk.
CAREER FORM FIGURES: 31
CAREER WINS: 2015: Aug NEWMARKET Good Mdn 6f

The Rossdales Handicap Stakes (81-100) for three year olds over six furlongs at Newmarket's Craven meeting (14th April) has been contested by some smart sprinters over the years. Group 1 July Cup winner Sakhee's Secret landed the event in 2007 by five lengths off a mark of 93. Twelve months later subsequent King's Stand Stakes winner Prohibit captured the prize off 86. Group 2 winner Es Que Love won it in 2012 off 91 and Danzeno, who has a Group 3 success on his CV, routed the opposition off 90 in 2014. Most recently, subsequent Stewards' Cup and Group 1 third Magical Memory was only fourth in last year's renewal off a mark of 87 (now rated 114).

Roger Varian has the race in mind for the promising Taneen who has the potential to develop into a Pattern horse himself. The son of Speightstown was purchased for $350,000 at Keeneland as a yearling and he held big race entries last summer. Green on his debut at Salisbury in August, he was sent off 13/8 favourite but was beaten four and a half lengths by Henry Candy's Vibrant Chords in third. Taneen was much more streetwise next time on the July course at Newmarket less than three weeks later. Well positioned under Paul Hanagan, he led on the approach to the final furlong and was pushed clear by the former dual champion to win by a couple of lengths from subsequent winners Fighting Temeraire (rated 82) and Wimpole Hall (rated 79). A minor setback prevented the Sheikh Hamdan Al Maktoum owned colt from running again but that may prove a blessing in disguise.

Kremlin House Stables is responsible for some tremendous young talent and there is a feeling that this twice raced colt will make a significant impact this summer. Look out for his reappearance on the Rowley Mile in that traditionally strong three year old sprint handicap.

POINTS TO NOTE:
Probable Best Distance - 6 furlongs
Preferred Going - Good/Firm
Connection's Comments: "Taneen had a wide draw on his debut at Salisbury, but ran a nice race and has come on since. He´s always been a nice horse." Roger VARIAN at Newmarket (29/8/15)

GOING:	R	W	P	TRACK:	R	W	P
Good	1	1	0	Right	2	1	1
Good/Firm	1	0	1	Galloping	2	1	1

TRIP:	R	W	P	JOCKEY:	R	W	P
6f	2	1	1	P.Hanagan	2	1	1

THE BLACK PRINCESS (FR)

3 b or br f Iffraaj – Larceny (IRE) (Cape Cross (IRE))
OWNER: R.J.H.GEFFEN
TRAINER: J.H.M.GOSDEN. Newmarket, Suffolk.
CAREER FORM FIGURES: 1
CAREER WINS: 2015: Nov KEMPTON Standard Mdn 1m

Owner Robin Geffen tasted Royal Ascot glory last summer when GM Hopkins won the Royal Hunt Cup. The same patron has enjoyed plenty of other big race successes with John Gosden over the years, most notably when Arctic Cosmos won the St Leger at Doncaster in 2010, and with Group 2 winner Western Hymn, who stays in training as a five year old.

The last named began his career on the polytrack at Kempton and another John Gosden trained inmate who carries the same colours, namely The Black Princess, did likewise in November. A daughter of Iffraaj who cost €170,000, she won a mile maiden at the Sunbury track by a couple of lengths under Jimmy Fortune. Overcoming a sluggish start, she made good progress with a quarter of a mile to run before being shaken up by her rider. She quickened up well and won going away from the Godolphin owned Bombilate. Despite being related to a twelve furlongs winner, The Black Princess appears to have plenty of speed and the fact she has been given entries in the English and French 1000 Guineas and Prix de Diane suggests she may be kept to shorter distances this year. She looks a highly promising filly who has reportedly wintered well. Her reappearance is one to look forward to because she could be anything.

POINTS TO NOTE:
Probable Best Distance - 1m – 1m 2f
Preferred Going - Good
Connection's Comments: "She is a nice filly. She travelled round good, quickened up nicely and put it to bed quickly." Jimmy FORTUNE at Kempton (4/11/15)

GOING:	R	W	P	TRACK:	R	W	P
Standard	1	1	0	Right	1	1	0
				Tight	1	1	0

TRIP:	R	W	P	JOCKEY:	R	W	P
1m	1	1	0	J.Fortune	1	1	0

TIME TEST

4 b c Dubawi (IRE) – Passage of Time (Dansili)
OWNER: PRINCE KHALID ABDULLAH
TRAINER: R.CHARLTON. Marlborough, Wiltshire.
CAREER FORM FIGURES: 212 - 11410
CAREER WINS: 2014: Aug SANDOWN Mdn 7f: 2015: May NEWBURY Good Hcap 1m 2f; June ROYAL ASCOT Good/Firm Group 3 1m 2f; Sept NEWMARKET Good Group 2 1m

"I loved that. I had that much horse. I stayed with them for a furlong in the straight and then said 'let's go,' and he flew," enthused Frankie Dettori following Time Test's explosive three and a quarter lengths win in the Group 3 Tercentenary Stakes at Royal Ascot in June. His trainer Roger Charlton added: **"He did a very good bit of work the other day and George Baker, who rode him, said: "This is a Group 1 horse." Last year, he was a bit fragile mentally and there was a bit of sweating between his legs today but he was brilliant. He loved the ground."** It was a sparkling performance in a fast time and one which suggested the son of Dubawi can score at the highest level this year. Indeed, the Prince of Wales's Stakes at the Royal meeting (15th June) over the same course and distance has been earmarked as his first major target of 2016.

Time Test began his three year old career with victory in the London Gold Cup at Newbury off a mark of 93. **"He's been working with Al Kazeem and we couldn't believe how well he was going with him,"** stated Roger Charlton afterwards. Ironically, four times Group 1 winner Al Kazeem won the same event four years earlier off 95. Following his Royal Ascot win, he was immediately stepped up further in class when contesting the Group 1 Juddmonte International Stakes at York. While he ran respectably in fourth behind Arabian Queen and Golden Horn, Time Test looked ill at ease on the slow ground with Charlton remarking afterwards: **"Pat (Smullen) said he came into it well but couldn't pick up – he floundered."** Given a break, he returned over a mile in the Group 2 Joel Stakes at Newmarket in late September and resumed winning ways with a length victory from Custom Cut. Ryan Moore, who partnered him at Newbury in May, was back on board and his partner quickened up smartly inside the final furlong to wear down David O'Meara's triple Group 2 winner. His jockey said: **"Time Test would not be out of place in any big race."** Roger Charlton also commented: **"I think York was down to the ground a bit and the way the race was run. They went very slowly down the backstraight and everyone was watching Golden Horn and it became a muddling race."** Only tenth in the Breeders' Cup Mile at Keeneland in October, he was drawn wide and the rain which arrived beforehand didn't suit him.

While Time Test looks quick enough to be competing at the highest level over a mile, which brings the Lockinge Stakes (14th May) into the equation, ten furlongs appears to be his optimum trip. Therefore something like the Group 3 Gordon Richards (22nd April) and Brigadier Gerard Stakes at Sandown (26th May) are possible early season targets, although the son of Dubawi will be forced to carry a Group 2 penalty. Later on, there is a strong possibility he will return to York for another crack at his owner's sponsored Juddmonte International Stakes in August. Granted ten furlongs and fast ground, there is a Group 1 race to be won with Roger Charlton's flagbearer.

POINTS TO NOTE:
Probable Best Distance - 1m 2f
Preferred Going - Good/Firm
Connection's Comments: "I think he'll end up being a better horse than Al Kazeem. Ryan (Moore) said the ground was a bit dead for him today." Roger CHARLTON at Newmarket (25/9/15)

GOING:	R	W	P	TRACK:	R	W	P
Good/Soft	2	1	0	Left Handed	4	1	1
Good	5	2	2	Right	4	3	1
Good/Firm	1	1	0	Galloping	7	4	2
				Tight	1	0	0

TRIP:	R	W	P	JOCKEY:	R	W	P
7f	3	1	2	Ryan Moore	3	2	0
1m	2	1	0	James Doyle	3	1	2
1m 2f	3	2	0	L.Dettori	1	1	0
				Pat Smullen	1	0	0

UAE PRINCE (IRE)

3 b c Sea The Stars (IRE) – By Request (Giant's Causeway (USA))
OWNER: Sheikh MOHAMMED OBAID AL MAKTOUM
TRAINER: R.VARIAN. Newmarket, Suffolk.

As discussed, owner Sheikh Mohammed Obaid Al Maktoum is responsible for some very talented horses in training with Roger Varian and this unraced son of Sea The Stars has a lofty reputation.

Entered in the Epsom Derby, French Derby (5th June) and Grand Prix de Paris (14th July), UAE Prince was purchased for 650,000gns as a yearling and he has reportedly pleased his new trainer since joining the yard last September. His homework is, by all accounts, very good and he is expected to make his racecourse debut at either Newmarket's Craven meeting (12th – 14th April) or Newbury (15th – 16th April). Varian's former boss, the late Michael Jarvis, introduced both subsequent Oaks winner Eswarah (2005) and Derby fourth Hala Bek (2006) at the Berkshire track, so don't be surprised if his protégé does likewise with UAE Prince. He could be an exciting prospect.

POINTS TO NOTE:
Probable Best Distance - 1m 2f – 1m 4f
Preferred Going - Good/Firm
Connection's Comments: "He will start in a maiden and then hopefully go for one of the Derby trials." Sheikh MOHAMMED OBAID AL MAKTOUM (4/2/16)

ZARAK (FR)

3 b c Dubawi (IRE) – Zarkava (IRE) (Zamindar (USA))
OWNER: H H AGA KHAN
TRAINER: A. DE ROYER-DUPRE. Chantilly, France.
CAREER FORM FIGURES: 1
CAREER WINS: 2015: Oct DEAUVILLE Heavy Mdn 1m

Rarely do I include a French trained horse in the *Top 40 Prospects*, but Zarak is bred to be something special being out of the brilliant and unbeaten filly Zarkava and the Aga Khan owned colt created a lasting impression when winning hard held on his debut at Deauville during the Autumn.

Zarkava, a daughter of Zamindar, won all seven of her races with her CV featuring Group 1 wins in the Prix Marcel Boussac, Poule D'Essai Des Pouliches, Prix de Diane, Prix Vermeille and Prix de L'Arc de Triomphe between 2007 and 2008. The Alain de Royer-Dupre trained filly didn't look straightforward when missing the break in the Prix Vermeille and her son is reportedly similar with an equal mix of brilliance and temperament.

The son of Dubawi was sent off 11/10 favourite at Deauville in October and didn't let his supporters down with an authoritative one and a quarter lengths win from Qatar Dream in a debutants event over a mile on testing ground. Racing down the middle of the track, Christophe Soumillon merely nudged his mount out for a ready success. The clock confirmed it was a very good performance with a winning time which was two and a half seconds quicker than the fillies' maiden on the same card, which was won by Andre Fabre's potentially exciting prospect Come Alive.

Significantly, Zarak was still in the 2000 Guineas at Newmarket when the latest forfeit stage was published in early March. Alain de Royer-Dupre rarely has entries in the opening British Classics suggesting the Dubawi colt must have thrived during the winter. His reappearance is eagerly anticipated.

POINTS TO NOTE:

Probable Best Distance	-	**1m – 1m 4f**
Preferred Going	-	**Good**

GOING:	**R**	**W**	**P**	**TRACK:**	**R**	**W**	**P**
Heavy	**1**	**1**	**0**	**Right**	**1**	**1**	**0**
				Galloping	**1**	**1**	**0**

TRIP:	**R**	**W**	**P**	**JOCKEY:**	**R**	**W**	**P**
1m	**1**	**1**	**0**	**C.Soumillon**	**1**	**1**	**0**

OWNERS' ENCLOSURE
HIGHCLERE THOROUGHBRED RACING & AL SHAQAB RACING

Harry Herbert, managing director of Highclere Thoroughbred Racing Ltd and Racing Advisor to HE Sheikh Joaan Hamad Al Thani's Al Shaqab Racing operation, has once again kindly passed on his thoughts regarding a select bunch of **UNRACED THREE YEAR OLDS**.

EL VIP (IRE) b c Pivotal – Elle Danzig (GER) (Roi Danzig (USA))
Trainer: L.M.CUMANI. Newmarket, Suffolk.
A seriously nice horse but, unfortunately, he has met with another setback which means that we won't be seeing him on the racecourse until later on in the season. He is a horse worth following if he stays sound.

COMMODITY (IRE) ch c Dutch Art – Royal Danehill (IRE) (Danehill (USA))
Trainer: Sir M.R.STOUTE. Newmarket, Suffolk.
We like him a lot. He was very immature last year but has transformed physically and could be a decent three year old in the making. He is the other half of Foundation, syndicate wise.

MAZAZ (IRE) b c Galileo (IRE) – Ice Mint (USA) (Awesome Again (CAN))
Trainer: J.H.M.GOSDEN. Newmarket, Suffolk.
I like this horse a lot. He has taken time to mature but you would expect that from his pedigree. I certainly think he will be one to follow this year.

MNEERAH (FR) ch f Giant's Causeway (USA) – Gointobegone (USA)
Trainer: Mrs C.HEAD-MAAREK. Chantilly, France.
I really like her and she has changed out of all recognition from two to three. She seems to go well and Criquette (Head-Maarek) expects her to make her debut any time now.

RASMIYA (IRE) b f Galileo (IRE) – Crystal Valkyrie (IRE)
Trainer: W.J.HAGGAS. Newmarket, Suffolk.
She is a very nice filly who has done everything easily so far. A half-sister to Above Average, who won the Sandown Classic Trial for Barry Hills, she could be anything is definitely one to watch out for.

I would also include **EL HAYEN**, a son of Invincible Spirit trained by **Sir Michael Stoute**. He is a really nice colt and seems to be doing everything right so far. **ZWAYYAN**, a son of Pivotal out of Mail The Desert trained by **William Haggas**, is also a nice unraced colt and finally **TRAINNAH**, a daughter of Pivotal out of Whazzat, also trained by William, is a filly who on looks and pedigree could be decent. All these have needed time to mature but are really nice individuals in the making.

The TWO HORSES HARRY HERBERT IS MOST LOOKING TO SEEING IN 2016
FOUNDATION (Highclere / John Gosden) & SHALAA (Al Shaqab / John Gosden)

TALKING TRAINERS

Henry CANDY

Stables: Kingston Warren, Wantage, Oxfordshire.
2015: 34 Winners from 241 Runners 14% Prize-Money £904,643

OLDER HORSES

CHAIN OF DAISIES 4 b f Rail Link – Puya
She enjoyed a very good season winning four times with her rating rising from 72 to 103. A courageous filly, I was delighted with her performance at Newmarket winning a Listed event. She has done well physically during the winter and we will be campaigning her in Listed and Group races this year. Yet to race beyond a mile and a quarter, I am hoping she will stay a bit further, which would help.

DINKUM DIAMOND (IRE) 8 b h Aussie Rules (USA) – Moving Diamonds
He has been a tremendous horse for us over the years. Placed in a Listed race at Windsor and fourth in the Stewards' Cup, we stepped him up to seven furlongs for the first time at Leicester in October and he duly won. It therefore gives us a few more options for this year.

GREENSIDE 5 b h Dubawi (IRE) – Katrina (IRE)
He is a useful horse on soft ground as he demonstrated at Newmarket during the Autumn when winning by five lengths. We then made a mistake by running him at Chelmsford three weeks later. The surface was riding quick and he never got to grips with it. Lightly raced, he didn't reappear last year until October, due to a split hind pastern. Despite the fact the handicapper raised him twelve pounds for winning at Newmarket, I think there is still room for improvement. We haven't any specific races in mind but we will be looking towards the decent handicaps.

HAROLD LLOYD 4 b g Cape Cross (IRE) – Silent Act (USA)
A huge horse who has only raced four times. He won at Sandown during the summer and then we felt it would be a good idea to give him a break and let him mature. I have been pleased with him during the winter and he looks in good order. Ideally suited by some cut in the ground, I think ten furlongs is his trip even though there is plenty of stamina on the dam's side of his pedigree. Officially rated 79, I feel he is on a fair mark.

ICONIC (IRE) 4 b f Kodiac – Christa Maria
She looked a promising filly on occasions last season winning her maiden at Salisbury and finishing second in a handicap at Ascot later in the year. Disappointing on her final run at Pontefract, that remains a mystery but she is a year older now and hopefully open to further improvement. A mile suits her well.

LIMATO (IRE) 4 b g Tagula (IRE) – Come April
He was very impressive when winning the Group 2 Park Stakes at Doncaster. That victory was gained over seven furlongs, which is an infuriating distance because there aren't enough high quality races over such a trip. Runner-up on his final start in the Prix de la Foret at Longchamp the following month, he ran well but the race came quick enough after his Doncaster win. Ideally, he wants a good three to four weeks between his races. If we had known the ground was going to be decent at Longchamp, we wouldn't have run him at Doncaster but we didn't expect such conditions in France at that time of year. The plan is to step him up to a mile this year because we are hoping he will stay. With that in mind, he will probably start off in the Lockinge Stakes at Newbury (14th May). He has done well during the winter and I think he will cope better with cut in the ground this year.

OAT COUTURE 4 b f Kyllachy – Oat Cuisine
Still a maiden, she has been a very backward filly who has been slow to mature. Runner-up at Salisbury and Bath, I hope she will improve as a four year old and win races at her level. We will be looking towards six and seven furlongs handicaps.

PERCEIVED 4 ch f Sir Percy – New Light
Twice a winner, she rarely runs a bad race but, as a result, is probably high enough in the ratings. A mile and a half possibly stretched her at Newbury during the summer. Ten furlongs on easy ground is ideal and she proved it when winning under such conditions at Ffos Las on her final start in September.

POSTBAG 4 b f Three Valleys (USA) – Postage Stampe
I am hoping she will have a good year because she has grown and matured from three to four. She won her maiden at Leicester when beating Journey, who subsequently won two Listed races and was runner-up in the Group 1 Fillies and Mares Stakes at Ascot's Champions day meeting. Placed on her next couple of starts, she remains lightly raced and appears to be on a manageable rating. We will almost certainly start her off over a mile but I am keen to see if she will stay a bit further.

SON OF AFRICA 4 b g Equiano (FR) – Generously Gifted
He won well at Newmarket during the summer but was raised nine pounds as a result, which made life much tougher. I thought he ran OK in a Group 3 at Sandown and we decided to geld him after his final run at Ascot. We are hoping that will help and bring about further improvement. Originally bought at the breeze-ups, it took him a while to settle down after that. Indeed, I am not a big fan of horses bought at the breeze-ups. There is no doubt he is a horse with plenty of ability and we will be looking to aim him at the big five and six furlongs handicaps.

SPRING FLING 5 b m Assertive – Twilight Mistress
From a family we know very well being a half-sister to Music Master and Twilight Son amongst others, she isn't the easiest mare to keep sound but she is good on her day. She only raced twice last year, including when finishing sixth in a Listed race at Doncaster on the final day of the season. In fact, I think she would have been even closer had she not been off the track for so long. It would be nice to think she could earn some black type this year.

STOIC BOY 4 ch g Paco Boy (IRE) – Dramatic Turn
He has once only raced three times because it took forever for the penny to drop. However, he ran very well on his final start at Kempton finishing a close third. He will be much more at home on a straight track on the turf this year and I will be disappointed if he can't win sprint races at a modest level.

TWILIGHT SON 4 b c Kyllachy – Twilight Mistress
He enjoyed a fantastic season winning three times, including the Group 1 Betfred Sprint Cup at Haydock in September. He is a horse I have always liked but I never thought he would win at the highest level as a three year old. Two lengths second behind Muhaarar in the Qipco British Champions Sprint at Ascot on Champions Day, the draw didn't do him any favours but he was never going to beat the winner. It was still a very good run, nevertheless. I have been delighted with him during the winter because he has grown and done very well. I am hoping he will improve again because I have always thought this would be his year. Six furlongs with some ease in the ground are his optimum conditions and, in all likelihood, he will start off in the Duke of York Stakes (11th May).

UELE RIVER 4 b f Refuse To Bend (IRE) – Baddi Heights (FR)
An enormous filly, she was still weak and backward last year even though she managed to win at Windsor during the summer. She has always worked nicely at home and I think she is better than she has shown thus far. Her best performances have been over ten furlongs but she is a big long striding filly who ought to stay further. She likes fast ground.

THREE YEAR OLDS

ARTISTS MODEL (IRE) b f Dutch Art – Zarwala (IRE)
We bought her at the breeze-ups during the spring last year and it took her a while to settle down after that. However, she ran well on both her starts on the all-weather at the backend of the year finishing third on each occasion. She has plenty of speed and I hope she will win races over six furlongs this season.

BEAR CHEEK (IRE) b f Kodiac – See Nuala (IRE)
A new addition, she joined us in January having shown a good level of form for Ger Lyons in Ireland last year. A Group 3 winner at the Curragh, she was beaten less than two lengths in the Flying Childers Stakes at Doncaster. Fifth on her final run in the Group 1 Cheveley Park Stakes, she is only small but looks very tough. She has settled in well and will be aimed at the good sprints.

BOUNCE b f Bahamian Bounty – Black Belt Shopper (IRE)
A nice filly who was very impressive when winning on her second start at Kempton in September. She ran well on her debut at Newbury despite the fact things didn't go to plan. James Doyle rode her that day and liked her a lot. She confirmed the promise at Kempton and hopefully she can develop into a black type filly. I would imagine we will enter her in a handicap during the spring and see what mark she is allocated. I think six furlongs will be her trip but she might not want the ground too quick.

FREE PASSAGE ch g Medicean – Free Offer
A half-brother to Cape Peron, he had three runs over seven furlongs at Newmarket last year. The handicapper has given him a mark of 68 and he will be heading down that route. We have gelded him since his last run and he has done very well physically during the winter. I think he will benefit from a step up to a mile and, while he isn't as good as his brother, I hope he will be competitive off his mark.

JACK NEVISON b g Dick Turpin (IRE) – Creative Mind (IRE)
I thought he ran well without winning as a juvenile being placed at Newbury and Sandown on his first couple of starts. Still very immature, especially in the knee department last year, we probably shouldn't have run him but his homework has always been good. He has come back in looking bigger and stronger and I think he is capable of winning a maiden before hopefully progressing as the year goes on. He is a sprinter.

JAUNTY JOH (IRE) b f Zoffany (IRE) – Don't Care (IRE)
Unraced, she is a well bred filly we bought at the breeze-ups. She was unable to run as a juvenile, due to a minor issue, but she is over that now and is a filly I like. I think a mile will be her trip.

LA RIOJA b f Hellvelyn – Talampaya (USA)
A very exciting filly who produced a tremendous performance to win the Group 3 Dick Poole Fillies' Stakes at Salisbury in September. I am keen to avoid very fast ground with her this year, although she doesn't necessarily need it as soft as it was at Salisbury. Andrea Atzeni rode her that day and was impressed with her and felt she was an out and out sprinter, hence we will be staying down that route this year. She may follow a similar programme to Limato last year with the Commonwealth Cup at Royal Ascot an obvious target, although we are obviously aware of the presence of Shalaa, who looked very good as a juvenile. She is a filly we have always liked and we weren't surprised by the progress she made last year.

LIMONATA (IRE) b f Bushranger (IRE) – Come April
A half-sister to Limato, she has developed well during the winter. We gave her one run at Windsor last year but I don't think she was quite right. She is better than she showed that day and, if she can win a race, she will be a valuable filly. I think seven furlongs will be her trip.

MEDICIMAN b c Medicean – Quintrell
Placed at Salisbury and Newmarket in decent maidens, he didn't have much luck at Goodwood in between. He is a nice horse and we will probably go straight down the handicap route and hopefully make the most of his mark, which I feel is reasonable. A mile on fast ground ought to suit him.

NICARRA (IRE) b f Kodiac – Nassma (IRE)
I thought she ran well on her only start at Salisbury finishing fourth. However, I was surprised how green she was during the race, but she finished well and looks a nice filly. We have given her a long break since and I think she will stay a mile this year because there is stamina on the dam's side of her pedigree.

NOBLE PEACE b g Kyllachy – Peace Concluded
He grew a lot last year and has developed into a huge horse. Placed in four of his six races, he ran well in defeat but I don't think he is a sprinter. I think he will come into his own over seven furlongs and a mile this year, although his mark is high enough for what he has achieved.

PAST MASTER b c Mastercraftsman (IRE) – Millestan (IRE)
I thought he ran very well on his debut at Sandown with the penny dropping late on and he finished strongly in third. He wasn't right following his next run at Salisbury and is better than he showed that day. I think he is a nice horse who has done well during the winter. He looks capable of winning his maiden before hopefully going on to better things.

ROSIE ROYCE b f Acclamation – Rebecca Rolfe
The form of her run at Yarmouth has worked out well with the winner subsequently being placed in a Listed race. She has shown enough to suggest she can win races over sprint trips.

SHOWING OFF (IRE) ch g Notnowcato – Walk On Water
He had worked well prior to running an encouraging race on his debut in a seven furlongs maiden at Newmarket during the Autumn. He was never going to be a precocious two year old and can only improve with age. A horse I like, he shouldn't have any problem staying a mile this year.

SQUIGGLEY b f Sir Percy – Oat Cuisine

A half-sister to Oat Couture, she ran a decent race at Salisbury finishing fourth behind Nathra (subsequently second in the Group 1 Fillies' Mile) and Light Music (won her next two, including the Listed Radley Stakes). Slow to mature, I think she will develop into a nice staying filly. She looks capable of winning a maiden before stepping up in grade over ten furlongs plus.

STAR JEANIE b f Kyllachy – Floating

She is a tough little filly who finished second on her debut at Goodwood before going one better at Lingfield next time. Not over big, she suffered a small chip fracture of her knee soon afterwards and missed the remainder of the season. However, she is back in work now and is a nice filly with a good attitude. Officially rated 73, she looks to be on a good mark and I hope she will make an impact in three year old sprint handicaps.

TERESAR (IRE) ch f Dandy Man (IRE) – High Chart

A quick filly who won her maiden at the second attempt at Kempton. She then took her chance in the Group 3 Cornwallis Stakes at Newmarket and, while she ran a respectable race in fifth, I feel she is better than she showed that day. Five furlongs is her trip and we are hoping to win some black type with her.

TIME TO EXCEED (IRE) b f Exceed And Excel (AUS) – In Your Time

Unraced, she was very weak and backward last year. However, she has come back in looking a nice, strong filly.

VIBRANT CHORDS b g Poet's Voice – Lovely Thought

Not very big, he is a nice tough horse who won his maiden at Salisbury before running well in defeat in a couple of nurseries. The form of his run at Haydock has worked out particularly well with the runner-up (Donjuan Triumphant) winning his next three races, including a Listed and Group 2 race. Rated 87, his pedigree suggests seven furlongs will suit him more than six this year. Although he is possibly high enough in the ratings, I hope he will make an impact in the decent three year old handicaps.

TRAINER'S HORSE TO FOLLOW: PAST MASTER

Roger CHARLTON

Stables: Beckhampton House, Marlborough, Wiltshire.
2015: 45 Winners from 280 Runners 16% Prize-Money £767,319
www.rogercharlton.com

OLDER HORSES

AYRAD (IRE) 5 ch h Dalakhani (IRE) – Sweet Firebird (IRE)
A new arrival during the winter, we haven't done a lot with him yet but he has some smart form winning at Listed level last year. I have been pleased with the way he has settled in and, whilst we haven't made any plans, we will obviously be looking towards Listed and Group races over ten furlongs plus.

CAPTAIN CAT (IRE) 7 b or br g Dylan Thomas (IRE) – Mother of Pearl (IRE)
He enjoyed a very good season in 2014 winning three times, including a couple of Group 3 events. However, he found it tough last year. It was therefore pleasing to see him get his head in front again at Kempton during the winter before he finished fifth at Lingfield on Good Friday. A strongly run mile is ideal because ten furlongs appears to stretch him. If things go right, he is a very capable horse.

CLOWANCE ONE 4 b g Oasis Dream – Clowance
Lightly raced, he won a maiden at Kempton towards the backend. We have gelded him and made a few adjustments since his last run, which will hopefully bring about improvement this year. He will be aimed at middle distance handicaps.

DECORATED KNIGHT 4 ch c Galileo (IRE) – Pearling (USA)
Along with Ayrad, he arrived during the winter and appears to have settled in well. Officially rated 107, I have watched a number of his races and he appeared to be quite keen on occasions last year. I think, if he learns to settle, there is no reason why he won't stay a mile and a quarter, although we will probably start him off over a mile. He needs to continue to improve but is still lightly raced.

HUNTSMANS CLOSE 6 b g Elusive Quality (USA) – Badminton
He has made great progress since joining us at the end of the 2013 season winning three times, including the Ayr Silver Cup in 2014 and a decent handicap at Windsor last summer. His form is very solid and being beaten a couple of lengths by Magical Memory in the Stewards' Cup when having too much daylight was a good effort. He got loose at Royal Ascot before the Wokingham, which unnerved him a little, so we have given him a long break and, provided he is happy mentally, he is a capable of winning another big six furlongs handicap.

OOTY HILL 4 gr c Dubawi (IRE) – Mussoorie (FR)
He is in good form at home and I hope he can put last season behind him because things didn't go his way. A winner on his debut at Newmarket as a juvenile, it was possibly a weaker race than we thought at the time. Unfortunately, the handicapper refused to give him a mark and we therefore started him off last season in a conditions race. Runner-up behind subsequent French Oaks winner Star of Seville at Newbury, he ran a race full of promise but the ground was firm and he incurred an injury, which kept him off the track until the Autumn. Disappointing in two runs at Newbury and Newmarket, he didn't finish off either of his races. A huge big backward horse, we have given him a good break and it is a case of a clean piece of paper this year and starting again. Hopefully, he will be on an upward trend this season with ten furlongs being his trip to start with, although I wouldn't rule out stepping him up to a mile and a half.

QUEST FOR MORE (IRE) 6 b g Teofilo (IRE) – No Quest (IRE)
We were delighted with him last season, winning two handicaps including the Northumberland Plate and finishing a neck second in the Goodwood Cup. Officially rated 90 at this time last year, I thought he was at an awkward level and may not be easy to place. However, he stepped up considerably and earned a lot of money last season. He also ran well in the Melbourne Cup getting over from a wide draw. The way the race was run didn't suit him because they crawled and then sprinted. He was still only beaten four lengths and ran up to his form. Two miles on fast ground is ideal and we will be looking towards Listed and Group races. Something like the Sagaro Stakes at Ascot (27th April) is a possible starting point.

TIME TEST 4 b c Dubawi (IRE) – Passage of Time
He had a good season winning three times, including successes at Group 2 and 3 level. The high point of the season came at Royal Ascot in the Tercentenary Stakes when he ran out a very impressive winner, in an impressive time. Ten furlongs on fast ground was ideal. Things didn't necessarily go to plan thereafter because the ground wasn't in his favour in the Juddmonte International Stakes at York. He bounced back in the Joel Stakes at Newmarket over a mile but then we took him to Keeneland for the Breeders' Cup Mile and nothing went right. Drawn wide, the rain arrived beforehand and the ground didn't suit him. We have given him a break since and he has done well from three to four. The majority of Dubawi's improve with age and his first main target is the Prince of Wales's Stakes at Royal Ascot (15th June) with the likelihood of one run beforehand. Although he has the speed for a mile, ten furlongs suits him very well, although it is not impossible he could stay a mile and a half. Granted his favoured conditions, I think there is a valuable race to be won with him.

THREE YEAR OLDS

BANHAM (USA) gr c Exchange Rate (USA) – Palisade (USA)
A half-brother to Sea Defence, who we previously trained before he went to Hong Kong, he isn't as good as him but he is a big scopey colt, who will hopefully progress as a three year old. Still inexperienced last year, he had a couple of runs at Newbury and Chelmsford. I am hoping he will stay ten furlongs.

BATTLEMENT b or gr f Dansili – Scuffle
She is a nice filly who met with a setback last year hence she didn't run as a juvenile. A well bred half-sister to Suffused, she was a promising second on her debut in a seven furlongs maiden at Wolverhampton in March. She will stay a mile, although there is speed in her pedigree.

BLAKENEY POINT b g Sir Percy – Cartoon
A half-brother to Lancashire Oaks winner Lady Tiana, we gave him three runs as a juvenile and he is now qualified for low grade handicaps. He is bred to improve with age and a step up in trip.

CHESTER STREET b c Invincible Spirit (IRE) – Expressive
He ran a promising race on his debut at Leicester but then made hard work of winning his maiden next time at Kempton. The fact he is quite an idle horse ought to help his mark because he is never going to win by a long way. Although he is a half-brother to the Ayr Gold Cup winner Don't Touch, he wasn't the fastest horse last year and it appears he will stay beyond a mile this year. However, if he switches on, that speed may appear.

EXECUTOR b c Cacique (IRE) – Star Cluster
Successful in a weak looking maiden at Bath, his win was gained on very fast ground. Either side of that performance he disappointed on soft ground at Newbury and Newmarket. We therefore feel he wants fast ground and, if that's the case, he is reasonably treated off a mark of 72. I think a mile to ten furlongs will be his trip.

HIGH SHIELDS (IRE) b c Shamardal (USA) – Marine City (JPN)
A big strong colt, he looked one paced over seven furlongs on his debut in a decent maiden at Ascot. Stepping up to a mile next time at Kempton, I thought he was unlucky not to win. There is plenty of stamina on the dam's side of his pedigree so I think he is likely to stay a mile and a half.

IMPERIAL AVIATOR b c Paco Boy (IRE) – Telescopic
He is a progressive horse who surprised us last year. He came into training late in the season but improved a lot in a short space of time. Placed in all three runs, I thought he should have won on his final start at Chelmsford. Only beaten half a length, he lost his position at a crucial stage before running on. Rated 83, we will probably aim him at another maiden. He has something of a mixed pedigree because he is by Paco Boy out of a Galileo mare. It is possible he will stay a mile and a half.

INTERMITTENT b f Cacique (IRE) – Innocent Air
Narrowly beaten on her debut at Leicester in testing conditions, she was runner-up again on her next couple of starts, too, at Lingfield and Wolverhampton. Thankfully, she got her head in front over a mile at the latter venue in March. Quite a free going filly, she is crying out for a step up in trip and is bred to want at least a mile and a quarter.

KINNI b f Dansili – Clowance
A well bred unraced filly who has always shown promise at home. We nearly ran her in the Autumn but decided to give her more time. She has size and scope and is a potentially nice filly out of Clowance and from a stout staying German family. Although she isn't slow, I would expect her to stay at least a mile and a half.

KUANTAN b g Acclamation – Gay Mirage (GER)
He made an encouraging start to his career when finishing second at Nottingham during the Autumn. The ground was soft and I don't know how strong the form is, but he ran a good race and looks capable of winning races. Despite the fact he is by Acclamation, there is stamina on the dam's side of his pedigree. I think a mile to ten furlongs will suit him.

KUMMIYA b or br g Dansili – Balisada
A half-brother to El Salvador and Galactic Star, we thought he would finish in the first four or five on his debut at Newbury but the ground was very soft and he disappointed. However, he stepped up considerably on that next time at Lingfield by winning comfortably. Still green, he didn't have a hard race and has the size and scope to progress as a three year old. His mark looks OK and, with a bit of luck, he will develop into a progressive three year old.

L'ETOILE (IRE) ch g Champs Elysees – Cross Your Fingers (USA)
An attractive unraced horse with a good stride, who should stay well.

MAKZEEM b c Makfi – Kazeem
An immature horse last year, but one that showed some promise. He is very strong and seems to take his work well. Being a half-brother to Al Kazeem, we hope that he progresses as much as he did through the years.

NOBLEWOMAN b f Showcasing – Rare Virtue (USA)
A very big imposing filly, she didn't run last year but I feel she is above average. Built like a sprinter, she has size and scope and ought to be making her debut in a five or six furlongs maiden in April/May.

PACIFIC SALT (IRE) gr c Zebedee – Villa Nova (IRE)
An attractive colt, he is better than he showed on his only run at Windsor in October. He appeared to be overwhelmed by the occasion, plus the ground wasn't ideal. We may look for a maiden on the all-weather with seven furlongs and a mile likely to suit him this year.

PALING b c Zamindar (USA) – Solar Pursuit
Showed very little on his debut at Kempton, but made significant improvement next time at the same track when being awarded the race in the stewards' room. Out of a Galileo mare, he has size and scope and will be running in three year old handicaps over ten furlongs plus.

PROJECTION b g Acclamation – Spotlight
He had a good season winning twice at Windsor and Salisbury and finishing fourth in a valuable sales race at Doncaster's St Leger meeting. He raced against some good opposition throughout the season and I was delighted with his win at Salisbury on his final run when beating some decent horses. Gelded during the winter, he is a fun horse who will be aimed at the good handicaps, plus conditions and Listed races. I think six and seven furlongs will be his trips this year.

PURE FANTASY b f Fastnet Rock (AUS) – Fictitious
She showed promise in three runs last year, including when third at Kempton last time. Bred to improve with age, she ought to stay further than a mile and will hopefully win a race or two off her mark.

PURE VANITY b f New Approach (IRE) – Miss Pinkerton
Bred to improve with age, she showed promise in two starts at Ascot and Wolverhampton. Provided she progresses this year, she ought to win races.

QUICK MARCH b f Lawman (FR) – Strut
From a very good family, being out of Strut, and therefore a half-sister to Mince, Skate and Stomp. She showed progressive form last year. She won her maiden in good style at Windsor but I think it was a rotten race and she lacks the scope of Mince. She will be running in six furlongs handicaps.

ROCKY STEADY (IRE) ch g Intikhab (USA) – Mannsara (IRE)
A fun horse who improved with each start last year, culminating in victory at Wolverhampton at the backend. The handicapper has given him a mark of 78 and it is difficult to say whether he is well treated or otherwise. He belongs to the Owners Group so the intention is to run him as often as possible. I think he will stay a mile.

TRAINER'S HORSE TO FOLLOW: KUMM!YA

Luca CUMANI

Stables: Bedford House Stables, Bury Road, Newmarket, Suffolk.
2015: 52 Winners from 267 Runners 19% Prize-Money £1,649,446
www.lucacumani.com

OLDER HORSES

AL 4 b g Halling (USA) - Incarnation (IRE)
A winner at Newmarket last summer, I thought he was a bit unlucky not to finish closer in the Melrose Stakes at York. Only beaten around four lengths, he found himself in a duel up front a long way from home. I would put a line through his final run at Nottingham because it was too soft for him. We have gelded him during the winter and hopefully that will bring about some more improvement. Trips around a mile and a half and a mile and six suit him and he is on the verge of the good middle distance and staying handicaps off his mark of 82.

BERMONDSEY 4 b g Galileo (IRE) - Barter
A half-brother to our winning juvenile Haggle (currently sidelined and unlikely to return until the second half of the season), he has been gelded during the winter. Still lightly raced, he won his maiden at Haydock before finishing third on his next two runs in handicap company. Ten and twelve furlongs ought to suit him this year, although he needs to improve if he is going to be competing in the big middle distance handicaps.

BESS OF HARDWICK 4 b f Dansili - Request
She is a very well bred filly being a half-sister to Ask but she didn't have much luck last year. A promising third behind Gretchen on her debut at Newmarket in late spring, she then incurred a splint problem which ruled her out for the majority of the season. Returning to action at Wolverhampton in October, she won easily. We were going to run her again at the backend but she suffered another splint on her other leg. She is a talented filly so we are hoping for an injury free year this time. Officially rated 87, we haven't decided which route she will take initially but the long-term aim is to gain some black type.

KOORA 4 b f Pivotal - Kithanga (IRE)
A good filly who was progressive last year winning twice, including the Group 3 St Simon Stakes at Newbury during the Autumn. Runner-up in the Galtres Stakes at York earlier in the season, she didn't stay a mile and six in the Park Hill Stakes at Doncaster. Despite winning over a mile and a half at Newbury, it wouldn't surprise me if she dropped back to ten furlongs this year. She will continue in Group races and, while she is untested on fast ground, I don't think testing conditions are a necessity for her. She proved at Doncaster when winning her maiden she has no trouble with good ground.

LAURENCE 4 b g Dubawi (IRE) - Victoire Celebre (USA)
He did nothing wrong as a three year old winning twice, including a decent handicap at Beverley. Effective over a mile and ten furlongs, he has been gelded since last year and I hope he can improve again. He will be aimed at the good handicaps.

MIZZOU (IRE) 5 b h Galileo (IRE) - Moments of Joy
A useful stayer, he won the Sagaro Stakes at Ascot during the spring before finishing seventh in the Ascot Gold Cup. Things didn't go to plan that day because it was a slowly run race and he found himself out of position. A good second in the Lonsdale Cup at York next time, he missed the Champions day meeting at Ascot due to a minor injury. Despite his win at Ascot, the track doesn't ideally suit him because he prefers a long home straight. I would think he will follow a similar programme this year.

PAMONA (IRE) 4 b f Duke of Marmalade (IRE) - Palanca

Third in the Ribblesdale Stakes at Royal Ascot, she was also placed three times at Listed level last year. I have been pleased with her during the winter because she appears to have matured. She is a Listed/Group 3 filly and will be campaigned accordingly. Ten or twelve furlongs suits her.

SECOND STEP (IRE) 5 b g Dalakhani (IRE) - My Dark Rosaleen

He enjoyed a very good season winning the Group 2 Jockey Club Stakes at Newmarket and a Group 1 in Germany during the summer. He picked up a minor injury in the Canadian International at Woodbine on his final run but he is 100% again now. A notch below top-class, he will follow a similar programme and there is every possibility he will reappear in the Jockey Club Stakes (30th April) once again.

SHAKOPEE 4 b g High Chaparral (IRE) - Tentpole (USA)

Lightly raced, he won at Leicester as a juvenile and then finished an encouraging second at Newmarket on his return to action last year. Unfortunately, he suffered an injury afterwards and missed the remainder of the season. Back in work, he is a decent horse who will be aimed at the good ten and twelve furlongs handicaps.

THREE YEAR OLDS

AL KHAFJI b c New Approach (IRE) - Wadaat

A winner on his final start at Lingfield over seven furlongs, the handicapper raised him eight pounds. However, he is the sort of horse to progress as a three year old and I think he will pay his way. We will be aiming him at ten furlongs plus handicaps.

BANKSEA b c Lawman (FR) - Stars In Your Eyes

He surprised us when winning on his debut at Yarmouth in September. Our more fancied runner was withdrawn at the start and I am not sure it was a particularly strong race. However, he ran OK in a nursery at Newmarket next time finishing third. He has the ability to progress and his mark looks fair. I would think he is most likely to start off over a mile this year.

BEAUTIFUL MORNING b f Galileo (IRE) - Date With Destiny (IRE)

A very promising filly who won well on her second start at York's Ebor meeting. We then aimed her at the Fillies' Mile at Newmarket in early October but she went weak beforehand. While she wasn't disgraced in fifth, she was going through a growing phase at the time. She has strengthened up during the winter and, while we haven't made any definite plans, I don't view her as a Guineas filly at this stage. I think she will want further than a mile, although she isn't guaranteed to stay a mile and a half because there is plenty of speed on the dam's side of her pedigree.

BLIND FAITH (IRE) ch f Zoffany (IRE) - Guajira (FR)

An unraced half-sister to Gabrial, she is a big filly who grew a lot last year. Too weak to run, she did a few nice pieces of work and pleased us. She is an unknown quantity but has shown ability at home.

CRYPTIC (IRE) br g Lord Shanakill (USA) - Privet (IRE)

Something of a surprise package, he disappointed on his first two runs but ran much better next time at Wolverhampton. He then won a nursery at Kempton on his handicap debut and has been raised five pounds since. A slow learner, we have gelded him and I hope he will be a fun horse over trips around a mile.

EL VIP (IRE) b c Pivotal - Elle Danzig (GER)

A promising unraced colt who is from a very good middle distance family. He was due to make his debut at Yarmouth in the same maiden won by Banksea but was lame beforehand and had to be withdrawn. His quality of work beforehand had been good and he has the potential to be a very nice horse. Unfortunately, he injured himself in February/March and therefore won't be running until much later in the year.

FARANDINE ch f Rock of Gibraltar (IRE) – Rivara
A nice filly who ran well on her debut at Newmarket finishing second. She didn't enjoy the all-weather at Kempton next time before winning in good style at Newmarket in October. She is a promising filly who we bought back at the December Sales for new clients and, while she is likely to reappear in a handicap, we are hoping she is another who can gain some black type later in the year. She shouldn't have any problem staying a mile and may get a bit further, too.

FOUR ON EIGHT gr c Lawman (FR) – Pocket Watch
A nice, genuine, straightforward colt who won his maiden at the third attempt at Windsor before finishing a creditable third in a nursery at Newmarket. Rated 81, he looks capable of winning more races this year and looks the sort to pay his way in handicaps.

MATERIALISTIC b f Oasis Dream – Pongee
A very nice filly from a family we know well, she won her only start at Newmarket last backend. We are hoping she will be one of our leading three year old fillies this year and the plan is to start her off in a Guineas trial. I have been pleased with her during the winter and I think a mile will suit her, although she is bred to stay further.

MYOPIC b f Teofilo (IRE) – Blinking
She is a big, long striding filly who ran very well at Leicester on her debut when finishing a close second. Only beaten half a length, she has potential to develop into a nice filly who is bred to stay. We will start her off in a ten furlongs fillies' maiden in the spring.

PACHARANA b f Oasis Dream – Cascata (IRE)
A full-sister to Richard of Yorke, she has always promised to do something but hasn't delivered in two runs so far. She was still weak last year though and is bred to improve as a three year old.

ROYAL MAHOGANY (IRE) b c Kodiac – Chiba (UAE)
Sixth on his sole outing as a juvenile at Lingfield, he isn't a black type horse in the making but I will be disappointed if he can't win races at his level. Seven furlongs or a mile ought to be his trip this year.

TIPTREE (IRE) b f Duke of Marmalade (IRE) – Taking Liberties (IRE)
A promising filly who finished seventh on her debut at Nottingham before winning in good style at Newmarket. She is a really likeable filly who has black type potential. Her pedigree suggests she will stay well and it is possible she will develop into an Oaks filly. She has pleased me during the winter and, being a big, long striding filly, she gives the impression she will come into her own over middle distances this year.

VERY DASHING br f Dansili – Dash To The Top
From a family we know well, she is a nice filly who I think bumped into a good one (Zest) at Doncaster on her second run. Beaten less than a length, she is a promising sort who ought to win her maiden without too much trouble. A mile and a half should be within her compass but she is likely to start off over ten furlongs.

VUELA ch f Duke of Marmalade (IRE) – Victoire Finale
An unknown quantity, she is well related but was too weak to race last year.

WAR STORY (IRE) gr c Myboycharlie (IRE) – America Nova (FR)
Beaten by a more experienced rival on his debut at Kempton, the form has worked out well with the third winning next time. He will be suited by a step up to a mile this year and ought to win races.

TRAINER'S HORSE TO FOLLOW: FOUR ON EIGHT

James FANSHAWE

Stables: Pegasus Stables, Snailwell Road, Newmarket, Suffolk.
2015: 45 Winners from 252 Runners 18% Prize-Money £548,353
www.jamesfanshawe.com

OLDER HORSES

ARTHENUS 4 b g Dutch Art – Lady Hen
Very immature as a young horse, he really got the hang of things towards the end of last year winning his final three races. We gelded him during the summer, he got stronger and has thrived ever since. He has got to a rating of 100 very quickly and, while we haven't made any plans, I hope he will make the transition to a higher level. A winner over nine furlongs at York in October, I think he may stay a mile and a quarter this year. He possesses a good turn of foot and enjoys some cut in the ground.

ESTEEMABLE 4 ch f Nayef (USA) – Ring of Esteem
She ran well on her second start at Kempton in August and the form looks strong (winner has won twice more since). She was unable to run again last year, due to a minor problem, but was back in action during the winter winning twice over a mile at Lingfield. Raised six pounds since her last win, she remains lightly raced and I hope she can win again before being covered. I think she may stay a bit further, too.

FLY 4 ch f Pastoral Pursuits – Hannda (IRE)
Unbeaten in three races, she is owned and bred by Tim Vestey, who has been with us since I started training. A half-sister to Gale Force and Seal of Approval, the dam has produced a lot of good horses and this filly is the latest one. She didn't make her debut until September but she got her act together in the Autumn winning all three of her races. Despite that, I feel there is still some mileage in her rating and she is from a family who improve with age. She may stay further in time but we will keep her to a mile for the time being.

HIGHER POWER 4 b g Rip Van Winkle (IRE) – Lady Stardust
Owned and bred by my sister, he ran two good races during the first half of last season but I wasn't happy with my horses during the spring. Runner-up at Nottingham last time, he jarred himself soon afterwards. We decided to geld him and give him plenty of time off. He has come back in looking much more the finished article and I am looking forward to seeing him run this year. Suited by some cut in the ground, he stays a mile and a quarter and may get further.

HIGH JINX (IRE) 8 b g High Chaparral (IRE) – Leonara (GER)
Fourth in the Prix De Barbeville at Longchamp in May, he suffered a stress fracture behind soon afterwards. While it wasn't a major injury, it was enough to keep him off for the remainder of the season. A Group 1 winner the previous season, he has been a great horse for the yard over the years earning nearly £500,000 in prize-money. He came back into work in March and the plan is to give him a late summer/Autumn campaign.

HORS DE COMBAT 5 ch g Mount Nelson – Maid For Winning (USA)
Even though he ran well when finishing second in the Listed Paradise Stakes and Group 3 Criterion Stakes at Ascot and Newmarket respectively, we never had him spot on last year. We gelded him at the end of the previous season and I think it took him a long time to get over it. Despite running such a good race in the Criterion Stakes over seven furlongs, a mile on good or fast ground is ideal. I have been pleased with him during the winter. He looks well and, granted a bit of luck, I am sure there is a Group race to be won with him.

KNIGHT OWL 6 b g Rock of Gibraltar (IRE) - Miss Ivanhoe (IRE)
Owned by Craig Bennett's wife Annabelle Condon, he is a horse with plenty of ability and he raced more consistently last year. A winner at Kempton at the backend, he is likely to start off in the Suffolk Stakes over nine furlongs at Newmarket's Guineas meeting (30th April).

LANDWADE LAD 4 b g Dansili - Sell Out
Not the biggest of horses, he is useful on his day and was a winner at Kempton last season. Raised ten pounds for that victory, he was consistent throughout the year and kept climbing the ratings. Owned by Simon Gibson, of Society Rock fame, we are hoping he will stay a mile and a half this time. His family loved soft ground so the plan is to run him on the turf during the spring. Officially rated 88, he is on a stiff enough mark so we may use our apprentice George Wood, who will take a few pounds off his back.

MISSED CALL (IRE) 6 b m Authorized (IRE) - Incoming Call (USA)
She always looked good at home after joining us during the second half of 2014 but never really reproduced it on the track. It also took her a while to come to herself last year. However, having been a bit unlucky at Goodwood, she was given a very good ride by Emma-Jayne Wilson to win at the Shergar Cup meeting at Ascot. She thrived thereafter finishing third in the Group 3 Cumberland Lodge Stakes behind Star Storm and then winning a Listed event at Kempton on her final run. The fact she is still rated 98 gives us a few options and there is every possibility she will return to Ascot because she loves it there. She seems to come into her own during the second half of the season.

MODERAH 4 b f Makfi - Meetyouthere (IRE)
I have been delighted with her during the winter because she has done well from three to four. Still a frame last year, she took forever to thrive. A five lengths winner at Leicester in September, we then had the Group 3 St Simon Stakes at Newbury in mind for a while and she finished a very creditable third and was only beaten a couple of lengths. She loves cut in the ground and is well suited by twelve furlongs. She will continue down the Pattern route. She is owned by Salem Bel Obaida. He and his father have been very good supporters of the yard over the years.

MR PICKWICK 4 b g Mount Nelson - Never Lose
A big, scopey horse (16.3hh), he ran one or two promising races last year but got himself in a state on more than one occasion. We have therefore gelded him and I hope that will bring about some improvement. A good moving horse, he has the scope to progress and, while his pedigree suggests he will be at his best over a mile, I am hoping he stays further.

RETURN ACE 4 b f Zamindar (USA) - Match Point
She improved as the season went on last year winning twice at Kempton before finishing third at Newmarket. Her family got better with age and we are hoping she will do likewise and gain some black type at some stage. The penny dropped halfway through last season and she didn't look back. She enjoys some cut in the ground and is in good form at home at the moment. A mile and a half is her trip at the moment but I don't see why she won't stay further.

SPEEDY BOARDING 4 b f Shamardal (USA) - Dash To The Front
A filly we have always liked and, having won her maiden at Goodwood from Journey (subsequently won 2 Listed races and finished runner-up in the Group 1 Fillies & Mares Stakes at Ascot), she won a Listed race at Newbury. We then ran her in the Irish Oaks and, while she ran well in fifth, the race may have come too soon in her career. She then suffered with a bout of ringworm and was never the same thereafter. Despite that, she was only beaten half a length in another Listed race at Yarmouth and then the ground was too soft at Ascot on her final run. A big, rangy filly, we are hoping she will progress again as a four year old. I think ten furlongs may be her optimum trip.

SPIRIT RAISER (IRE) 5 b m Invincible Spirit (IRE) - Macadamia (IRE)
A dual winner over a mile at Kempton last season, she is owned by Lord Vestey and is from the family of Macadamia, who won the Royal Hunt Cup and Falmouth Stakes for us. She is a big, strong filly and we are going to try and win some black type with her this year. She has the ability to do so and we feel a mile is her optimum trip.

STAR STORM (IRE) 4 b c Sea The Stars (IRE) - Sayyedati Storm (USA)
Still a maiden in early September, he ended last season with three wins, including in the Group 3 Cumberland Lodge Stakes at Ascot. It took forever for the penny to drop, although he endured a hard race in the Listed Glasgow Stakes at Hamilton in July. He won his maiden at Haydock before following up in a handicap at Yarmouth less than a fortnight later. Stepped up in grade, it may not have been the strongest renewal of the Cumberland Lodge but he hacked up and couldn't have been more impressive. We haven't mapped out his programme yet but a race like the Coronation Cup at Epsom (4th June) is a possibility. He has the scope to improve again and we are looking forward to his four year old career.

THAI NOON (IRE) 4 b f Dansili - Alsace Lorraine (IRE)
Out of Alsace Lorraine, who we trained to win the Listed Upavon Stakes a few years ago, she is a strong scopey filly who took a long time to come to herself and didn't start racing until October last year. She had a few niggles, too, but she won her maiden at the backend of the year and we have given her a break since. Her dam didn't win until she was four and improved with age. We are hoping this filly will do likewise.

THE TIN MAN 4 b g Equiano (FR) - Persario
A progressive horse, he is a half-brother to Deacon Blues and is from a family who take a bit of time to reach their peak. Sixth on his debut at Doncaster, we decided to geld him because he wasn't concentrating. He has always looked nice and we considered entering him in the Commonwealth Cup at Royal Ascot but the race came too soon in his career. He won his maiden at Doncaster and followed up at the same track in a handicap. A bit flat next time at York, he returned to form at Ascot in another handicap and hacked up by nearly five lengths. We then decided to supplement him (had been entered originally but took him out following his run at York) for the Group 1 Qipco British Champions Sprint Stakes at Ascot and he ran a cracking race in fourth. While he wouldn't have beaten the winner, Tom (Queally) felt he would have finished closer had he got a bit more cover and experience. Still lightly raced, his family improved with age and he is an exciting prospect for this year. I think it is a case of aiming him at the Diamond Jubilee Stakes at Royal Ascot (18th June) and working backwards in the first half of the season. I have been pleased with him during the winter and he looks well.

UP IN LIGHTS (IRE) 4 ch f Makfi - Spotlight
Twice a winner last season, she surprised us when making a winning debut at Nottingham because she had been free beforehand. However, she grew up a lot and won a handicap at Yarmouth later in the summer. She has a nice pedigree being from the family of Dust Dancer and I think she will stay a mile and a quarter this year. The aim is to get some black type but she doesn't want firm ground. A bit of ease is ideal without it being bottomless.

THREE YEAR OLDS

ALWAYS SUMMER b f Flatter (USA) - Air Kiss
Owned by Dr Catherine Wills, she is from a good staying family including Invermark, who won the Group 1 Prix du Cadran for us. Unraced, she has shown ability at home and will improve as the year goes on.

BLUES SISTER b f Compton Place – Persario
From a family which has been very good to the yard, she is an unraced full-sister to Deacon Blues and a half-sister to If So and The Tin Man. She had a few niggles last year but she looks well and has developed during the winter. Built like a sprinter, she is strong and has inherited some of the family's ability. Bred to improve with age, I think she will want some ease in the ground. All being well, she will make her debut in the spring.

COLUMN b c Mount Nelson – Tottie
Following an encouraging run on his debut at Leicester, he won impressively at Beverley next time scoring by eight lengths. Indeed, I could have killed Freddie (Tylicki) afterwards for winning by too far! The form of the race hasn't worked out but he couldn't have won any easier. The handicapper hasn't given him a mark so we haven't made any plans for him yet. Light framed last year, he has filled out during the winter and is a nice prospect. I think he will be suited by a mile this year because I am not sure he will stay much further even though he is out of a Fantastic Light mare. He is a very good moving horse and one with plenty of talent.

ENMESHING ch g Mastercraftsman (IRE) – Yacht Club (USA)
He is a nice unraced horse who had a minor niggle last year hence he didn't race. However, he had been going well prior to that. Owned by Mr (Ben) Wong, he will ultimately end up in Hong Kong but hopefully he will win races beforehand.

FILUMENA ch f Pivotal – Phillipina
She comes from the family of Cesare and is an attractive unraced daughter of Pivotal. A big, strong filly, her dam was runner-up in the Cheshire Oaks for Sir Michael Stoute. I think she will favour some ease in the ground.

INDULGED b f Teofilo (IRE) – Fondled
A tall, rangy unraced filly who is from the same family as Filumena. She is a very good mover and a nice filly. She has shown ability but has taken time to come to herself. I think she will improve as the season goes on. We will probably start her off over ten furlongs but she ought to stay a mile and a half.

KING OF NAPLES b g Excellent Art – Avon Lady
Out of a very tough mare who improved with age, he is owned by Paul Ryan who is a financial director of Tattersalls. He showed promise on his only outing at Wolverhampton and will come into his own over seven furlongs and a mile with some cut in the ground this year.

LORD GEORGE (IRE) 3 gr c Sir Percy – Mahima (FR)
Third on his debut at Salisbury, we then had the option of running him at Wolverhampton or York in early October and decided on the former. He won by a neck but the handicapper hasn't taken any chance giving him a mark of 81. However, he has got plenty of scope and I think he will stay ten furlongs this season. A very good moving horse, he may not want it too soft on the turf.

MAZZINI ch c Exceed And Excel (AUS) – Firenze
Owned and bred by Peter Hopper and Mike Morris, he is from a family we know very well, including Frizzante and Zidane. A laid back colt, we hadn't done a great deal with him prior to his debut at Kempton in December. He fluffed the start but flew home and was only beaten a neck by a more experienced winner. By a good sire, he is a powerful colt who looks a sprinter. He is a nice prospect.

NOBLE STAR (IRE) b c Acclamation – Wrong Answer
A nice unraced colt, a small problem prevented him from running last year. However, he has shown ability at home and has a good pedigree.

PERMISSION b f Authorized (IRE) – Continua (USA)
An attractive unraced half-sister to Charlie Hills' smart sprinter Cotai Glory, she is owned and bred by Julia Scott. Unlike her brother, I don't think she is going to be a sprinter and she may need a bit of time. Indeed, I am expecting her to improve as the season goes on.

PRINCESSE EVA (FR) b f Manduro (GER) – Wing Stealth (IRE)
A half-sister to dual Group 1 winner Covert Love, Philippa Cooper bought her at the Arqana Sale in France in December. She only raced four times over there and her pedigree and make and shape suggest she will stay at least ten furlongs. I think she will progress once the warmer weather arrives.

REGICIDE b c Archipenko (USA) – Armoise
Owned by Chris Van Hoorn, he was unable to run as a juvenile due to a small setback. He is 100% now though and we are hoping he will be making his debut in April. Although he is bred to stay ten furlongs, he shows speed at home and I would think he will start off over a mile.

REPLENISH (FR) ch c Le Havre (IRE) – Brambleberry
We bought him at the breeze-ups during the spring last year having been recommended to us by his consignor Con Marnane. He improved with every run and produced a tough performance to win his maiden at Kempton in the Autumn. A winner over seven furlongs, he will be suited by a return to a mile now he is a year older. We will be looking towards one mile handicaps but he may not want very fast ground.

SAM MISSILE (IRE) b c Smart Strike (CAN) – Kitty Matcham (IRE)
Purchased by Federico Barberini and Apple Tree Stud at the breeze-ups, he is a horse with one of the best pedigrees in the book. It took a while for him to come to himself and he hadn't done much before making his debut at Kempton in January. He couldn't have won much easier though when scoring by six lengths. We are hoping he could develop into a black type horse. He will be back in action in the spring and we are likely to start him off over a mile and a quarter.

STONEY BROKE b f Dansili – Alvee (IRE)
Owned and bred by Craig Bennett, she hails from a very successful family and I am a big fan of her sire. I thought she produced a really tough performance to win on her debut at Nottingham and she has the pedigree to progress as a three year old. I would expect her to reappear over ten furlongs but a mile and a half ought to be well within her compass.

TEGARA ch f Hard Spun (USA) – Damaniyat Girl (USA)
She slightly surprised us when running so well on her debut in a seven furlongs maiden at Newmarket because she doesn't show a lot at home. By Hard Spun, there is speed in her pedigree and she is a filly with a lot of quality. I think fast ground will bring out the best in her because she is a very good mover. We will look for another seven furlongs maiden to begin with.

ZEST (IRE) b f Duke of Marmalade (IRE) – Affinity
Beaten a short head on her debut at Haydock, she did everything wrong next time at Doncaster but still won comfortably. There was no pace and she was keen early on and what pleased me the most was the fact Freddie (Tylicki) had a job pulling her up afterwards. She comes from a superb family, including Soviet Song and Ribbons. She is owned and bred by Elite Racing Club, who have produced some wonderful horses for the yard over the years. Her dam won over a mile and a half for Sir Henry Cecil and she is bred to stay ten furlongs but I am not certain she will. Officially rated 84, we haven't made any plans but black type is obviously the aim. Both her races have been on easy ground and I don't think she would want it too firm. Having said that, I don't think it will be as crucial as it was for Ribbons.

TRAINER'S HORSE TO FOLLOW: SAM MISSILE

William HAGGAS

Stables: Somerville Lodge, Fordham Road, Newmarket, Suffolk.

2015: 102 Winners from 508 Runners 20% Prize-Money £2,287,979

OLDER HORSES

ADAAY (IRE) 4 b c Kodiac - Lady Lucia (IRE)

He is a smart horse who enjoyed a good season last year winning three times, including the Group 2 Sandy Lane Stakes at Haydock and Hungerford Stakes at Newbury. His win in the latter event was his first run over seven furlongs and Sheikh Hamdan (Al Maktoum) is keen to step him up to a mile this year. The Lockinge Stakes at Newbury (14th May) is his first big target but he will have a run beforehand. The Bet365 Mile at Sandown (22nd April) or King Richard III Stakes at Leicestershire (23rd April) are possible starting points. He has a nice way of racing and we feel he could improve again when tackling a mile. Ideally, he likes a bit of cut in the ground.

AFJAAN (IRE) 4 b g Henrythenavigator (USA) - Elusive Galaxy (IRE)

A fine big horse, he is lightly raced and talented. He, unfortunately, fractured his pelvis in the spring last year hence he didn't reappear until early October. Twice a winner at Beverley and Wolverhampton, he won in good style on the latter occasion but was lame afterwards. Back in work, we haven't made any plans but we feel there is some mileage in his mark and he will be campaigned in seven furlongs and one mile handicaps.

DAWN MISSILE 4 b g Nayef (USA) - Ommadawn (IRE)

He is a decent horse who likes fast ground. Successful in three of his first four races, he is rated 94 which means he will get in the good middle distances handicaps this year. Suited by a mile and a half and a mile and six, he looks tailormade for something like the Old Newton Cup at Haydock (2nd July).

FOREVER POPULAR (USA) 4 b or br f Dynaformer (USA) - Pussycat Doll (USA)

I like her and feel she is well treated off a mark of 82. Runner-up on her first two runs, including behind subsequent Listed and Group 2 winner Gretchen at Newmarket in May, she then won at Chepstow. Disappointing next time at Ascot, she suffered a fracture which sidelined her for the remainder of the season. She is 100% now and has done well during the winter. A lurker for this season, her dam was a good filly and we have kept her in training because we would love to gain some black type with her this year.

HATHAL (USA) 4 ch c Speightstown (USA) - Sleepytime (IRE)

He is a smart horse who was never right last year, although he came good on his final start in a Listed race at Newbury. He showed what a good horse he is that day. Prior to that, he had run well in a competitive three year old handicap at York's Ebor meeting. Earlier in the season, he suffered an injury which meant he didn't reappear until June. He wants some cut in the ground and I think he is definitely a Group horse in the making. His win at Newbury was gained over seven furlongs but I think a mile suits him better. If he stays sound, he has the potential to be a very good horse.

MITRAAD (IRE) 5 ch g Aqlaam - Badweia (USA)

A very talented horse, he has had his problems over the years but I thought he was impressive when winning at Newmarket last summer. Unlucky not to follow up at Chelmsford, he is good fresh and enjoys nice ground. We will be aiming him at the big one mile handicaps with the Royal Hunt Cup (15th June) an obvious target.

MUFFRI'HA (IRE) 4 b f Iffraaj - Grecian Dancer
She is a useful filly who won at Lingfield last season and was fourth in a couple of Listed races at Newmarket and Ascot. We have kept her in training to contest more Pattern races and hopefully enhance her value. The Group 3 Chartwell Stakes at Lingfield (7th May) is one race we have in mind for her and then, all being well, the Duke of Cambridge Stakes at Royal Ascot (15th June).

MUTAKAYYEF 5 ch g Sea The Stars (IRE) - Infallible
I have always loved him even though he has only won one race throughout his career. Despite that, I haven't lost faith in him and a gelding operation during the winter will hopefully help. Placed in his three races last year, he is a galloper who wants fast ground. We have been running him over nine and ten furlongs, but I think he will benefit from dropping back to a mile. He may even reappear over seven furlongs in the Listed King Richard III Stakes at Leicester (23rd April) and then he will probably be given an entry in the Queen Anne Stakes at Royal Ascot.

MUTHMIR (IRE) 6 b g Invincible Spirit (IRE) - Fairy of The Night (IRE)
I was pleased with him last year winning a couple of Group 2 races, including the Qatar King George Stakes at Glorious Goodwood. It was his first season competing in Pattern races and he was only beaten half a length in the King's Stand Stakes at Royal Ascot and was also third in the Prix de L'Abbaye at Longchamp. Five furlongs on fast ground is ideal and he wants plenty of cover in his races. Third in a Listed race at Lingfield in February and a running on fifth in the Group 1 Al Quoz Sprint at Meydan the following month, he will follow a similar programme, although he may contest the Temple Stakes at Haydock (21st May) this time before heading back to Royal Ascot. He is capable of winning a Group 1 race this season.

PICK YOUR CHOICE 4 b g Elusive Quality (USA) - Enticement
Although I don't think he is a stakes horse in the making, he is a nice handicapper who has only raced four times. A winner at Chelmsford last year, he was inclined to be keen in his races but isn't short of ability. We decided to operate on his wind because he was making a noise and he sprung a rib during the winter, which means he won't be running until later in the season. Seven furlongs and a mile is ideal.

PREDOMINANCE (IRE) 4 b g Danehill Dancer (IRE) - Gilded Vanity (IRE)
He didn't make his debut until September last year having suffered a fracture early on, plus he was slow to come to hand. A six lengths winner at Chepstow, he was unlucky not to follow up at Newbury next time. Fourth on his final run over seven furlongs at Doncaster, he likes soft ground and wants a mile. A race like the Spring Cup at Newbury (16th April) could suit him. I think he will develop into a very solid one mile handicapper on soft ground.

SEALIFE (IRE) 4 b f Sea The Stars (IRE) - Bitooh
She has only raced four times, winning twice at Windsor and Nottingham. We have kept her in training because we feel she has more to offer and we think she will do well this year. Although she is effective over a mile, ten furlongs is her optimum trip.

SQUATS (IRE) 4 b g Dandy Man (IRE) - Light Sea (IRE)
A useful juvenile, he struggled a bit last season but I think he will do well as a four year old and develop into a solid handicapper. He loves Ascot and the Wokingham Stakes at the Royal meeting is his target (18th June).

VALLEY OF FIRE 4 b g Firebreak – Charlie Girl
He, too, was a useful two year old but wasn't right last season and only raced twice. We have always liked him and I think he could have a good four year old season. He has been gelded and we feel he will benefit from stepping up to seven furlongs and even a mile this year. I can see him developing into an Ascot handicap type. He wants quick ground.

WONDER LAISH 4 b c Halling (USA) – Wonder Why (GER)
One of my favourites, I love him. Things didn't go to plan on his final start at Newmarket but he still had a good year winning at Lingfield and dead heating in a heritage handicap at Ascot in September. We will be aiming him at the good twelve furlongs handicaps and, although he is possibly better racing left-handed, the Duke of Edinburgh Stakes at Royal Ascot (17th June) is an obvious target. He does prefer some cut in the ground though.

YORKER (SAF) 6 b h Jet Master (SAF) – Little Indian (SAF)
A three times Grade 1 winner in South Africa, he joined us last Autumn and is a very good horse. He has had a few issues since arriving but, if we can keep him right, I think he will have a good season. He likes fast ground and a mile is his minimum trip. Something like the Group 2 Summer Mile at Ascot (9th July) and the Group 3 Strensall Stakes at York (20th August) are races we will consider for him.

THREE YEAR OLDS

AJAYA b c Invincible Spirit (IRE) – Nessina (USA)
A useful juvenile last year, he won twice at York, including the Group 2 Gimcrack Stakes. Fourth in the Middle Park Stakes on his final run, he is very fast and sprinting is his game. Not over big, his main summer target is the Commonwealth Cup at Royal Ascot (17th June) with the Duke of York Stakes (11th May) a likely stepping stone. Five and six furlongs on fastish ground is ideal.

ASAMA BLUE (IRE) b f Fastnet Rock (AUS) – Butterfly Blue (IRE)
She is a big scopey galloping filly who was too backward to race last year. Physically, she has changed a lot from two to three and, while we are hoping to start her off over a mile, she should stay further.

BARJEEL (USA) br c Speightstown (USA) – Listen To My Song (USA)
He is a big, strapping, unraced colt who cost $500,000 as a yearling. He goes well and we will probably start him off over seven furlongs or a mile. I like him and he should enjoy fast ground.

BEDROCK b g Fastnet Rock (AUS) – Gemstone (IRE)
He hasn't done a lot wrong and is a horse with a lot of bone. Despite the fact he won on easy ground at Newbury on his final run, I don't think he is a soft ground horse. He basically outstayed the opposition at Newbury and wants further than six and a half furlongs. I think he will improve when tackling a mile this year. We ran him in a valuable sales race at Newmarket on his second start, but it was too much for him at that stage in his career.

BESHARAH (IRE) b f Kodiac – Dixieland Kiss (USA)
A very good juvenile, she won four times and was really impressive in the Lowther Stakes at York. She likes to race and the fact she had to wait nearly six weeks between the Lowther and Cheveley Park Stakes didn't suit her. Beaten less than a length at Newmarket, she kept on at the finish and, while she isn't certain to stay a mile, we are going to train her with the Guineas in mind. She will either reappear in the Nell Gwyn at Newmarket (12th April) or Fred Darling Stakes at Newbury (16th April) and then we will decide whether to run in the Guineas or not. Ease in the ground holds no fears for her and she likes a flat track. Physically, she hasn't changed much during the winter. If she doesn't stay, then the Commonwealth Cup at Royal Ascot (17th June) is an obvious summer target.

BREDA CASTLE ch f Dutch Art – Ice Palace
An unraced half-sister to Queen of Ice, she hasn't shown much at home but is a well bred filly. She is likely to start off over a mile.

CARENOT (IRE) b f Iffraaj – Sahara Sky (IRE)
Another well bred filly being a half-sister to Group 1 winner Dick Whittington, the first priority is to win a race with her. She is not a bad filly finishing second on both her starts last year at Salisbury and York. She got further back than ideal on the latter occasion before running on at the finish. I would expect her to stay a mile this season.

COHERENT (IRE) b c Rip Van Winkle (IRE) – Hold Off (IRE)
Tall and leggy last year, he has improved physically during the winter. Runner-up at Kempton on his second run, he won an ordinary maiden at Wolverhampton next time and needs to improve this year. Having said that, his mark looks OK and I think he will stay a mile and a quarter.

CURRICULUM b g New Approach (IRE) – Superstar Leo (IRE)
From a very good family being out of Superstar Leo, he is a half-brother to Enticing and Sentaril amongst others. He ran well finishing fourth on his only start at Newmarket, although I don't think it was a strong maiden. In fact, we were keener on our other runner in the race who only finished ninth (Mujaamil). Backward last year, he is a useful horse who is capable of winning a maiden. He should stay a mile this year.

DAPHNE b f Duke of Marmalade (IRE) – Daring Aim
She is a nice filly who was very green on her debut at Newbury last backend. I was pleased with the way she finished though and I think she will stay well this year. A half-sister to Bold Sniper, who was placed twice at Royal Ascot, she will reappear in a ten furlongs maiden but will have no trouble staying a mile and a half plus. I think she is a useful filly.

DAWN HORIZONS b f New Approach (IRE) – Hidden Hope
A nice unraced half-sister to our Listed Galtres Stakes winner Our Obsession, she was backward last year and then had a minor setback at the end of the season. She therefore didn't come back into work until later than the others and won't be running until the summer. A very nice mover, she will make her debut in a ten furlongs maiden.

DUTCH DESTINY b f Dutch Art – Danehill Destiny
I think she is a useful filly who is rated 81. A fast finishing second on her debut at Kempton, she confirmed the promise at Salisbury next time and won well. We toyed with the idea of running her in a Listed race at the backend but she went lame so we put her away for the winter. She will start off in a handicap or two but I feel she could be a stakes filly in the making. Both her races last year came over seven furlongs but she could get faster as she gets older. She clearly handles soft ground well but I don't know about a quicker surface.

DWIGHT D b c Duke of Marmalade (IRE) – Almatinka (IRE)
A strong galloping horse, he won his maiden by nine lengths at Wolverhampton in January. The handicapper has given him a mark in the low 80s but he could take his chance in the Sandown Classic Trial (22nd April). He is a middle distance horse in the making.

EASY CODE b g Bahamian Bounty – Skirrid
We have always liked him and I think he is a nice horse. Well made, he won at Pontefract on his third run and we gelded him afterwards. I have always liked the way he goes at home and I am expecting him to improve when stepped up in trip this year.

ELJEEMI (IRE) b c Shamardal (USA) – Arthur's Girl
We were keen to run him last backend and took him to Redcar in November but he disappointed. It is possible the soft ground was against him. Pat (Cosgrave) liked him beforehand and I think he will be a nice horse this year. His dam stayed a mile and a half and I am hoping he will win a maiden before going handicapping.

FADILLAH b f Monsun (GER) – Sasuela (GER)
A €1,200,000 purchase at the 2014 Arqana Yearling Sales. She has the most attractive page and is a half-sister to Seismos and a full-sister to Soberania (a German Oaks runner-up). Like her siblings, she was always going to be better at three and will hopefully make up into a nice middle distance prospect this season. I think she will prefer a bit of ease in the ground, although she does not get her feet very high off the ground.

FASTNET TEMPEST (IRE) b g Fastnet Rock (AUS) – Dame Blanche (IRE)
A big, raw plain horse, he ran a very promising race at Newmarket on his only run in October. Clueless early on, the penny dropped during the latter stages and he finished strongly in fifth. He can only improve as a three year old. We will start him off in a one mile maiden but he should stay at least a mile and a quarter this year. I would view him as a handicapper at the moment but he has the potential to be better.

FIELD OF STARS b f Acclamation – Map of Heaven
Runner-up a couple of times, she then won her maiden by six lengths at Kempton in December. The handicapper has given her a mark of 83, which means she will have to be quite good to defy such a rating. She has plenty of speed and I am not sure she will stay much further than six furlongs. Six furlongs fillies' handicaps will be on her agenda to begin with.

FLEETING DREAM (IRE) b f Dream Ahead (USA) – Flanders (IRE)
A half-sister to G Force, she was disappointing at Windsor on her only run last year. She showed a lot of speed early on before fading. Still weak last year, she has strengthened up and will hopefully improve. She is a fast filly.

GOLDEN REIGN (IRE) ch f Champs Elysees – Fleche D'Or
A full-sister to the talented Eastern Belle (rated 104), she is, of course, also a half-sister to last season's horse of the year, Golden Horn. We didn't get to do too much with her last season but hopefully she will improve as much as her half-brother did from two to three. She is obviously now very valuable as a broodmare but she should hopefully win a race this season and then progress to stakes races. She is likely to be best at around 10 furlongs. We hope she will be as good as her siblings.

GRAVITY FLOW (IRE) ch f Exceed And Excel (AUS) – Landela
She ran two good races finishing runner-up at Windsor and Kempton. Quite keen, she has done well physically from two to three and ought to win her maiden in the spring. I think six or seven furlongs will be her trip.

GUY FAWKES b g Big Bad Bob (IRE) – Flight of Fancy
A half-brother to Fabricate, he is bred to stay and I think he will develop into a nice staying handicapper over a mile and six plus. Very weak as a juvenile, he raced twice finishing third at Wolverhampton last time. I hope he will win a maiden before going handicapping.

IMPRISON (FR) b c Sea The Stars (IRE) – Lockup (IRE)
He came from Mike de Kock this winter. He was an expensive yearling who has been quite backward, but he moves well and is quite playful at the moment. He will likely stay a mile and a half in time.

IN THE CITY ch c Exceed And Excel (AUS) – Soft Morning
He is a nice horse who finished fourth in a very good maiden won by Emotionless at Newmarket in August. We were unable to run him again because he had problems with his feet. However, he is doing very well now and will reappear in a seven furlongs maiden. He should stay at least a mile this year.

INTILAAQAH b f Oasis Dream – Quan Yin (IRE)
She is a kind, sweet natured filly who is out of an unraced Sadler's Wells mare, whose dam, East Of The Moon, was Champion three-year-old in France in 1994, who, herself, was out of Miesque. She is bred on the same lines as Approve and I hope she will be as tough and as good as he was.

ISTANBUL BEY ro g Exceed And Excel (AUS) – Starfala
He only joined us late last year and we gelded him straight away but I have liked what he has shown us so far. His pedigree is quite mixed as there is some speed there but also quite a lot of stamina on the female line, with his half-sister Star Rider (rated 85) winning a two mile Newmarket handicap at the end of last season. Despite that, he isn't slow and will probably start off over seven furlongs, possibly at the Craven meeting.

IZMIR (IRE) b f Sir Percy – Limit (IRE)
A filly with a bit of temperament, she has done nothing wrong in two runs. Third at Newmarket on her debut, she won well next time at Wolverhampton and I think she is better than her mark of 73. I am expecting her to improve as a three year old. She ought to stay a mile and may even get ten furlongs.

JULIA DREAM b f Montjeu (IRE) – Winds of Time (IRE)
A half-sister to The Paddyman, who finished second in the Richmond Stakes for us a few years ago. I thought she ran a good race at Newmarket finishing seventh and she is a filly with a bit of substance. While she is unlikely to be top-class, I think she is useful and will appreciate trips around a mile and a quarter.

LAPILLI b g Bahamian Bounty – Blue Lyric
He is a lovely unraced horse who we thought was our best juvenile last spring. Unfortunately, he suffered with ringworm and then chipped a bone in his knee, which meant he was unable to run last year. We have gelded him and he has developed into a big strong horse. He looks a sprinter.

LIGHT MUSIC b f Elusive Quality (USA) – Medley
A very nice filly who won her maiden by fourteen lengths at Leicester before scrambling home in the Listed Radley Stakes at Newbury. The runners raced on the far side that day and, having shot clear, she probably hit the front too soon. If she had been ridden more patiently, I think she would have won easier. She is obviously useful and, being a big scopey filly, I hope she will do very well this year. She needs to learn to relax but she ought to stay a mile and we are hoping she is a Guineas filly. Like Besharah, the plan is to run her in either the Nell Gwyn (12th April) or Fred Darling Stakes (16th April). All three of her races have been on easy ground but I will be staggered if she needs testing conditions.

MUJAAMIL b c Dansili – Muwakleh

I like him. He disappointed us on his debut at Newmarket when finding the ground too soft. However, he wasn't beaten far and I think he will do well this year. I will be disappointed if he doesn't win his maiden with trips around a mile and ten furlongs likely to suit him.

MUSAANADA b f Sea The Stars (IRE) – Gaze

From the family of Fame And Glory, she is unraced but looks a nice staying filly in the making. Her pedigree suggests she will improve with age. She will have no trouble staying a mile and a half.

MUZDAWAJ b c Dansili – Shabiba (USA)

A half-brother to Ertijaal, he is a beautiful moving horse who could be useful. Fourth on his debut at Newmarket, he then finished second at Redcar. He will stay further than a mile and ought to win a maiden before developing into a nice three year old.

NOBEL DUKE (IRE) ch g Duke of Marmalade (IRE) – Dowager

I believe that Duke Of Marmalade's progeny are better at three than they are at two and, adding to that, the geldings tend to win more than the colts so we had him gelded at the end of last year. He goes nicely and, although he does possess some speed, he should get ten furlongs in time. He may well start over a mile.

NOVALINA (IRE) b f Galileo (IRE) – Baraka (IRE)

Out of a Lingfield Oaks Trial Winner, Novalina is a full-sister to Min Alemarat (rated 92) and Beyond Conceit (rated 93) who are both useful staying types and this filly fits in with that profile. Quite backward last year, I think she will prefer some give in the ground and should be able to win races this season. She should stay very well.

OLYMPIC RUNNER ch f Exceed And Excel (AUS) – Lochridge

A fast filly who I thought did well to win at Lingfield on her last run. She had disappointed on her previous outing at Ripon but she made amends next time. She is a sprinter who will enjoy fast ground this year. I don't think she is a bad filly.

ORIENTAL CROSS (IRE) b f Cape Cross (IRE) – Orion Girl (GER)

An unraced filly who is owned by HM The Queen, she looks a stayer. A big galloping filly, she isn't the quickest.

ORNATE b c Bahamian Bounty – Adorn

He has run some very good races, including when finishing a head second in the Group 2 Flying Childers Stakes at Doncaster. Third and second at Wolverhampton and Lingfield respectively on his next two runs, Pat (Cosgrave) thought his wind was bothering him when he came under pressure. We therefore cauterized his palate. He is a horse with a lot of speed with five furlongs being his trip.

OUT AND ABOUT (IRE) b g Fastnet Rock (AUS) – Starship (IRE)

A very nice horse who I like a lot. He is a beautiful looking horse who wants top of the ground. A half-brother to Bilimbi who finished fourth for us in the Britannia Stakes at Royal Ascot a couple of years ago, he is a better horse than him. Fourth on his debut at Newbury, he won next time at Redcar and has been given a mark of 84. I am hoping he will also develop into a Britannia Stakes horse (16th June) but he may need a bit more experience beforehand. He will have at least one run before Royal Ascot.

QORTAAJ b g Kyllachy – Cardrona

Made a satisfactory start to his career when finishing fourth on his debut at Doncaster on the final day of the turf season in November. We found it difficult to keep weight on him last year but he has the ability to win a maiden.

RASMIYA (IRE) b f Galileo (IRE) – Crystal Valkyrie (IRE)

A beautifully bred filly who is a half-sister to the Group 3-winning pair of Above Average and Sent From Heaven. She is a filly with huge potential and was always going to be better at three and gives the impression she will stay well. Depending on her work, she will make her debut in a mile or ten furlongs maiden, possibly at the Newbury Spring Meeting (15th April).

RAUCOUS b c Dream Ahead (USA) – Shyrl

A nice horse who has done well during the winter. He won his first couple of races at Sandown and Newmarket before finishing third in the Gimcrack and Mill Reef Stakes. There is a lot of speed in his pedigree, especially on the dam's side. However, we may try him over seven furlongs with the Free Handicap at Newmarket (13th April) a possible target. We have given him an entry in the French 2000 Guineas but he may prove best over shorter trips. The Group 3 Pavilion Stakes at Ascot (27th April) over six furlongs is another race we will consider, plus the Listed Carnarvon Stakes at Newbury (14th May). If six furlongs proves to be his trip then we will obviously have the Commonwealth Cup at Royal Ascot (17th June) in mind. Still quite leggy last year, he has really developed from two to three.

RELATIONSHIP ch f Pivotal – Courting

An unraced full-sister to Fury, she is a filly I like. The Bridget Fillies' Maiden Stakes over seven furlongs at Newbury (15th April) looks an ideal starting point.

RUSSIAN FINALE b f Dansili – Russian Rhythm (USA)

A big, tall unraced leggy filly who has done well during the winter. She will make her debut in a seven furlong or one mile maiden. I think she is a nice filly.

SAINTED ch f Dutch Art – Blithe

She is a full-sister to Telmeyd and is a useful filly. We have had a bit of luck with her family and I feel she is on a very good mark having won first time out at Doncaster on the final day of the season. The family tend to prefer a bit of cut in the ground and I think this is a lovely filly.

SELECTION (FR) ch c Siyouni (FR) – Perspective (FR)

A really nice unraced horse but, unfortunately, he has suffered a fracture and won't be running until the second half of the season. He is a beauty though who will make a very nice four year old next season.

SHUFOOG b f Mawatheeq (USA) – Hamloola

We trained her dam and she was quite a nice filly. I thought she won her maiden in good style at Lingfield and appears to have been given a fair mark. She walks her box but has ability and is a nice filly. I would expect her to stay a mile because she finished off well on her debut over seven furlongs.

SKY KINGDOM (IRE) b c Montjeu (IRE) – We Can Say It Now (AUS)

A very good looking unraced colt who joined us towards the end of last year. He is a nice horse who is still in the Derby and we like him. All being well, he will make his debut at the Craven meeting at Newmarket (12th - 14th April) either over a mile or ten furlongs, depending on his homework at the time.

SMASHED (IRE) b g Beat Hollow – Sel
Smashed's dam, Sel, is out of Frog, and is therefore very closely related to Beaten Up (also by Beat Hollow) as well as Harris Tweed and Vow. Sel hasn't been quite as illustrious as her mother in the breeding shed but Smashed is a handsome gelding with a good nature, although he is quite a gross horse. He has been quite backward, stemming mainly from the fact he was a May foal, but he gives the impression he will stay well.

SOUNDSTRINGS b f Oasis Dream – Straight Lass (IRE)
An unraced full-sister to Group 1 winner Naaqoos, she is not too dissimilar to him. A leggy filly, I like her and I think she will be suited by top of the ground. She could make her debut in the seven furlongs fillies' maiden at the Craven meeting (14th April).

STRAW HAT (IRE) b f Galileo (IRE) – Velouette
A lovely unraced filly who is a full-sister to Telescope. She is a good mover and is doing nicely now having earlier sprung a curb, which held her up. She will start off in a ten or twelve furlongs fillies' maiden, possibly at Newbury (15th April). She is a potentially very nice filly.

SYMPOSIUM ch f Exceed And Excel (AUS) – Soodad
We have always liked her but she was disappointing at Newmarket in a nursery because we thought she was well handicapped. A strong filly, I think six furlongs will be her trip and I hope she will do well this year.

TASLEET b c Showcasing – Bird Key
A very genuine and tough colt, he was a smart juvenile winning a Listed race at Newbury and the DBS Premier Yearling Stakes at York. We are hoping he will train on and the plan is for him to reappear in either the Free Handicap at Newmarket (13th April) or the Greenham Stakes at Newbury (16th April). I think the latter is more likely and seven furlongs is probably as far as he will want to go this year.

TUTU NGURU (USA) b f Blame (USA) – Haka Girl (USA)
Twice a winner last year, I don't think she will be easy to place this season even though she ran well on her reappearance in a Listed race at Lingfield in March. Seven furlongs or a mile ought to suit and something like the Listed Michael Seely Memorial Stakes at York (13th May) is a possible target.

VICTORY BOND b c Medicean – Antebellum (FR)
He ran very well on his debut in a mile maiden at Newbury finishing a close second. We had hoped he would run well because his homework beforehand had been encouraging. He should stay ten furlongs comfortably and may get a bit further. I don't know whether he will be a stakes horse but we will look for a maiden at a nice track in the spring.

WAVE REVIEWS b c Fastnet Rock (AUS) – Critical Acclaim
Bred to stay being a half-brother to William of Orange, I like him a lot and feel he could develop into a King George V Stakes horse at Royal Ascot (16th June). Fifth and second in maidens at Newmarket last year, he will hopefully go one better in the spring and then go on to better things. He is a lovely horse.

WRAPPED ch f Iffraaj – Muffled (USA)
Third on her debut at Newbury, she was a bit disappointing on her next two starts but we found she had an issue with one of her hind legs. That has been sorted now and hopefully she will make her mark in seven furlongs and one mile fillies' handicaps.

TRAINER'S HORSES TO FOLLOW: OUT AND ABOUT
MAUREEN HAGGAS' HORSES TO FOLLOW: FOREVER POPULAR

Mark JOHNSTON

Stables: Kingsley House Stables, Middleham, North Yorkshire.
2015: 204 Winners from 1208 Runners 17% Prize-Money £2,748,949
www.markjohnstonracing.com

OLDER HORSES

DONNA GRACIOSA (GER) 4 b f Samum (GER) - Donna Alicia (GER)
She did very well last year winning four times with her rating rising from 59 to 79. We are hoping she will improve again and I see no reason why she won't stay further. Her owner believes she wants fast ground so we will be aiming her at middle distance/staying handicaps on a sound surface.

FIRE FIGHTING (IRE) 5 b g Soldier of Fortune (IRE) - Savoie (FR)
He had a good season winning three times, including a Listed race at Dundalk and the Zetland Gold Cup at Redcar. A close third in the Wolferton Stakes at Royal Ascot, he also ran well in defeat at the likes of Epsom and Glorious Goodwood. Sixth in the Winter Derby in late February, he was only beaten a length at Lingfield on Good Friday. He will follow a similar programme.

FREIGHT TRAIN (IRE) 4 b g Manduro (GER) - Sigonella (IRE)
He has changed owners during the summer. Having previously belonged to Alan Spence, I bought him back at the Newmarket October Sales on behalf of his son Michael. A winner at Redcar in the Autumn, we have given him the winter off. We loved him as a two year old and, while he largely failed to live up to expectations last year, he did OK and remains lightly raced and hopefully open to more improvement.

MAMBO PARADISE 4 b f Makfi - Mambo Halo (USA)
She had a good year winning three times before disappointing on her final run at Newmarket in August. However, she was found to have fractured a pastern hence she didn't run again. Back in work, we are hoping she will resume winning ways and the dream is to gain some black type at some stage.

MISTER UNIVERSE 4 br c Cape Cross (IRE) - Miss Ivanhoe (IRE)
Things need to go his way but he is a horse with a lot of ability. A winner at Ascot last season, he also ran well when finishing second in a Listed race at Epsom in June. Seven furlongs appears to be his optimum trip, although he won over a mile on his first run on the all-weather at Lingfield in March. A Listed winner at Wolverhampton on his next start, he then finished sixth at Lingfield on Good Friday. The plan is for him to follow a similar programme to last year, although he is higher in the ratings now.

NOTARISED 5 b g Authorized (IRE) - Caribbean Dancer (USA)
He has been a good horse over the years and it was great to see him win over two miles for the first time at Chelmsford in early March, although he disappointed at Lingfield next time. A three times winner last year, including the Old Newton Cup at Haydock, he clearly stays well but is probably at his best over a mile and a half or a mile and six. He will be running in the big middle distance/staying handicaps once again.

NOVANCIA (IRE) 4 b f Fastnet Rock (AUS) - Ceoil An Aith (IRE)
From the family of Yavana's Pace and Littlepacepaddocks, she is bred to improve with age. Twice a winner last season, she disappointed on her final couple of runs but we are hoping she will get back on track this time. Rated 82, she is still lightly raced and will be aimed at middle distance handicaps.

ORIENTAL FOX (GER) 8 ch g Lomitas – Oriental Pearl (GER)
He did us proud once again last year when winning the Queen Alexandra Stakes at Royal Ascot before being placed three times in Group races subsequently. He is going to be a difficult horse to place this year but the Queen Alexandra is his main target once again. Anything else he achieves is a bonus.

REVOLUTIONIST (IRE) 4 b c Pivotal – Mysterial (USA)
A half-brother to Dubai Destination, he has won three of his five career starts and is a horse we have always liked. He disappointed on his final run at Lingfield and we don't have an explanation for it. We gave him a good break and he was back to winning ways at Chelmsford in March. While he needs things to go his way, he is a useful horse.

RHYTHMICAL 4 b f Halling (USA) – Caribbean Dancer (USA)
A half-sister to Notarised, her pedigree suggests she will improve with age. She won on her debut at Leicester last year before finishing runner-up at Goodwood and Newmarket. Bred to stay well, she remains lightly raced and open to further improvement.

SALIERIS MISS 4 b g Mount Nelson – Sunley Gift
He is a nice horse who won at Ripon on his debut last season before running some good races in defeat at Haydock and Ayr. There was talk of selling him at the end of last season but he incurred an injury after his final start at Nottingham. He is 100% now and we will be aiming him at the good middle distance handicaps. Then, there is every chance he will be going to the pre Royal Ascot sale in mid June. Lightly raced, he is open to further improvement.

SEA THE SKIES 5 b g Sea The Stars (IRE) – Model Queen (USA)
Having missed the whole of 2014, he won twice last year at Leicester and Ripon. Unfortunately, he suffered another injury after his latter win in July and missed the rest of the season. Given a break, he is back in work now and is a nice horse. He remains fairly treated and is another who will be running in middle distance handicaps.

SENNOCKIAN STAR 6 ch g Rock of Gibraltar (IRE) - Chorist
He had another busy campaign (19 races), including four races in Meydan at the start of last year. A dual winner at Chelmsford and Chester, he was only beaten half a length in the Wolferton Stakes at Royal Ascot. An injury after his last run prevented him from going to the sales at the end of the season so he will follow a similar campaign this year. A mile and a quarter is his trip. He gives the impression he will stay further but every time we try him over a mile and a half, he doesn't get home.

THINK SNOW (USA) 4 ch f Giant's Causeway (USA) – Snow Forest (USA)
Despite being a four year old, she has only raced once finishing second at Haydock as a juvenile. Absent last year, due to a number of niggly problems, we have always thought a lot of her, hence she remains in training. A fine, big filly, we will hopefully get a clear run with her this time.

THREE MERRY LADS 4 b g Danehill Dancer (IRE) – Obsessive (USA)
Similar to Think Snow, he has only raced once and missed the whole of his three year old season due to injury. Very well bred being a half-brother to Excellent Art and Double Obsession, he finished second at Musselburgh as a two year old. He is another we have always thought very highly of, hence he is still with us.

VIVE MA FILLE (GER) 4 b f Doyen (IRE) – Vive Madame (GER)
Consistent last year, she won on her debut at Lingfield before finishing fourth in the Queen's Vase at Royal Ascot, fifth in the Goodwood Cup and being Listed placed. She has had a long break since her last run in September and, with a rating of 97, the chief aim is to gain some more black type this year. A mile and a half plus is ideal.

WATERSMEET 5 gr g Dansili – Under The Rainbow
He enjoyed a good season last year winning four times and a close second behind Notarised in the Old Newton Cup at Haydock. Already a winner at Dundalk this season, too, he will continue in the top middle distance handicaps even though he ran below par at Lingfield on Good Friday.

YORKIDDING 4 b f Dalakhani (IRE) – Claxon
A well bred filly who won at York and Sandown last spring. She ran some good races in defeat thereafter and it will be a case of more of the same. Bred to improve with age, she stays well and doesn't look too badly treated.

THREE YEAR OLDS

ABAREEQ ch c Haatef (USA) – Hafawa (IRE)
He was unable to race last year, due to an injury, but he made a pleasing start to his career when finishing second on his debut at Lingfield in early March. Showing signs of greenness, he hung towards the rail late on but wasn't beaten far. He confirmed the promise next time at the same track over a mile. Making all, he won by six lengths and we will see what sort of mark he is given before making plans. He clearly stays a mile well but he isn't short of speed either. Still quite raw, he can only improve.

ADVENTUROUS (IRE) b c Invincible Spirit (IRE) – Rosia (IRE)
The third highest rated three year old in the yard, he looks an exciting horse for the future. Placed a couple of times at Group 3 level, he was used as a pacemaker in the Dewhurst Stakes at Newmarket last time and is better than he showed that day. Prior to that, I had been pleased with his juvenile season, although he had disappointed in the Acomb Stakes at York. Seven furlongs or a mile ought to suit him this year and, although he disappointed on his reappearance at Lingfield in March, I would imagine we will be looking towards a Guineas trial in the spring.

ALEKO b c Cape Cross (IRE) – Monnavanna (IRE)
Having won on his debut at Haydock, we ran him in the Woodcote Stakes at Epsom on Derby Day and thought he may be our best chance ahead of Buratino. However, it wasn't the case and he disappointed us during the second half of the season, too. While he failed to live up to that initial promise, the handicapper has dropped him as a result and he is now only rated 75. He has been working well during the winter/early spring so hopefully he will bounce back.

BAILEYS ESQUIRE b c Halling (USA) – Silversword (FR)
An unknown quantity, he has yet to race having had a few problems last year. He is very well bred though being a full-brother to Cavalryman.

BATHOS (IRE) b c Poet's Voice – Santolina (USA)
He enjoyed a very good season winning four times with his handicap mark rising from 62 to 87. Seventh on his reappearance at Wolverhampton on Good Friday, he lost his chance by starting very slowly. We will be aiming him at the good three year old handicaps over trips around a mile or possibly a bit further.

BEAVERBROOK b c Cape Cross (IRE) – Bint Almatar (USA)
We have a number of three year olds, including this colt, who earned ratings around 100 as juveniles based on their early season form. It is therefore a worry that some of them have been over rated and will struggle as a result. Fourth in the Coventry Stakes at Royal Ascot behind Buratino, he found it tough in his subsequent races. We gave him a break after his run in the Champagne Stakes at Doncaster and I thought he ran well on his return in a competitive handicap at Wolverhampton on Good Friday finishing third, That was his first run over a mile and he saw the trip out well.

BURATINO (IRE) ch c Exceed And Excel (AUS) – Bergamask (USA)
He is in good form at home and I have been delighted with him during the winter because he has done very well physically. Even though he had a great season with some tremendous form, I feel he is something of a forgotten horse. We are excited by the prospect of running him in Group 1 races this year as an underdog. An impressive winner of the Coventry Stakes at Royal Ascot from Air Force Blue, he then finished behind the same rival in the Phoenix Stakes at the Curragh. The ground was softer than described that day. He was back to his best on his final run when only half a length behind Shalaa in the Middle Park Stakes. Despite the fact he is by Exceed And Excel, he gave the impression at Newmarket that he will stay further. We haven't made any definite plans but I am hoping he will be a miler this year and we go straight to Newmarket for the 2000 Guineas (30th April). He enjoys fast ground.

BYRES ROAD ch c Pivotal – Croeso Cariad
Placed on his first couple of runs, he won his maiden at Chelmsford in late January. The handicapper hasn't done him any favours though giving him a mark of 80. Indeed, I think he has set him a stiff task and it will be a case of attempting to defy it.

CAPE SPEED (FR) b c Cape Cross (IRE) – At A Great Rate (USA)
We thought he would go close on his debut at Ayr in June and we were devastated when he only finished fifth. However, it transpired that he had fractured a hock and he didn't run again until December. A three times winner on the all-weather since, we felt he deserved an entry in the 2000 Guineas but he disappointed at Lingfield on Good Friday and we don't know why. His next target is the £200,000 Tattersalls Millions 3YO Trophy at Newmarket (14th April) over a mile and a quarter. Physically, he doesn't look like a ten furlongs horse but the manner in which he finished at Kempton over a mile suggested it is worth a try. He looked a progressive horse, prior to his run on Good Friday.

CHAMPAGNE CITY ch g Tobougg (IRE) – City of Angels
A half-brother to Royal Ascot winner I'm So Lucky, he spent the winter with his owner Roger Brookhouse. A decent horse, he won three times as a juvenile and was runner-up at Listed level, too. Disappointing on his final run at Ayr, he is rated 98 and we will be looking towards more Listed races at some stage.

DALEELAK (IRE) b c Arcano (IRE) – Alshamatry (USA)
A maiden winner at Musselburgh, he disappointed last time at Doncaster so we have given him a good break. He seems in good form at home and hopefully he will improve as a three year old. Rated 77, he will be going down the handicap route.

DAWAA ch f Tamayuz – Athreyaa
A dual winner at Nottingham and Goodwood over six furlongs, she may not have been suited by the step up in trip at Newmarket last time. We will therefore be looking towards six furlongs handicaps, although she might not be the easiest to place off a rating of 94.

DEODORO (USA) b f Medaglia D'Oro (USA) - Anna Wi'Yaak (JPN)
She could be an interesting filly stepping up in trip this season. A comfortable winner of her maiden at Beverley, she wasn't disgraced when finishing second in a nursery at Windsor. She doesn't look badly treated, especially when tackling longer distances.

DESSERTOFLIFE (IRE) gr f Mastercraftsman (IRE) - Cranky Spanky (IRE)
Already a Group 3 winner in Germany, she had a decent juvenile season. We ran her in the Group 1 Fillies Mile at Newmarket but it proved a step too far, at that stage in her career. I think she will appreciate stepping up in trip as a three year old and, while she is already a valuable filly being a Group 3 winner and Listed placed, it would be nice to enhance her still further.

EQLEEM b g Acclamation - Blessing
He won on his debut at Haydock and we thought he would go on to better things. However, he only finished third of four on his next two starts at Newmarket and Ripon. Both those races were on soft ground, so it is possible he wants a sound surface.

FIREGLOW b f Teofilo (IRE) - Fading Light
A tremendous filly last year, she was a dual Listed winner at Sandown and Newmarket and was a close second in the Group 3 Sweet Solera Stakes at Newmarket and Prestige Stakes at Goodwood. She is one of our big hopes for Group races this season and we feel she will benefit from stepping up in trip as a three year old. With that in mind, we will be looking towards one of the Oaks trials in the spring.

FOUR MILE BEACH gr c Dalakhani (IRE) - Rappel
Third at Southwell on his debut in February, he was then runner-up at Wolverhampton ten days later. Third at the same track in early March last time, he looks capable of winning handicaps.

GALESBURG (IRE) b g Shamardal (USA) - Calista
Twice a winner at Leicester and Epsom, he disappointed at Newbury on his final run. Considering he has already won a couple of races, he doesn't look overburdened off his mark and we will be aiming him at one mile three year old handicaps.

GOLD MERLION (IRE) b f Alhaarth (IRE) - Sea of Time (USA)
She only raced three times last year, winning on her debut at Thirsk before finishing a close third at Goodwood. Well held in a sales race at the Curragh last time, she looks capable of making her mark in fillies' handicaps.

HALEY BOP (IRE) ch f Dream Ahead (USA) - Hallie's Comet (IRE)
Had a good season winning a couple of times at Redcar and Hamilton. I would forgive her run in the Two Year Old Trophy at Redcar and, while she looks exposed, she ought to be competitive in handicaps this year. She has plenty of speed.

HAWATIF (IRE) b f Royal Applause - Excellerator (IRE)
A six lengths winner of her maiden at Carlisle, she wasn't beaten far in the Weatherbys Super Sprint at Newbury before producing a moderate performance in a valuable nursery at Newmarket. Officially rated 80, she is still lightly raced and can win more races at handicap level.

HERALDIC (USA) b or br c Discreet Cat (USA) - Chilukki's Song (USA)
He showed great promise early on finishing third behind Easton Angel on his debut at Musselburgh before winning by six lengths at Lingfield. Disappointing thereafter, he has always gone well at home and we are hoping he will progress as a three year old. He will reappear in handicaps.

HUNTLAW b g Oasis Dream – Attraction
Out of Attraction, we fancied him first time out at Ayr but he was very green throughout the race. We were going to run him again but got cold feet because he didn't thrive at home. He has had a good break since though and looks capable of winning a maiden.

ISHARAH (USA) b c Kitten's Joy (USA) – Menekineko (USA)
A well bred colt, he was narrowly beaten on his debut at Kempton in February before scoring by a short head at Wolverhampton during the same month. We feel he is better than he has shown so far and hopefully he will make his mark in handicaps on the turf.

JAAMEH (IRE) b c Iffraaj – Miss Gibraltar
I was disappointed he didn't win last year but he was only beaten a couple of lengths at Newmarket last time when finishing fifth. He is capable of winning a maiden before hopefully progressing as a three year old.

JINTSHI b c Poet's Voice – Ivory Gala (FR)
Disappointed on his latest start at Chelmsford towards the end of February, we know he is better than that. Prior to that, he had won his maiden at Wolverhampton and had looked progressive. He will continue in one mile handicaps for the time being.

JUSTE POUR NOUS b c Pour Moi (IRE) – Steam Cuisine
A promising colt who improved from his debut at Chelmsford to winning at Hamilton next time. Bred to stay well, he will appreciate a step up to at least a mile and a quarter plus. I have been pleased with him during the winter and he looks to be fairly treated off a mark of 81. I hope he will develop into a nice middle distance three year old.

KING'S PAVILION (IRE) b c King's Best (USA) – Embassy
A very consistent horse, he had a busy season racing nine times. Twice a winner at Wetherby and Ripon, he never finished out of the first three. He got on edge on occasions last year but he is a nice horse who should have another good season in three year old handicaps.

LEYBURN ch f Shamardal (USA) – Lurina (IRE)
A well bred unraced filly who had a lot of issues last year. In terms of ability, it is too early to say because we haven't done enough with her. However, she has a nice pedigree.

LUMIERE gr f Shamardal (USA) – Screen Star (IRE)
She is in very good form at home and we are excited about seeing her again this year. Indeed, I think she is the best horse I have trained since Attraction and Shamardal. A Group 1 winner last year in the Cheveley Park Stakes, we haven't made any definite plans but I would imagine she will go straight to the 1000 Guineas. We have always thought she was a very good filly. Russ Kennemore, who works for Godolphin during the winter and us during the summer, rode her one morning in a piece of work and came back in and said she was the fastest horse he had sat on. She promptly won as she liked on her debut at Newmarket's July meeting. We then ran her in the Lowther Stakes at York and I feel greenness beat her. Returning a month later in the Cheveley Park at Newmarket, I was more than hopeful she would turn the tables on Besharah and she did and won by half a length. Physically, she hasn't grown dramatically or put on much weight during the winter. Indeed, she currently weighs 476kg compared to 468kg when she won at Newmarket. The intention is to have her weighing the same in the Guineas as she was in the Cheveley Park. I would like to think there is more to come from her. If she stays a mile, and I believe she will, I don't think the others who raced against her last season will have any chance of beating her this year because our filly has more scope. In terms of ground, she handles a fast surface very well and she had no trouble with Autumn good ground at Newmarket as well. She is an exciting prospect.

MARIEE b f Archipenko (USA) – Maria Di Scozia
She started her career well with two wins on the all-weather at Chelmsford and Wolverhampton during the winter. It was therefore disappointing to see her lose her unbeaten record at the former venue last time. However, she is a filly with plenty of scope and I think she will be more suited by racing on the turf.

MARY BEALE (IRE) ch f Shamardal (USA) – What A Picture (FR)
A half-sister to Art History, who we used to train, she showed a lot of promise at home last year but was unable to run due to a few issues. However, she made her debut at Wolverhampton in March but was very green and never got involved. I hope she will improve for the experience because she has ability.

MINIATURIST (FR) b g Shamardal (USA) – Herboriste
She peaked in the middle of the summer when winning her maiden at Sandown. Disappointing in three races subsequently, she is bred to stay further than a mile being out of a Hernando mare. Hopefully she will improve when stepping up in trip.

MONTSARRAT (IRE) br c Poet's Voice – Flying Flag (IRE)
I was delighted with him last season winning three of his five races. While he came unstuck on his final run at Doncaster, I thought he ran well on his return in a good three year old handicap at Wolverhampton on Good Friday. It showed he has benefited from a good break during the winter and I think he will progress further this year.

MUATADEL b c Exceed And Excel (AUS) – Rose Blossom
At the start of last season, we thought he was one of our sharpest juveniles and was very much our benchmark. Unfortunately, he never managed to win any of his four races but was placed on each occasion. A horse with a lot of speed, he looks a sprinter and hopefully it won't be long before he gets his head in front.

NEW CALEDONIA (IRE) b c Cape Cross (IRE) – Tessa Reef (IRE)
He looked a promising colt when winning at York and finishing runner-up in nurseries at Windsor and Newmarket. However, he disappointed on his final run at Catterick and there was no explanation forthcoming. It looked a case of it being too bad to be true. We will be targeting him at decent three year old handicaps over trips around a mile.

ODE TO EVENING ch r Poet's Voice – Ever Love (BRZ)
A nice horse who had some very good form during the first half of the season. A nine lengths winner of his maiden at Ripon, he then finished fifth in the Coventry Stakes at Royal Ascot behind Buratino. Unfortunately, he flopped in the Gimcrack Stakes at York next time and we don't know why. We have given him a break since and hopefully he will return to form this year. He is bred to stay further than six furlongs but I am not certain he will because he isn't short of speed. He is a rig.

PLAGIARISM (USA) b f Lonhro (AUS) – Journalist (IRE)
She is a nice filly who won on her debut at Newcastle before finishing third in the Listed Rose Bowl Stakes at Newbury. Disappointing in her next couple of runs, she suffered an injury soon afterwards but is OK again now. Officially rated 88, she may not be the easiest filly to place but she has plenty of ability.

POWDERHORN (IRE) b c Raven's Pass (USA) – Innclassic (IRE)
He had a good consistent season winning twice at Lingfield and Chester. Rated in the mid 80s, he may stay beyond seven furlongs and will be going down the three year old handicap route.

RAH RAH b f Lonhro (AUS) – Rahiyah (USA)
She won on the first day of last season at Kempton before following up in the Lily Agnes Stakes at Chester. In and out in good races thereafter, she suffered an injury in the Princess Margaret Stakes at Ascot and missed the remainder of the season. She incurred a fracture which required a screw to be inserted. Returning at Wolverhampton on Good Friday, she won in good style over five furlongs against older horses. Given her lofty rating, she will continue to run in good sprints.

RENFREW STREET b f Iffraaj – Malpas Missile (IRE)
She started off well last year winning her maiden at Beverley on her second start. However, it was disappointing that she failed to progress in her next three races. As a result, she is only rated 75 and there ought to be plenty of opportunities for her.

RICHIE McCAW b c Zamindar (USA) – Cochin (USA)
A lovely horse who is named after a New Zealand Rugby Union player. Fifth on his debut at Beverley, the plan was for him to win while the player was in the country during the World Cup and he duly did so at Chelmsford in October. He, unfortunately, came back lame afterwards having been struck into. We found that he had split his hoof but he is 100% again now and is one to look forward to in three year old handicaps. He looks reasonably treated and ought to stay at least a mile and a quarter.

RIFLESCOPE (IRE) b g Raven's Pass (USA) – Red Intrigue (IRE)
He did well last year winning twice, including the Listed Dragon Stakes at Sandown in July. We never thought he would develop into a sprinter on pedigree but it looks the case and that's the route he will continue racing down. He won't be easy to place though off a mark of 99.

ROSAMARIA (IRE) gr f Rip Van Winkle (IRE) – Rosa Grace
She ran well on her first couple of starts at Doncaster and Chepstow and wasn't disgraced at Ascot either. However, I was disappointed she didn't manage to win in four starts. Having said that, she was still quite weak as a juvenile and has developed during the winter. Bred to stay well being out of a Lomitas mare, she will hopefully improve once stepped up in trip.

SAMAAWY b c Alhaarth (IRE) – Tasheyaat
He only raced once last season finishing fifth in a seven furlongs maiden at Leicester. I thought he showed enough that day to suggest he can win a similar event before stepping up in grade.

SECOND SERVE (IRE) b c Cape Cross (IRE) – Aguinaga (IRE)
A half-brother to the Gimcrack and Stewards Cup winner Conquest, he had a minor medical issue last year and only raced once. Making his debut at Catterick, he was very green before running on at the finish. A big, tall rangy horse, he improved during the winter and I thought he ran well at Wolverhampton on Easter Sunday when running on to finish third over nine furlongs. I expect him to continue to improve with experience.

SHADOW GAME b c Shamardal (USA) – Victoria Star (IRE)
Consistent last year, he was placed on four occasions before getting his head in front at Newmarket in August. Well held last time, the handicapper has given him a chance by dropping him four pounds. Effective over six and seven furlongs, he may stay a mile this year.

SIGNED AND SEALED b g Authorized (IRE) – Broken Peace (USA)
A nice big scopey horse owned by Roger Brookhouse. Placed at Pontefract and Nottingham, we have gelded him and he looks a promising middle distance three year old in the making. He appears to be on a fair mark.

SIXTH SENSE (IRE) ch c Shamardal (USA) – Shinko Hermes (IRE)
A good horse on his day, he won twice, including a Listed event at Ascot in July. Third in the Chesham Stakes at Royal Ascot, we used him as a pacemaker towards the end of the season. Officially rated 100, he isn't going to be easy to place and we will be looking to drop him in class because he was found out at Group 1 and 2 level as a juvenile.

SOLDIER IN ACTION (FR) ch c Soldier of Fortune (IRE) – Ripley (GER)
Runner-up on his first two starts, he won at Wolverhampton at the third attempt. I thought his rating of 80 was harsh considering he had only won at Wolverhampton and he promptly only finished sixth in a nursery at Chelmsford next time. I do, however, think he is better than he showed that day and expect him to improve when tackling longer trips. He is the type to progress with age, too.

STAR OF LOMBARDY (IRE) b f Cape Cross (IRE) – Million Waves (IRE)
I was disappointed she didn't manage to win last year because every time she ran I thought she would go very close. Runner-up at Leicester and Chelmsford, she is a half-sister to Blue Wave, who has done well for us over middle distances. However, she has more speed than him and hopefully it won't be long before she wins races because she has the ability to do so.

STREET DUEL (USA) b or br c Street Cry (IRE) – Fifth Avenue Doll (USA)
A half-brother to St Leger winner Arctic Cosmos, he was runner-up in three of his four races as a juvenile. Given a break since his last run at Kempton in August, he won on his reappearance at Southwell in March. Even though he won over seven furlongs, he is bred to come into his own over middle distances.

TARTAN BUTE b g Azamour (IRE) – On A Soapbox (USA)
Half-brother to our dual Group winner Soapy Danger, he took a long time to show anything and is a laid back and lazy individual. Thankfully, he ran OK at Lingfield and Wolverhampton in January. Gelded since, he will appreciate a return to longer trips and ought to win races in handicap company.

TAWAKKOL b c Firebreak – Dayville
Consistent without winning last year, he was placed in five of his six races. It was frustrating because we have always thought he was a very nice horse. Injured when finishing second at Wetherby in July, he returned at Wolverhampton in March and won by five lengths. Raised eight pounds as a result, it won't be easy off a mark of 88 but he has plenty of ability.

TEMPLIER (IRE) b g Mastercraftsman (IRE) – Tigertail (FR)
We fancied him a few times last season but he failed to win any of five races. Runner-up on three occasions, the handicapper hasn't done him any favours with a mark of 79. We will probably try and win a maiden before going handicapping.

THOLEN (USA) b f Lonhro (AUS) – Zelanda (IRE)
Despite the fact he remains a maiden after five starts last year, I will be disappointed if he can't win a race or two this season. Only rated 74, we have the option of going down the handicap route.

TURBINE (IRE) b c Cape Cross (IRE) – Chiquita Linda (IRE)
All three of his races have been on the all-weather during the winter. A winner on his debut at Wolverhampton in November, he hasn't really backed it up with two defeats, including at Dundalk last time. He looks high enough on a mark of 90 but hopefully he can win a handicap or two on the turf.

TWOBEELUCKY b g Tobougg (IRE) – She's The Lady
He spent the winter with his owner Roger Brookhouse and, while he remains a maiden, he looks a promising type. Placed in all three starts over a mile, including twice at Nottingham, I was pleased with him last season. He looks capable of winning a maiden before going handicapping over ten furlongs plus.

WHITMAN b or br c Poet's Voice – Sundrop (JPN)
A good two year old, he won three times including the Listed Champion Two Year Old Trophy at Ripon. Well held in the Mill Reef Stakes last time, he is high in the ratings off 97 but we are hoping he will stay further this year. Yet to race beyond six furlongs, it would certainly help if he stayed seven furlongs or a mile.

TWO YEAR OLDS

Kingsley House Stables was responsible for a magnificent 92 juvenile winners in 2015, including Buratino's victory in the Coventry Stakes at Royal Ascot and Lumiere won the Group 1 Cheveley Park Stakes. Mark has kindly offered me a list of the new intake of two year olds for this season. Here is just a selection of this year's crop.

ALWALAA b f Elzaam (AUS) – Aljana (IRE) (Exceed And Excel (AUS))
Owned by **Sheikh Hamdan Al Maktoum**. Date of Birth: 1/4/14

FRANKUUS gr c Frankel – Dookus (IRE) (Linamix (FR)
Owned by **Lootah & Hussain**, he was bought for **€130,000** at the Goffs Orby Sale and is a half-brother to Group 3 winner US Law. DOB: 18/4/14

KAHRAB gr c Dark Angel (IRE) – Dance Club (IRE) (Fasliyev (USA))
Owned by **Sheikh Hamdan Al Maktoum**, he was purchased for **110,000gns** at Tattersalls in October and is a half-brother to Online Alexander. DOB: 13/3/14

KHAMAARY b f Tamayuz – Nufoos (Zafonic (USA))
Owned by **Sheikh Hamdan Al Maktoum**, she is a half-sister to Awzaan, Hajras and Muteela. DOB: 14/3/14

LOVE POWER (IRE) b c Power – Royal Fizz (IRE) (Royal Academy (USA))
Owned by **Mick Doyle (Crone Stud)**, he was bought for **€50,000** at the Goffs Orby Sale and is a half-brother to Hitchens and Tanzeel. DOB: 25/4/14

MAKKAAR b c Raven's Pass (USA) – Beneventa (Most Welcome)
Owned by **Sheikh Hamdan Al Maktoum**, he cost **85,000gns** at the Tattersalls October Sale and is a half-brother to former stablemate Bow Creek. DOB: 3/2/14

MARQOOM ch c New Approach (IRE) – Night Frolic (Night Shift (USA))
Owned by **Sheikh Hamdan Al Maktoum**, he was bought for **200,000gns** in December and is a half-brother to Bonfire and Joviality. DOB: 15/2/14

RUSUMAAT b c Arcano (IRE) – Queen Wasp (IRE) (Shamardal (USA))
Owned by **Sheikh Hamdan Al Maktoum**, he was bought for **45,000gns** at the Doncaster Premier Yearling Sale in August. His dam is a half-sister to the high-class Naheef (triple Group 3 winner). DOB: 7/3/14

THE LAST LION (IRE) b c Choisir (AUS) – Mala Mala (IRE) (Brief Truce (USA))
Owned by **John Brown & Megan Dennis**, he was purchased for **€82,000** and is a half-brother to Contest (won 5 times), Russian Rock (11) and Silvanus (15). DOB: 12/2/14

Unnamed b c Cape Cross (IRE) – Chantilly Pearl (USA) (Smart Strike (CAN))
Owned by **Sheikh Hamdan Bin Mohammed Al Maktoum**, he was bought for **€90,000** at Goffs in October. DOB: 14/2/14

Unnamed b c Cape Cross (IRE) – Desert Gazelle (USA) (Smart Strike (CAN))
Owned by **Sheikh Hamdan Bin Mohammed Al Maktoum.** DOB: 24/3/14

Unnamed b f Distorted Humor (USA) – Cheeky Charm (USA) (A P Indy (USA))
Owned by **Sheikh Hamdan Bin Mohammed Al Maktoum.** DOB: 18/3/14

Unnamed b c Exceed And Excel (AUS) – Lacily (USA) (Elusive Quality (USA))
Owned by **Sheikh Hamdan Bin Mohammed Al Maktoum.** DOB: 19/3/14

Unnamed ch c Exceed And Excel (AUS) – Screen Star (IRE) (Tobougg (IRE))
Owned by **Mark Johnston Racing Ltd**, he is a half-brother to Group 1 winning stablemate Lumiere and was bought for **105,000gns** at the Tattersalls October Sale. DOB: 13/3/14

Unnamed b c Hard Spun (USA) – House of Grace (USA) (Limehouse (USA))
Owned by **Sheikh Hamdan Bin Mohammed Al Maktoum.** DOB: 16/3/14

Unnamed b f Invincible Spirit (IRE) – Missisipi Star (IRE) (Mujahid (USA)
Owned by **Sheikh Hamdan Bin Mohammed Al Maktoum**, she was bought for **150,000gns** in December and is a half-sister to Listed winner Baileys Jubilee. DOB: 13/2/14

Unnamed ch f New Approach (IRE) – West Wind (Machiavellian (USA))
Owned by **Sheikh Hamdan Bin Mohammed Al Maktoum.** DOB: 28/2/14

Unnamed b c Pivotal – Camlet (Green Desert (USA))
Owned by **Sheikh Hamdan Bin Mohammed Al Maktoum.** DOB: 4/5/14

Unnamed b c Poet's Voice – Duniatty (Green Desert (USA))
Owned by **Sheikh Hamdan Bin Mohammed Al Maktoum**, he was acquired for **€160,000** at the Goffs Orby Yearling Sale. DOB: 19/1/14

Unnamed b c Shamardal (USA) – Illandrane (IRE) (Cape Cross (IRE)
Owned by **Sheikh Hamdan Bin Mohammed Al Maktoum**, he was bought for **120,000gns.** DOB: 17/1/14

TRAINER'S HORSE TO FOLLOW: LUMIERE

David O'MEARA

Stables: Willow Farm Upper Helmsley, York, North Yorkshire.
2015: 119 Winners from 931 Runners 13% Prize-Money £1,688,245
www.davidomeara.co.uk

OLDER HORSES

ALEJANDRO (IRE) 7 b g Dark Angel (IRE) - Carallia (IRE)
He didn't manage to win last year and, as a result, has dropped to a mark which he ought to be competitive off this season. A sharp seven furlongs on a turning track is ideal and he wants fast ground. Indeed, it seemed to rain the night before every time he raced last season.

ALFRED HUTCHINSON 8 ch g Monsieur Bond (IRE) - Chez Cherie
A lovely big horse who joined us during the winter. An eight times winner, he won the Listed Hambleton Stakes at York last season and the race is likely to be on his agenda once again (12th May).

ALL ABOUT TIME 4 b f Azamour (IRE) - Up And About
A lovely big filly who has grown again during the winter and I think she has more to offer. In fact, it wouldn't surprise us if she gained some black type this year. She only raced three times last season winning on her most recent start at Ripon over a mile and a quarter. I think she will stay further this year, which could bring about further improvement.

AMAZING MARIA (IRE) 5 gr m Mastercraftsman (IRE) - Messias Da Silva (USA)
She only joined us last year and enjoyed a great season winning two Group 1s, namely the Falmouth Stakes at Newmarket and the Prix Rothschild at Deauville, plus the Group 2 Duke of Cambridge Stakes at Royal Ascot. Prior to Royal Ascot, she had run well in a handicap at Ascot when hitting the front too soon, and she wasn't beaten far in the Group 2 Lanwades Stud Stakes at the Curragh. We therefore thought she would run well in the Duke of Cambridge Stakes and she produced a very good performance. A length winner of the Falmouth, she followed up in the Prix Rothschild and the form worked out very well with the runner-up Ervedya subsequently winning the Prix du Moulin against the colts. She appears to be suited by a straight mile on fast ground. Below par in the Matron Stakes at Leopardstown, the ground was on the slow side. She spent the winter at Sir Robert Ogden's Sicklinghall Stud and she has come back in looking very well. I would think she will follow a similar programme during the middle of the summer with the Duke of Cambridge Stakes (15th June), Falmouth Stakes (8th July) and Prix Rothschild all likely targets again. There are also races such as the Dahlia Stakes at Newmarket (1st May), Lockinge Stakes at Newbury (14th May) and Lanwades Stud Stakes at the Curragh (21st May) is consider beforehand.

BIRDMAN (IRE) 6 b g Danehill Dancer (IRE) - Gilded Vanity (IRE)
He had a very good season winning five times with his rating going from 70 to 104. Suited by seven furlongs and a mile, he will continue in the big handicaps but we are hoping he might be able to progress to Pattern level later in the year.

BURANO (IRE) 7 ch g Dalakhani (IRE) - Kalimanta (IRE)
A new addition, we bought him at the Newmarket October Sales. Gelded since arriving, he is a nice horse with some decent form. A mile to ten furlongs appears to be his trip and he is eligible for 0-85 handicaps having dropped to a mark of 83.

CARPE VITA (IRE) 4 b f Montjeu (IRE) – Dance Parade (USA)
A full-sister to Leading Light, she is a very well bred filly who joined us last summer. She won on her first run for us at Redcar and then bumped into one at Ayr's Western meeting when finishing second. Lightly raced and a filly with plenty of scope, she stays a mile and six and I don't see why she won't stay further and could be one for those long distance handicaps at Pontefract.

CHANCERY (USA) 8 b or br g Street Cry (USA) – Follow That Dream
He had a great season winning three times, including off a mark of 98 at York in October, which is a career best performance. Effective over ten and twelve furlongs, he is arguably at his best over a mile and a quarter. He likes a bit of ease in the ground and, while he will follow a similar programme, he could start off at Ripon in a 96-110 handicap over a mile and a half (23rd April).

CUSTOM CUT (IRE) 7 b g Notnowcato – Polished Gem (IRE)
I was delighted with him last year winning two Group 2 races at Sandown and Leopardstown. He won the Bet365 Mile at the former track and it is possible he will head back there (22nd April). Eight and nine furlongs around a bend is ideal because a mile and a quarter seems to stretch him. With that in mind, we may consider the Group 1 Prix d'Ispahan at Chantilly (24th May) over nine furlongs. We ran him in the Lockinge Stakes last year but it didn't suit him. He is in good form at home and is capable of winning more Pattern races this year.

DANDYLEEKIE (IRE) 4 b g Dandy Man (IRE) – Cockaleekie (USA)
Bought cheaply at the Newmarket October Sales, he had some smart juvenile form for Ger Lyons in Ireland before losing his way last year. He has settled in well and is in great form at home. Hopefully a fun horse, he appears to like good ground with seven furlongs being his optimum trip.

DUTCH ARTIST (IRE) 4 ch g Dutch Art – Baltic Princess (FR)
We also purchased him at Newmarket during the Autumn having only raced once as a two year old for David Wachman. Sixth in a hotly contested maiden at the Curragh in September 2014, he missed the whole of his three year old season. It is early days but he looks OK and I have been pleased with him.

ETERNITYS GATE 5 b g Dutch Art – Regency Rose
He joined us last summer and nearly won on his first run at Pontefract when headed close home. Fifth next time at Thirsk, he suffered a hairline fracture above his joint soon afterwards and missed the remainder of the season. Back in work, he is effective over five and six furlongs and ought to win races off his mark.

FIRMAMENT 4 b g Cape Cross (IRE) – Heaven Sent
Bought out of Jeremy Noseda's yard in October, he was placed in both his runs for us on the all-weather in December. Only beaten half a length by Volunteer Point (won twice more since) at Chelmsford, his form looks strong and we have purposely given him a break during the winter. Suited by good ground on the turf, he has plenty of speed and will be campaigned in one mile handicaps.

FLYMAN 6 b g Pastoral Pursuits – Satin Bell
A winner at Ripon last season, he also ran well in the Bronze Cup at Ayr finishing fourth. Six furlongs on soft ground are his conditions and he could be the sort who goes back to Ayr in September.

FOREIGN DIPLOMAT 4 b g Oasis Dream – Longing To Dance

A winner on the all-weather at Chelmsford in December, I think he will want six furlongs on fast ground on the turf and will benefit from a bit of cover during his races. He has ability but is difficult to win with.

FORT BASTION (IRE) 7 b g Lawman (FR) – French Fern (IRE)

An easy winner at Ayr in May, the handicapper raised him seven pounds which made it tough for him thereafter. However, he still ran well at Ascot in a heritage handicap in July. We will be aiming him at races like the Thirsk Hunt Cup (30th April), which he won a couple of years ago, and the Listed Hambleton Stakes at York (12th May). Even though he has run some good races over seven furlongs, I think a mile is his ideal trip.

HARD TO HANDEL 4 b g Stimulation (IRE) – Melody Maker

A half-brother to Haaf A Sixpence, Middleham Park Racing bought him at the Newmarket October Sales. A dual winner for Ralph Beckett, he appears to be effective over seven furlongs and a mile and looks a fun horse.

HARWOODS VOLANTE (IRE) 5 ch g Kheleyf (USA) – Semiquaver (IRE)

A great big horse, I think he is the sort to improve again this year. He won twice last season at York and Wetherby and has enough speed for six furlongs, although he stays seven. Dropped a couple of pounds since his last run, I don't think he is on a bad mark because given his size, he is open to further improvement.

HE'S NO SAINT 5 b g Dutch Art – Stellar Brilliant (USA)

He is a decent horse on his day and proved it when winning easily at York in July. Fitted with a visor for the first time, he was granted a soft lead on that occasion and it is possible he was slightly flattered. Raised eleven pounds as a result, he struggled in his subsequent three races. A mile is probably his ideal trip, although he is quick enough for seven furlongs. We will be looking towards 0-95 handicaps. He wants fast ground.

HIGHLAND ACCLAIM (IRE) 5 b g Acclamation – Emma's Star (ITY)

A horse with a lot of ability, he isn't the easiest to train. Narrowly beaten at York in August, he ran a good race in the Portland Handicap at Doncaster. There is no doubt he is a well handicapped horse, if he put his best foot forward, but he isn't straightforward and needs things to go his way. A strongly run six furlongs is ideal, although he would stay seven furlongs, if he gave himself a chance. I would think he will reappear in the six furlongs handicap at York's Dante meeting (11th May).

HIT THE JACKPOT (IRE) 7 ch g Pivotal – Token Gesture (IRE)

He won over ten furlongs at Ayr last summer and will follow a similar programme this year. A mile and a quarter is his optimum trip but he possesses the speed to be competitive over a mile as well.

KING TO BE (IRE) 4 b g Myboycharlie (IRE) – Becuille (IRE)

We purchased him out of Richard Hannon's yard at the Newmarket Horses In Training Sale in October. A winner at Goodwood last year, he also ran well at York and wasn't disgraced in the Britannia Stakes at Royal Ascot. We haven't made any plans but he is likely to be aimed at the decent seven furlongs and one mile handicaps.

LOAVES AND FISHES 4 b f Oasis Dream - Miracle Seeker

Won her maiden well first time out as a juvenile, but she has faced some tough opposition since. Dropped to a mark of 90, she joined us during the winter and we will look at handicaps during the early part of the season with some tilts at black type to enhance her paddock value likely at the backend of the year.

LORD OF THE LAND (IRE) 5 b h Shamardal (USA) - Lady Vettori

George Turner bought him at the Arqana Arc Sale in early October having won five of his nine races for Andre Fabre. A full-brother to French 2000 Guineas and Derby winner Lope De Vega, he is very well bred and was recommended to us before the sale. A winner over six and a half and nine furlongs, we are hoping he will develop into a Pattern horse one day. We have been pleased with him since arriving and we're looking forward to seeing him run.

LUSTROUS 5 b m Champs Elysees - Tamzin

A Listed winner, she is a nice filly who finished second in the Group 2 Ribblesdale Stakes at Royal Ascot a couple of years ago and runner-up in the Lancashire Oaks last summer. She joined us during the winter and we will be looking towards conditions and Pattern races over ten and twelve furlongs.

MADAME BUTTERFLY (IRE) 4 b f Rip Van Winkle (IRE) - Messias Da Silva (USA)

A half-sister to Amazing Maria, she finished second on both starts last year. Runner-up on her debut at Thirsk, we thought she would win next time at Newcastle. Beaten eight lengths, she suffered a setback shortly afterwards and missed the rest of the season. Back in work, she looks to have a bright future and ought to win a maiden before stepping up in grade. Even though she was quite gassy on her debut, she should stay a mile.

MARAAKIB (IRE) 4 b g Dark Angel (IRE) - Mrs Cee (IRE)

He has proved a very good buy having acquired him at the Newmarket July Sales. Once stepping up to a mile and a quarter, he never looked back winning three of his last four races. I think he will stay further, too, if necessary. He also enjoys soft ground.

MIME DANCE 5 b g Notnowcato - Encore My Love

A solid genuine handicapper, we bought him out of Andrew Balding's yard at the Horses In Training Sale in the Autumn. A four times winner over seven furlongs and a mile, he has won off higher marks than his current rating and will hopefully pay his way.

MONDIALISTE (IRE) 6 b h Galileo (IRE) - Occupandiste (IRE)

He had a fantastic season winning three times, including the Grade 1 Woodbine Mile and finishing a very good second in the Breeders' Cup Mile at Keeneland. He had a long season, too, finishing second in the Lincoln in late March and ending the year by contesting the Hong Kong Mile in mid December. His run in the Breeders' Cup was as good as any of his career performances. This time last year we were looking forward to the Lincoln at Doncaster and he was unlucky not to win it having hit the front soon enough. This season we are looking to start him off in something like the Lockinge Stakes at Newbury (14th May) or the Prix D'Ispahan at Chantilly (24th May). A mile with a bit of cut in the ground are his optimum conditions, although he proved in the Group 3 Strensall Stakes at York last August, he stays nine furlongs. He is likely to be given an entry in the Queen Anne Stakes at Royal Ascot as well.

MOVE IN TIME 8 ch g Monsieur Bond (IRE) – Tibesti
Once again, he had a good season winning a conditions event at Hamilton and a Group 3 at Longchamp in September. Beaten less than three lengths in the Prix de L'Abbaye, he doesn't want the ground too firm and will have an early and late season campaign. Fifth in a Listed race at Lingfield in February, we may consider taking him to France during the spring.

MUSTAQQIL (IRE) 4 b g Invincible Spirit (IRE) - Cast In Gold (USA)
A lightly raced gelding we bought out of John Gosden's yard at the Newmarket October Sales. A winner on the all-weather at Kempton, he has only raced four times and we have given him a good break since joining us. A mile on a sound surface may bring out the best in him and we are hoping to have him in action by mid to late April.

OSARUVEETIL (IRE) 5 b g Teofilo (IRE) – Caraiyma (IRE)
A nice big horse who has yet to run for us having been acquired at the Newmarket July Sales. Held up by a few minor niggles, he has only raced twice in his career but he seems in good form at home at the moment. Already a winner on the all-weather, he may go back down that route at some stage. Middle distance handicaps will be on his agenda.

OUT DO 7 ch g Exceed And Excel (AUS) – Ludynosa (USA)
He really surprised and impressed us last season showing a lot more speed than we thought he had. Having won at Pontefract over six furlongs on his reappearance, we decided to experiment and drop him back to the minimum trip at York. He never looked back winning there and also the Listed City Walls Stakes over the same course and distance in July. We then ran him in the Group 2 King George Stakes at Goodwood but the track didn't suit him. He is at his best on flat tracks such as Haydock and York. We thought he would run well in the Nunthorpe Stakes at York in August but he suffered an injury to his jaw which ruled him out for the rest of the season. Thankfully, he is 100% again and we will probably give him one run, possibly in the Temple Stakes at Haydock (21st May), before aiming him at the King's Stand Stakes at Royal Ascot (14th June). A horse with loads of speed, he wants plenty of cover in his races.

PANDORA (IRE) 4 ch f Galileo (IRE) – Song of My Heart (IRE)
A lightly raced filly who joined us during the winter. She won a maiden for Charlie Hills before finishing third in the Musidora Stakes at York. We haven't made any plans but she is rated 98 and we could start her off in a handicap. Ten furlongs appears to suit her.

PROVIDENT SPIRIT 5 b g Invincible Spirit (IRE) – Port Providence
Although he didn't manage to get his head in front last year, he ran some very good races in defeat. Runner-up in the Carlisle Bell, he was unlucky in the Summer Cup at Thirsk leading until getting headed close home. Although he stays a mile, he is possibly better suited by seven furlongs. He will be campaigned in the same sort of races and I think he could do well this year.

REGAL DAN (IRE) 6 b g Dark Angel (IRE) – Charlene Lacy (IRE)
A winner over seven furlongs at York last summer, the key to him is fast ground. Runner-up behind Rex Imperator at Doncaster's St Leger meeting, he is effective over six and seven furlongs.

REX IMPERATOR 7 b g Royal Applause – Elidore
Not the easiest horse to train but he won twice last season at Thirsk and Doncaster. Thankfully, he behaved better in the stalls but he has had his share of problems. However, he is capable of winning more races. Six furlongs on quick ground and plenty of cover is what he wants.

SALATEEN 4 ch c Dutch Art – Amanda Carter
He only arrived a week before having his first run for us at Doncaster in late October. Although he ran well enough in third, the ground was too soft for him. He likes fast ground and seems to enjoy racing prominently. Tracks like Haydock and York suit him and we will be aiming him at conditions and Listed races over seven furlongs.

SAVED BY THE BELL (IRE) 6 b g Teofilo (IRE) – Eyrecourt (IRE)
A good staying horse, he isn't straightforward but improved again last season winning at York and finishing second a couple of times at the same track. He will follow a similar programme and be aimed at one mile six plus handicaps.

SIGNORE PICCOLO 5 b g Piccolo – Piccolo Cativo
Good fresh, he won first time out for us at Ripon last season and also won at Catterick during the summer. A solid horse, he can be slowly away at times, which doesn't help his cause. Effective over six and seven furlongs, he ran well from a wide draw at Thirsk over the latter trip.

SO BELOVED 6 b g Dansili – Valencia
He is a very good horse who enjoyed an excellent season winning a decent handicap at York and the Group 3 Supreme Stakes at Goodwood. Despite pulling hard, he still ran well in a Listed race at Redcar and was then only beaten a length in the Group 2 Challenge Stakes at Newmarket. He didn't have the best of reputations as a young horse because he was inclined to flash his tail. However, he has really got his act together and, being a huge horse, he could improve again this year. Seven furlongs is his trip and there are plenty of options for him, including the Listed King Richard III Stakes at Leicester and the Listed Spring Trophy at Haydock (7th May). There is also the Group 3 John of Gaunt Stakes at Haydock (28th May) to consider. Later in the year, the Lennox Stakes at Glorious Goodwood could be an option because we know he likes the track. He seems to handle any ground and there is no reason why he couldn't end up in something like the Prix de la Foret at Longchamp on Arc day in October. He looks well at the moment.

STEEL TRAIN (FR) 5 b g Zafeen (FR) – Silent Sunday (IRE)
Ex-French, he is a solid handicapper who won at Thirsk last spring. Runner-up at the same track later in the year, he ought to remain competitive off his mark and will continue at the same level.

SUEDOIS (FR) 5 b g Le Havre (IRE) – Cup Cake (IRE)
An exciting new addition, we bought him at the Arqana Sale in October. A six times winner, he has already won at Listed and Group 3 level and wasn't beaten far in the Group 1 Prix de la Foret at Longchamp on his final start. He has settled in well and we will be looking towards races like the Group 3 Abernant Stakes at Newmarket (14th April). Six and seven furlongs appear to be ideal. We are very pleased with him.

TADAANY (IRE) 4 b g Acclamation – Park Haven (IRE)
A fun horse, we acquired him at the Newmarket Horses In Training Sale in October. Previously trained by Dermot Weld, he won over a mile at Listowel in September and he reminded us of Bartack, who we used to train. He looks well and we will be aiming him at seven furlongs and one mile handicaps with some cut in the ground.

TAWDEEA 4 b g Intikhab (USA) – Sharedah (IRE)
Bought out of Richard Hannon's yard in October, he has only raced three times but was placed at Sandown and Nottingham last summer and is officially rated 87. We are hoping he is open to improvement and a step up to a mile and a quarter may suit him this year.

TERHAAL (IRE) 4 b g Raven's Pass (USA) – Silk Trail
Lightly raced, we bought him at the Newmarket July Sales and he was placed at Catterick and Newmarket in October. Beaten by a good horse on the latter occasion, he likes plenty of cut in the ground with seven furlongs and a mile being his trips.

THAT IS THE SPIRIT 5 b g Invincible Spirit (IRE) – Fraulein
A nice horse who started last season very well by winning the Listed Spring Trophy at Haydock in May. His form tailed off thereafter but he seems in good form at home. Seven furlongs around a bend is ideal with Haydock really suiting him. He will follow a similar campaign to Salateen, although we may start him off over six furlongs. He does like a bit of cut in the ground.

TREASURY NOTES (IRE) 4 b g Lope De Vega (IRE) – Elegant As Well (IRE)
Previously trained in Ireland, he arrived in late summer and has only had four runs for us. Placed at Beverley and Pontefract, he won at Hamilton in between over a mile. He likes some ease in the ground and we bought him back at the October Sales because he looks progressive and remains reasonably treated. Narrowly beaten over a mile on his reappearance at Redcar on Easter Monday, I think ten furlongs will be his trip this year.

USTINOV 4 b g Exceed And Excel (AUS) – Tamzin
He only joined us in August but he won twice at Ayr and Wolverhampton over six and seven furlongs. A talented horse who wants plenty of cover in his races, he likes a strongly run six furlongs.

WATCHABLE 6 ch g Pivotal – Irresistible
He looks well and, although he didn't manage to win last year, he ran some very good races in defeat. Runner-up in the Abernant Stakes at Newmarket in April, he was only beaten a couple of lengths when finishing fourth in the Group 1 Prix Maurice de Gheest at Deauville during the summer. Six furlongs with some cut in the ground are his optimum conditions and we will be giving him an early and late season campaign.

THREE YEAR OLDS

ALSVINDER b c Footstepsinthesands – Notting Hill (BRZ)
A lovely unraced colt who is going very well at home. He has developed during the winter and will probably start off in a six furlongs maiden in early April.

AREEN (IRE) b c Kodiac – Falcolnry (IRE)
He was a smart juvenile for Kevin Ryan last season winning at York on his debut before finishing a close second in the Windsor Castle Stakes at Royal Ascot and he was also third in the Group 2 Prix Robert Papin at Maisons-Laffitte. A lovely big horse, we may aim him at the Listed Westow Stakes at York (12th May) over five furlongs. He joined us during the winter and has settled in well.

CAPE LOVE (USA) ch c Cape Blanco (IRE) – Matroshka (IRE)
He is a nice horse who won his maiden at the second attempt at Thirsk. Stepping up in grade next time, he didn't give his running in a Listed race at Haydock. Officially rated 80, I think he is on a fair mark and, while we will probably start him off over a mile, there is every chance he will stay further in due course.

FLYBOY (IRE) b c Zoffany (IRE) – In Dubai (USA)
A very nice colt who showed a lot of speed at the breeze-ups last spring when we bought him. We gave him plenty of time and we thought he would run well on his debut at Musselburgh in October. Beaten around three lengths in third, we feel he will benefit from dropping back to seven furlongs. He is a half-brother to Earth Drummer, who we trained to win twice. He stayed a mile and a half but was by Dylan Thomas. This colt isn't slow.

HARAZ (IRE) b g Acclamation – Hanakiyya (IRE)
Bought at Goffs in November, he was quite consistent last year for Mick Halford without getting his head in front. Placed three times in decent maidens, he has done well during the winter and we are hoping he will be a fun horse who may develop into a Saturday horse. He has only raced over seven furlongs but we may drop him back in distance.

MON BEAU VISAGE (IRE) br g Footstepsinthesand – Hurricane Lily (IRE)
A half-brother to Kool Henry, who we used to train, he won at Redcar on his debut last year. While he didn't really progress in the manner we had hoped, he appears to have grown up a lot mentally during the winter. Still immature last year, he is the type to improve with age and I think he may stay further this season.

MUROOR ch g Nayef (USA) – Raaya (USA)
Previously trained by Marcus Tregoning, we acquired him cheaply at the Newmarket Sales in late October. A keen, quirky sort, he has only raced twice finishing fourth at Leicester last time. If he learns to settle down, he could be quite a nice horse because he has ability.

NORTH SPIRIT (IRE) b g Zebedee – Zara's Girl (IRE)
He ran well behind Poet's Prize on his first run for us at Beverley before having another couple of outings on the all-weather. Five furlongs on sharp tracks suit him because he possesses a lot of speed. Good ground is ideal.

SUNGLIDER (IRE) b g High Chaparral (IRE) – Desert Ease (IRE)
We bought him at Goffs in February having been placed in three of his four maidens for Dermot Weld last year. He has some very good form on fast ground before disappointing on his final run on soft ground. A nice big horse, we will try and win a maiden with him before hopefully progressing. Seven furlongs suited him last year but he ought to stay at least a mile being by High Chaparral.

TAWAYNA (IRE) b f Invincible Spirit (IRE) – Bratislava
A half-sister to three times Listed winner Katla, she has joined us from William Haggas during the winter. She was an expensive yearling and is well thought of. Quite a keen going type, she won her maiden over five furlongs at Ripon last August and hopefully she is open to plenty of improvement. The handicapper has given her a mark of 70 and she will be going sprinting.

TOLSTOY (IRE) b c Galileo (IRE) – Song of My Heart (IRE)
An unraced full-brother to Pandora, he is a lovely big horse who we quite like. He possesses plenty of scope and is hopefully one to look forward to.

TRAINER'S HORSE TO FOLLOW: SUEDOIS
TRAINER'S ASSISTANT (Jason Kelly) HORSE TO FOLLOW: FLYBOY

Hugo PALMER

Stables: Kremlin Cottage Stables, Snailwell Road, Newmarket.
2015: 34 Winners from 197 Runners 17% Prize-Money £1,042,340
www.hugopalmer.com

OLDER HORSES

ASCRIPTION (IRE) 7 b g Dansili – Lady Elgar (IRE)

A soft ground horse who is still relatively lightly raced considering he is a seven year old. I still believe there is a big day in him. Second a couple of times last season, he was only beaten two lengths in the Group 2 Lennox Stakes at Glorious Goodwood and will follow a similar programme this time. Seven furlongs is his trip and the natural starting point is the Group 3 John of Gaunt Stakes at Haydock (28th May), a race in which he was only beaten half a length by Cable Bay in last year. Given his preference for easy ground, it wouldn't surprise me if he ended the season in the Group 1 Prix de la Foret.

COVERT LOVE (IRE) 4 b f Azamour (IRE) – Wing Stealth (IRE)

She looks tremendous having grown and matured during the winter. A Group 1 winner over ten and twelve furlongs, the world is her oyster this season. She is currently 45kg heavier than when she won the Prix de L'Opera at Longchamp in October. We have always liked her but we knew she was going to be very good when winning the Listed Hoppings Stakes at Newcastle against the older fillies in June. She never looked back thereafter winning the Irish Oaks and at Longchamp on Arc day. We will be avoiding slow ground this year though because it didn't suit her in the Yorkshire Oaks or on Champions Day at Ascot on her final run. The obvious race to start her off in this time is the Group 2 Middleton Stakes at York (12th May), where she will carry a three pounds penalty. Races like the Pretty Polly Stakes at the Curragh (26th June), Nassau Stakes at Goodwood and Yorkshire Oaks again will all be strongly considered but we would like to take on the colts at some stage. That means the Prince of Wales's Stakes at Royal Ascot, Eclipse and King George are possibilities, too. It would be nice to think she could end up in the Prix de L'Arc de Triomphe because we know she stays and likes Longchamp. She doesn't need a lot of work and we are looking forward to seeing her running again.

EXTREMITY (IRE) 5 ch g Exceed And Excel (AUS) – Chanterelle (IRE)

He endured a frustrating year last season and we don't know why. Rated twelve pounds lower than this time last year, he is very well handicapped if we can get him right. He has always worked well at home but over raced early on last season. We have given him a change of scenery at home and put him in a different yard. He looks great and is moving well following a long break. We might try him in a hood because he needs to switch off early on in his races. We may also fit him with a stalls blanket this time around.

HOME OF THE BRAVE (IRE) 4 ch c Starspangledbanner (AUS) – Blissful Beat

Last year's Free Handicap winner, he is so much bigger than he has ever been. He weighed 425kg when winning his maiden as a two year old and is over 500kg now. The most confusing thing about him is his trip. James McDonald rode him in the Commonwealth Cup at Royal Ascot last year and said he didn't have the change of gear over six furlongs at that level and I wish we had run him in the Jersey Stakes instead. When he ran over seven furlongs at the Curragh (won but later disqualified) he looked as though he would stay a mile. If he is going to be a Group 1 horse this year, I think it will be over a mile. With that in mind, the Lockinge Stakes at Newbury (14th May) is the obvious starting point followed by the Queen Anne Stakes at Royal Ascot. Due to the fact he is 75% owned by Australians, there is every chance he will run over there at some stage.

NOT NEVER 4 ch g Notnowcato – Watchoverme

He had a very good season winning at Chester's May meeting and finishing second in the Melrose Stakes at York in August. I shouldn't have run him at Newmarket on his final start but he has grown a few inches during the winter and he could be an exciting staying horse this year. An old fashioned stayer, he needs cut in the ground and I am hoping he will be at least an Ebor horse, having run well at York in the past. The fact he has already won at the track means we could also consider the Chester Cup (4th May). I see no reason why he won't stay two miles or further.

SPANISH SQUEEZE (IRE) 4 ch g Lope De Vega (IRE) – Appetina

I have always rated him very highly and thought he was the best of our two year olds in early 2014, in a batch which also included Aktabantay and Covert Love. I think he is a lot better than he has shown so far and feel he remains a potential Group horse in the making. There hasn't been anything major wrong with him but he has been unsound on occasions and has only raced a handful of times. However, we have gelded him and he has finally matured and looks a beast. Narrowly beaten over ten furlongs at Chelmsford in November, he wasn't right next time at Kempton. It wasn't the trip which beat him but I am not convinced he will stay a mile and a half, even though Martin Harley was adamant he would. He wants fast ground and the Listed Wolferton Stakes at Royal Ascot (18th June) could be a lovely race for him.

TAMGA (IRE) 4 b c Azamour (IRE) – Miss Beatrix (IRE)

European bred, he is a very good looking horse who has been racing in Istanbul. He has done well over there with a mile appearing to be his trip. It is possible he will stay a bit further, too, and could be one for something like the Zetland Gold Cup at Redcar (30th May).

TWITCH (IRE) 4 b f Azamour (IRE) – Blinking

She has always done her work at home with Covert Love but has only managed one win so far from a dozen races. Placed at Listed level on her final start in France, she matured last year and that has continued during the winter. She is twice the size now and the main priority in 2016 is to try and win a Listed race. A mile and a half suits her and she may even stay further. She does like cut in the ground.

WALPOLE (IRE) 4 b g Rock of Gibraltar (IRE) – Serena's Storm (IRE)

A really interesting horse who, despite being a half-brother to Rizeena, is a staying handicapper in the making. He won a bumper at Huntingdon in October and then we decided to switch him to the Flat. A length and a half winner at Wolverhampton in February, Jamie Spencer rode him and feels he will develop into a 90 horse on the Flat. Currently rated 77, we have given him a break since his last run but he will be in action on the turf during the spring.

THREE YEAR OLDS

ARCHITECTURE (IRE) b f Zoffany (IRE) – Brigayev (ITY)

She has done very well during the winter and, while we don't view her as a Classic contender at the moment, we are hoping she will gain some black type at some stage this season. Third on her debut at Haydock, she won next time at Nottingham and I think the further she goes this season, the better she will be. She has grown and strengthened since last year and we view her as a middle distance filly for this season. Indeed, if she stays a mile and a half, she could be very good. Officially rated 82, we have the option of running in a handicap or aiming her at an Oaks trial. In terms of ground, she has only raced on an easy surface and it is hard to say whether she will be as effective on a quicker one. We are still learning about her.

BAYDAR b c Rock of Gibraltar (IRE) – Splashdown
A half-brother to Aktabantay, he looks very promising having won his maiden at Lingfield on his second start. It didn't appear a strong race but he couldn't have won any easier. He doesn't have the speed of his brother but Martin Harley, who rode him on both starts last year, feels he will stay ten furlongs as a three year old. I have been pleased with him during the winter because he is stronger now. Depending on his work during the spring, he could start off in a handicap but I think he is at least a Listed class horse. He could be a Britannia Stakes horse or he may come into his own over a bit further. Very green on his debut at Haydock, he had an easy time of it on his second run and is therefore lightly raced and lacks experience.

DRIVE FASTER b c Invincible Spirit (IRE) – Fowey (USA)
A winner of his only start in Istanbul, he looks a really nice colt. We haven't made any plans but he has settled in well and I am very pleased with him.

GALILEO GOLD ch c Paco Boy (IRE) – Galicuix
Another very exciting horse who has developed tremendously during the winter. Despite the fact it was his fourth race, he still looked immature when winning the Group 2 Vintage Stakes at Goodwood in late July. It may not have been the strongest renewal but he did it well and then finished a very good third in the Group 1 Prix Jean-Luc Lagardere at Longchamp. He was drawn wide that day and the ground was quick enough but he finished strongly and was only beaten a length and a quarter. Both Frankie (Dettori) and I immediately said afterwards that the French Derby could be his race this year. In all likelihood, he will start in either the English or French 2000 Guineas but he doesn't want rattling fast ground. I think he is sure to stay ten furlongs because he is one of those horses who only does enough.

GIFTED MASTER (IRE) b g Kodiac – Shobobb
He must be the highest rated three year old gelding in Europe with a mark of 111. Successful in four of his six races last year, he has settled down and grown up a lot. The decision to geld him after his third run at Newmarket in May proved to be the right thing to do and he won over five, six, seven and eight furlongs as a juvenile. An easy winner at Newcastle in June, he suffered an injury soon afterwards and didn't canter again until August. Reappearing at Newmarket in early October, he won the £500,000 Tattersalls Millions 2YO Trophy and then produced a great performance to win the Group 3 Autumn Stakes at the same track over a mile. He has already achieved a lot and his first big target is the Jersey Stakes at Royal Ascot (15th June). In the meantime, he will run in the Tattersalls Sprint Stakes at Newmarket (13th April) over six furlongs. I think a mile will prove to be his optimum trip this year and I view him a potential Group 1 or 2 miler, especially abroad.

GOLD TRADE (IRE) b g Raven's Pass (USA) – Trading Places
Placed in all four of his races, I was not convinced he was going through with his effort and therefore decided to geld him in February. He also had a high testicle, which was pinching him, and hopefully the gelding operation will make a big difference. A big, strong horse, he could win a maiden early on or we go down the handicap route. It wouldn't surprise me if he developed into a Silver Bowl at Haydock (21st May) and Britannia Stakes at Royal Ascot type horse.

HARRY CHAMPION b g Cockney Rebel (IRE) – Nine Red
He is another we have gelded since his last run. Fourth at Windsor on his second run, he suffered a fracture soon afterwards and therefore missed the majority of the season. He returned in early December and won at Wolverhampton and I thought he should have followed up at the same track in a nursery a fortnight later. Rated 81, I feel he has more to offer off his mark and he is another who could develop into a Britannia horse. He should stay a mile.

HAWKSMOOR (IRE) b f Azamour (IRE) – Bridal Dance (IRE)
She is a really exciting filly who won twice last season, including the Group 3 Prestige Stakes at Goodwood and was Group 1 placed in the Fillies Mile. Last year was very encouraging because she was still immature and grew throughout the season. She doesn't want extremes of ground and I think ten furlongs will be as far as she wants to go this season. We have given her the right entries, namely the English/Irish and French 1000 Guineas, plus the French Oaks and Prix Saint Alary, which is being run at Deauville (16th May) this year. Physically, she has done particularly well from two to three and she has a very high opinion of herself – she goose steps on to the gallops. In all likelihood, she will reappear in one of the Guineas.

MENGHLI KHAN (IRE) b c Lope De Vega (IRE) – Danielli (IRE)
A half-brother to Fillies' Mile and Breeders' Cup Juvenile winner Chriselliam, he has always been a giant of a horse but has really filled out during the winter. An exciting prospect, he won his maiden at Nottingham but then I made a mistake by running him in the *Racing Post* Trophy at Doncaster less than three weeks later. He appeared to have the right profile beforehand but he went a bit weak and the ground was too soft for him. Although he handled easy ground at Nottingham, it probably wasn't a great race and he definitely doesn't want a bog. We haven't made any definite plans but I think he is most likely to reappear in a Derby trial, possibly the Feilden Stakes over nine furlongs at Newmarket (12th April) or he could go to Chester for the Dee Stakes (6th May). Due to his size, I don't see him as an Epsom Derby horse and he isn't certain to stay a mile and a half in any case. However, he could be a French Derby horse or perhaps one for the Tercentenary Stakes at Royal Ascot (16th June).

MURAD KHAN (FR) b c Raven's Pass (USA) – Lady Elgar (IRE)
He is a half-brother to Ascription but I think he will stay further than him and prove at his best around a mile and a quarter. We thought he would win on his debut at Kempton but he only finished third and suffered with a sore shin afterwards. He has turned inside out since and shouldn't have much trouble winning a maiden in the spring. His owner isn't keen on handicaps so we will probably be going down the stakes races route with him thereafter. He has a low quick action and will be suited by fast ground on the turf.

NESSITA ch f Shamardal (USA) – Neshla
I think she is a really exciting prospect and, of all my three year old fillies, she could be anything. We have given her entries in the French and Irish Oaks and, being out of a Singspiel mare, I think she will stay a mile and a half. She won her maiden at Kempton on her second run and has improved markedly during the winter. Even though she is only rated 77, we will be looking towards an Oaks trial in the spring. She floats across the ground so probably doesn't want it too soft.

PARIS MAGIC b c Champs Elysees – Belgooree
Runner-up on his debut at Wolverhampton, he should have won next time at Kempton but the race didn't work out as planned. He has come back in from his winter break looking bigger and stronger and I will be disappointed if he doesn't win races this year. The further he goes, the better he will be and I can see him staying beyond a mile and a half, if necessary. He may emerge as a King George V Handicap horse for Royal Ascot (16th June). I think he will handle most types of ground.

PERU b f Motivator – Bolsena (USA)
She is not over big but is broader and heavier than last year. A winner at Haydock, she should have won next time in a nursery at Pontefract. Over the top by the time she contested the Listed Montrose Stakes at Newmarket, plus the ground was possibly too soft, she has been given an entry in the French Oaks at her owner's request. There are so many Oaks trials to consider during the spring. We are obviously keen to win some black type with her.

SACRED TRUST b c Acclamation – Paracel (USA)
Placed in two runs at Lingfield, the form of his half length second behind Hombre Rojo looks strong with the winner subsequently landing his next two starts and finishing third in the UAE 2000 Guineas at Meydan. We have given him a break since and the first aim is to win a maiden. His owner is from Hong Kong, which is where this horse will end up. Beforehand, he could be another Silver Bowl/Britannia type horse.

THEY SEEK HIM HERE (IRE) b or br c Elusive Pimpernel (USA) – Spiritville (IRE)
A big horse who did well as a juvenile considering his size. Having won his maiden at the first time of asking at Kempton, he finished fourth in the Group 2 Superlative Stakes at Newmarket and also the Group 3 Solario Stakes at Sandown. With hindsight, I wish we had put him away for the winter after that but we were preparing him for a Group 1 in France over ten furlongs at the end of the season and he pulled a muscle five days before the race. It took him a long time to get over that. Thankfully, he is fine now and looks really well. Trips around ten and twelve furlongs will suit him this year and we are hoping he develops into a Saturday horse.

TO BE WILD (IRE) br c Big Bad Bob (IRE) – Fire Up
Very green when finishing a promising fifth on his debut at Newmarket in late September, he has unfortunately suffered a stress fracture to his pelvis since and won't be running until the middle of the summer. However, the prognosis is good and he is potentially a very nice horse. A well bred colt, it would be nice to think he could develop into a Great Voltigeur/St Leger horse later in the year but he needs to win his maiden first and we will go from there. We will start him off over ten or twelve furlongs with a bit of ease in the ground. He has been a slow learner at home and, as discussed, he was green on his first run and then he coughed afterwards. Physically, he has grown and filled out since last year and is a horse with a lot of ability.

WE ARE NINETY (IRE) b f Thewayyouare (USA) – Brigids Cross (IRE)
She won nicely at Wolverhampton on her only start and I think she is well treated off a mark of 70. Still very weak last year, she has changed physically during the winter and could be anything. We will make the most of her rating initially but she could be black type material later on. She has really strengthened up and is a lovely prospect.

ZODIAKOS (IRE) b g Kodiac – Zonic
A huge horse, he won by four and a half lengths on his debut at Sandown but then hated the soft ground at Salisbury next time. Runner-up at Kempton on his final run, he is yet another who could contest the Silver Bowl at Haydock and the Britannia Stakes at Royal Ascot. There is every chance he will be heading to Hong Kong after Royal Ascot. I think a mile will be his trip because he isn't short of speed.

TWO YEAR OLDS

Hugo was responsible for 22 juvenile winners in 2015 at an impressive strike-rate of 22%. They included Galileo Gold (Group 2 Vintage Stakes), Hawksmoor (Group 3 Prestige Stakes) and Gifted Master (Group 3 Autumn Stakes). The Newmarket based handler has kindly hand picked 22 of his new crop to keep an eye on during 2016. Hugo nominated the likes of Baydar, Gifted Master, Hawksmoor and Zodiakos in this feature last year, so I strongly suggest readers keep a close eye on the following.

BEE CASE br f Showcasing – Binabee (Galileo (IRE))
Owned by Prince Khalid Abdullah. Date of Birth: 3/2/14.

EXPRESS LADY (IRE) b f Helmet (AUS) – Star Express (Sadler's Wells (USA))
Owned by Dr Ali Ridha, she was bought for **40,000gns** at the Tattersalls October Sale. DOB: 11/4/14.

FORTITUDE (IRE) b f Oasis Dream – Sweepstake (IRE) (Acclamation)
Owned by Mr Isa Salman, she is a half-sister to Horseshoe Bay and was bought for **240,000gns** at the Tattersalls October Sale. DOB: 25/1/14.

IBN ALEMARAT (IRE) b c Zoffany (IRE) – Trois Graces (USA) (Alysheba (USA))
Owned by Ahmad Abdulla Al Shaikh, he was acquired for **42,000gns** at the Tattersalls October Sale. DOB: 29/4/14.

KODIAC KHAN b c Kodiac – Mirwara (IRE) (Darshaan)
Owned by Mr Hussain Alabbas Lootah, he is a half-brother to 11 times winner Dunaskin and was bought for **€65,000** at the Goffs Orby Sale. DOB: 3/5/14.

NILE EMPRESS b f Holy Roman Emperor (IRE) – Temple of Thebes (IRE) (Bahri (USA)
Owned by Mr & Mrs A.E.Pakenham, she cost **20,000gns** at the Tattersalls October Sale. DOB: 16/2/14.

ROSELAND (USA) b f First Defence (USA) – Aviate (Dansili)
Owned by Prince Khalid Abdullah. DOB: 24/1/14.

UNFORGETABLE FILLY b f Sepoy (AUS) – Beautiful Filly (Oasis Dream)
Owned by Dr Ali Ridha, she was bought for **50,000gns** at the Tattersalls October Sale. DOB: 1/3/14.

WEDDING BREAKFAST (IRE) ch f Casamento (IRE) – Fair Countenance (IRE) (Almutawakel)
Owned by De La Warr Racing, she was bought for **26,000gns** at the Doncaster Premier Yearling Sale. DOB: 21/2/14.

Unnamed b f Canford Cliffs (IRE) – Tencarola (IRE) (Night Shift (USA))
Owned by Rebels With A Cause, she cost **36,000gns** at the Tattersalls October Sale. DOB: 20/4/14.

Unnamed br c Dark Angel (IRE) – Karliysha (IRE) (Kalanisi (IRE))
Owned by Sun Bloodstock SARL, he was purchased for **115,000gns** at the Tattersalls October Sale. DOB: 17/4/14.

Unnamed ch c Dutch Art – Cantal (Pivotal)
Owned by Al Shaqab Racing, he was acquired for **350,000gns** at the Tattersalls October Sale. DOB: 12/2/14.

Unnamed ch c Exceed And Excel (AUS) – Anna Amalia (IRE) (In The Wings)
Owned by Mr Sultan Ali, he is a half-brother to Grade 1 winner Ave and cost **78,000gns** at the Tattersalls October Sale. DOB: 3/4/14.

Unnamed b c Excelebration (IRE) – Blissful Beat (Beat Hollow)
Owned by Mr V.I.Araci, he is a half-brother to Home of The Brave and was purchased for **€160,000** at the Arqana Deauville Yearling Sale. DOB: 23/3/14

Unnamed b c Frankel – Drops (IRE) (Kingmambo (USA))
Owned by Al Asayl Bloodstock Ltd. DOB: 14/2/14.

Unnamed b or br c Intense Focus (USA) – Jouel (FR) (Machiavellian (USA)
Owned by MPH Racing, he cost €**55,000** at the Tattersalls Ireland September Sale. DOB: 11/3/14.

Unnamed b f Invincible Spirit (IRE) – Dalasyla (IRE) (Marju (IRE)
Owned by Al Shaqab Racing, she is a half-sister to Listed winner Dalkova and was bought for **300,000gns** at the Tattersalls October Sales. DOB: 30/1/14.

Unnamed b c Mayson – Hypnotize (Machiavellian (USA))
Owned by Al Shaqab Racing, he is a half-brother to Group 1 Cheveley Park Stud Stakes winner Hooray and was bought for **115,000gns** at the Tattersalls October Sale. DOB: 3/2/14.

Unnamed b f Oasis Dream – Virginia Waters (USA) (Kingmambo (USA))
Owned by Mr V.I.Araci, she was bought for €**295,000** at the Arqana Deauville August Sales. DOB: 29/3/14.

Unnamed b f Rock of Gibraltar (IRE) – Maid For Winning (USA) (Gone West (USA))
Owned by Mr V.I.Araci, she is a half-sister to Hors De Combat and was acquired for **45,000gns** at the Tattersalls October Sale. DOB: 31/3/14.

Unnamed b c Sir Prancealot (IRE) – Mystic Dream (Oasis Dream)
Owned by Anglia Bloodstock Syndicate VIII, he was bought for **30,000gns** at the Doncaster Premier Yearlings Sale. DOB: 15/1/14.

Unnamed b c Vale of York (IRE) – Al Mahmeyah (Teofilo (IRE))
Owned by Mr Hamad Rashed Bin Ghedayer. DOB: 12/2/14.

TRAINER'S HORSE TO FOLLOW: SPANISH SQUEEZE

Roger VARIAN

Stables: Kremlin House Stables, Fordham Road, Newmarket, Suffolk.
2015: 100 Winners from 474 Runners 21% Prize-Money £1,541,465
www.varianstable.com

OLDER HORSES

AJMAN BRIDGE 6 b g Dubawi (IRE) - Rice Mother (IRE)
His form is in the book and he boasts some strong form in the big middle distance handicaps. Narrowly beaten in the Duke of Edinburgh Stakes at Royal Ascot last summer, he also ran well in the John Smith's Cup. He joined us in the Autumn and has enjoyed a good winter. We haven't made any plans but I would expect him to follow a similar route this year.

AMERICAN ARTIST (IRE) 4 ch c Danehill Dancer (IRE) - American Adventure (USA)
A consistent horse who improved as the season went on last year, winning three times. His best performance was at Doncaster's St Leger meeting when he appreciated the step up to a mile and a quarter for the first time. I thought he was a bit unlucky in the Silver Cambridgeshire next time because they went no gallop and it didn't suit him. Still progressive, I think there is more improvement to come from him.

BARSANTI (IRE) 4 b g Champs Elysees - Silver Star
A progressive horse who has won twice on the all-weather at Chelmsford and Kempton since joining us. I think he appreciated the step up in trip last time and he should stay a bit further, too. Third behind Decorated Knight at Haydock last summer, his form looks solid and I hope he will continue to improve.

BATTERSEA 5 b h Galileo (IRE) - Gino's Spirits
I am pleased with him and it was good to see him get his head in front again at Meydan during the winter, having endured an unlucky season last year. He is a good horse when he encounters fast ground. It was too soft at Haydock and Goodwood on his first two runs last year and then he was unfortunate not to win the Mallard Handicap at Doncaster in September having experienced traffic problems. Still lightly raced, he will either continue in the big middle distance or staying handicaps or we will step him up in class and look towards the Cup races. Effective over a mile and a half and a mile and six, he should stay two miles, although he is quite an exuberant horse. Depending on how he performs between now and then, the Melbourne Cup is a possible long-term target.

BELARDO (IRE) 4 b c Lope De Vega (IRE) - Danaskaya (IRE)
A top-class Group 1 winning two year old, he shaped with a lot of encouragement on his final two runs last season and it was enough to keep him in training as a four year old. He was only beaten three parts of a length by Solow in the Queen Elizabeth II Stakes at Ascot on Champions Day and he has thrived during the winter. Following the Doncaster Mile, the plan is to run him in the Group 2 Bet365 Mile at Sandown (22nd April) and then the Lockinge Stakes at Newbury (14th May).

CENTRAL SQUARE (IRE) 4 b g Azamour (IRE) - Lucky Clio (IRE)
Despite being a four year old maiden, he remains a promising horse. Only beaten a length by subsequent Group winner Koora at Doncaster on his debut, he wasn't quite right next time when disappointing at Chester. He is capable of winning a maiden before hopefully going on to better things.

DOUBLE UP 5 b g Exceed And Excel (AUS) – My Love Thomas (IRE)
He has developed into a very good sprinter winning three times last year and producing some excellent performances in defeat. Indeed, I thought his stand out run last season came at Goodwood when he finished second behind Ridge Ranger (subsequently placed at Listed and Group 3 level) conceding seventeen pounds. Prior to that, he was very good when winning a heritage handicap at Ascot. I regretted running him in the Shergar Cup at the same track and then we decided to put him away because he isn't suited by Autumn ground. Officially rated 107, he is still relatively lightly raced and we are hoping he can make the transition to Pattern races this year. He may start off in a 96-110 five furlongs handicap at Newbury (15th April).

INTILAAQ (USA) 4 b c Dynaformer (USA) – Torrestrella (IRE)
He is a very good horse who we are hoping will develop into a Prince of Wales's Stakes at Royal Ascot (15th June) and Eclipse Stakes (2nd July) horse this year. Then, it would be nice to think the King George at Ascot will come under consideration. We feel he will develop into a Group 1 horse. A three times winner last season, he won his maiden at Newbury during the spring by eight lengths but endured a harder race than it looked at the time. He was supplemented for the 2000 Guineas but it came very early in his career. Given a break, he produced two good performances at Newbury and Haydock, including in the Group 3 Rose of Lancaster Stakes at the latter. We considered running him in the Champions Stakes at Ascot but he is a top of the ground horse and he didn't sparkle on good to soft in a racecourse gallop at Newmarket beforehand so we decided to put him away for the winter. He has done very well during the winter and, having run creditably in the Group 1 Dubai Turf over nine furlongs at Meydan in late March, the plan now is to aim him at Royal Ascot. He has improved physically and, while we feel ten furlongs will be his ideal trip, I see no reason why he won't stay a mile and a half, if necessary.

KING BOLETE (IRE) 4 b g Cape Cross (IRE) – Chanterelle (FR)
A winner at Newbury last year, he ran some good races in defeat, including when fourth in the King George V Handicap at Royal Ascot. We have gelded him since arriving and hopefully that will help him. Officially rated 90, he will be running in the good middle distance handicaps this summer.

LADY OF DUBAI 4 b f Dubawi (IRE) – Lady of Everest (IRE)
A Listed winner, she was placed in the Oaks at Epsom last year. We have given her a good break since joining us and, in all likelihood, she will have her first run for us in the Group 2 Middleton Stakes at York (12th May). Andrea (Atzeni) feels ten furlongs is her best trip but I don't think she wants over racing.

MALJAA 4 ch g Paco Boy (IRE) – Kerry's Dream
He is not over big but extremely tough and he enjoyed a very good season winning three times. I must admit he surprised me a bit, although we did feel he may be a Royal Ascot two year old at one stage but he was unhealthy. Having finished second a couple of times, we decided to fit him with blinkers and it clearly helped because he won his next three races. He handles any ground and could be ideal for the Dash at Epsom (4th June) with one run beforehand. A very fast horse, he could even develop into a Prix de L'Abbaye horse.

MEDIATION 4 b f Azamour (IRE) – Macleya (GER)
A very late maturing filly, I think she could do well as a four year old. She has only raced three times, winning at Chelmsford on her most recent outing. Her mark looks OK and we are hoping she will gain some black type this year. She will continue over a mile and a quarter for the time being but she should stay further.

MINDUROWNBUSINESS (IRE) 5 b h Cape Cross (IRE) – Whos Mindin Who (IRE)
He has surprised me since we bought him at the end of 2014 winning five times, including at Wolverhampton in February. He tends to keep a bit back for himself at home and clearly saves it for the track. Third at Lingfield on Good Friday, we have given him a break since with a view to bringing him back in June/July. Suited by turning tracks, I think he wants fast ground on the turf.

MONOTYPE (IRE) 4 b g Makfi – Mill Guineas (USA)
A staying type who has only raced three times, we are still learning about him but it is possible he could develop into an Ebor type horse. He won his maiden at Doncaster last year before running in the Bahrain Trophy. Soft ground appears essential to him and he may have found it quick enough at Newmarket last time. We have gelded him since arriving and he looks a nice prospect for this year.

MOUNT LOGAN (IRE) 5 ch h New Approach (IRE) – Vistaria (USA)
A winner at Glorious Goodwood last summer, he also ran well in the Wolferton Stakes and John Smith's Cup at Royal Ascot and York respectively. His form is in the book but life is going to be tough for him this year off a mark of 110. A very likeable horse, he may be better off in Listed races off level weights.

MUJASSAM 4 ch g Kyllachy – Naizak
Something of a Jekyll and Hyde character, I think there is a big handicap to be won with him this year. The decision to geld him last year was a wise one and he won by eight lengths at Salisbury during the summer. Disappointing next time at Newbury, we decided to fit him with a visor at Yarmouth and he returned to form and won in good style. I think the Victoria Cup at Ascot (7th May) with one run beforehand could suit him. I wouldn't rule out dropping him back to a stiff six furlongs either because he isn't short of speed.

POSTPONED (IRE) 5 b h Dubawi (IRE) – Ever Rigg
He is in great form at the moment having enjoyed a very profitable spring. A three lengths winner of the Group 2 Dubai City of Gold at Meydan in early March, he then produced another very good performance when winning the Group 1 Sheema Classic during the same month. It was fantastic effort by the whole team and it was just the best feeling to have a winner on the greatest night of racing on a world stage. The King George (23rd July) is once again his main target with the likelihood of one race beforehand. The Coronation Cup at Epsom (4th June) is a possibility. Despite the fact he won the King George last year on soft ground, Andrea (Atzeni) thinks he is at his best on a quick surface. It would be nice to think he will end up in the Prix de L'Arc de Triomphe at the end of the season.

QUEEN'S PEARL (IRE) 4 b f Exceed And Excel (AUS) – Gimasha
I really like her and feel she is capable of winning a Group race. Six furlongs on fast ground are her conditions and I thought she was very good when winning at Nottingham last summer. She could return there for the Listed Kilvington Fillies' Stakes (7th May) and there are other options at Haydock during the first half of the season. She likes a flat track.

REALTRA (IRE) 4 gr f Dark Angel (IRE) – Devious Diva (IRE)
A very good filly who joined us during the second half of last season, winning twice, including the Group 3 Sceptre Stakes at Doncaster. Fifth in the Group 1 Sun Chariot Stakes at Newmarket, I thought she ran very well and shaped like the third best filly in the race. The Group 2 Duke of Cambridge Stakes at Royal Ascot (15th June) is her first main target and she will have one run beforehand. She appears to handle any ground.

ROSEBURG (IRE) 5 ch g Tamayuz – Raydaniya (IRE)
Runner-up in a valuable handicap at York's Ebor meeting, it won't be easy for him this year off 106. He appears to like some cut in the ground and we could step him up in trip this season. He will be aimed at the big middle distance handicaps.

SPANGLED 4 ch f Starspangledbanner (AUS) – Zykina
A lovely big filly who we are hoping will make the step up into Pattern races this year. Twice a winner last season, she is a monster who looks capable of progressing again as a four year old. She needs to be ridden quietly because we rode her too handily at Newmarket on her final run. We will start her off in a fillies' handicap but it wouldn't surprise me if she developed into a contender for the Duke of Cambridge Stakes at Royal Ascot (15th June).

SPIRITING (IRE) 4 b g Invincible Spirit (IRE) – Gold Bubbles (USA)
We haven't done a great deal with him but he looks a nice horse who has some good form in the book. A winner over a mile at Leicester, he looks like a sprinter and has form over shorter trips. We have gelded him during the winter and hopefully that will help him. He will continue down the handicap route.

STEPS (IRE) 8 br g Verglas (IRE) – Killinallan
He looked as good as ever last season winning the Portland Handicap at Doncaster and a Group 3 at Newbury. He has run two very good races in the Dash at Epsom finishing fourth on each occasion. Each time, he has been slowly away before finishing strongly. He may go back there in early June with the Palace House Stakes at Newmarket (30th April) a possible target en route. Already a Group 3 winner, he needs to be ridden bravely and enjoys cut in the ground. He usually needs his first run and wants a strong gallop. I am convinced he could be a Prix de L'Abbaye horse, if he gets his ground.

STEVE ROGERS (IRE) 5 b g Montjeu (IRE) – Three Owls (IRE)
Very genuine, he handles any ground and is a horse I love. A five times winner last season, I would dearly like to win the Chester Cup with him (4th May). The fact he has already won at the track is a bonus but he needs a further rise in the ratings to be assured of getting in. Even though he only finished ninth in the Cesarewitch, I thought he ran very well because he was drawn in stall 33 and was beaten less than four lengths. He stays well and I feel he is open to further improvement.

WHITE LAKE 4 b g Pivotal – White Palace
A horse with a lofty reputation, he held Group 1 entries last season but we haven't done a lot with him since arriving. Even though he ran well in the Heron Stakes at Sandown over a mile, I am tempted to drop him back to seven furlongs. With that in mind, he could be one for the Listed King Richard III Stakes (23rd April), which we have won a couple of years ago with Eton Forever. He has been gelded since his last run.

THREE YEAR OLDS

ABSOLUTE ZERO (IRE) b g Cape Cross (IRE) – Emsiyah (USA)
I was disappointed he didn't win as a two year old because I have always liked him. Placed at Sandown and Beverley, he is on a realistic mark and I hope he will develop into a fun handicapper over seven furlongs and a mile.

AGHAANY gr f Dubawi (IRE) – Hathrah (IRE)
A half-sister to Hadaatha, who was a Listed winner and Group 1 placed for us a couple of years ago, I liked her early on last year. However, she didn't progress as much as we hoped and only finished sixth on her sole outing at Newmarket at the backend. Given her pedigree, the first priority is to win a race with her.

AJMAN PRINCESS (IRE) b f Teofilo (IRE) – Reem Three
Unraced, she is a filly I like, who moves well at home. The plan is to start her off in a ten furlongs fillies' maiden during the spring.

ALJULJALAH (USA) b f Exchange Rate (USA) – Ruler's Charm (USA)
I like her a lot and she won on her debut at Newmarket in late September. We then stepped her up in class a fortnight later in the Group 3 Oh So Sharp Stakes at the same track but she disappointed. I am hoping a combination of soft ground and the fact she wasn't healthy afterwards explains her performance. I think she is quite smart and, although she may not be ready to run early in the spring due to a little setback, she could be one for something like the Sandringham Handicap at Royal Ascot (15th June). She works very well at home and I think seven furlongs or a mile will be her trip this year.

CHOREOGRAPHER (IRE) ch c Sea The Stars (IRE) – Evensong (GER)
An expensive yearling, he looks the part and could be anything. He is a nice type who was too immature to race as a juvenile but we liked him last year. I would expect him to start in a ten furlongs maiden but he ought to stay further. He is a colt with potential.

DAILY NEWS b c Street Cry (IRE) – Zeeba (IRE)
An unraced half-brother to Dandana, who won a Listed and Group 3 a few years ago. He is a promising type for the second half of the season.

DAWN OF HOPE (IRE) ch f Mastercraftsman (IRE) – Sweet Firebird (IRE)
A half-sister to Ayrad, she was an impressive winner of her maiden at Ascot on her second start. We then rushed her up in grade next time when contesting the Group 1 Fillies Mile at Newmarket. She was too fresh and raced up with the pace. With hindsight, we should have switched her off. Despite that, she is a filly we like and the intention is to aim her at an Oaks Trial in the spring. She won over a stiff mile at Ascot as a juvenile, so ought to stay ten and twelve furlongs this year. I don't think she would want the ground any quicker than good though.

ENNAADD b c King's Best (USA) – Zayn Zen
I like him. Having run well on his first two starts at Windsor and Lingfield, he returned to the latter venue and won his maiden by six lengths. He appears to be getting better and proved it when winning on his handicap debut at Chelmsford in February off a mark of 91. Raised seven pounds, he may develop into a contender for something like the Britannia Stakes at Royal Ascot (16th June). Long-term, we are hoping he could be better than a handicapper.

EX LOVER ch c Monsun (GER) – Tu Eres Mi Amore (IRE)
Another nice unraced colt, he is one for the second half of the season.

FACTS AND FIGURES (IRE) gr c Galileo (IRE) – Laddies Poker Two (IRE)
A well bred unraced colt, he is out of a Wokingham Stakes winner and is a decent type. Held up by niggly problems last year, he could start off in something like the Wood Ditton Stakes at Newmarket (13th April).

FIRST RATE b c Kyllachy – Hooray
Bred to be speedy being out of a Lowther and Cheveley Park Stud Stakes winner, he disappointed on his debut at Haydock where the ground was too soft and he was too fresh. Third next time at Bath, he will hopefully win a five or six furlongs maiden before going sprint handicapping.

FOURTH WAY (IRE) b f Iffraaj – Spiritual Air
She is a nice filly. Having won her maiden at Yarmouth, she ran a good race in the Listed Radley Stakes at Newbury finishing third. She could be another for the Sandringham Handicap at Royal Ascot (15th June).

HAALICK (IRE) ch c Roderic O'Connor (IRE) – Lucky Pipit
I thought he was very good first time out when winning at Haydock and then he did nothing wrong in a Listed event at Doncaster's St Leger meeting finishing second. However, he was disappointing in the Group 3 Somerville Tattersalls Stakes at Newmarket and I don't know why. Thankfully, he has returned to his best during the winter/spring winning a Listed race at Lingfield in March before finishing an unlucky third in the 3 Year Old Mile Championships Conditions Stakes at the same track on Good Friday.

HEART SPRINKLED (IRE) b f Galileo (IRE) – Heart Shaped (USA)
Unraced, I quite like her but she was still immature last year. All being well, she will make her debut in a ten furlongs fillies' maiden in April.

HIGH COMMAND (IRE) b c High Chaparral (IRE) – Plaza (USA)
A likeable colt, he didn't race last year due to immaturity but we have been pleased with him during the winter. He is another who will start off in a mile and a quarter maiden but he should stay twelve furlongs later on.

KARISMA (IRE) gr f Lawman (FR) – Lucky Clio (IRE)
She ran OK on her only outing at Ascot as a juvenile but suffered a setback afterwards. I think she is better than she showed that day and will be suited by a step up to ten furlongs this year. She is a half-sister to Central Square.

MAJDOOL (IRE) b c Acclamation – Maany (USA)
Unbeaten on the all-weather last year at Wolverhampton and Kempton, he didn't manage to win on the turf but I don't envisage any problems. He may prefer some ease in the ground and we will be aiming him at the good three year old handicaps over seven furlongs and a mile.

MUTARAJJIL (IRE) b c Acclamation – Rouge Noir (USA)
I like him and I feel he could be progressive as a three year old. Beaten a nose at Kempton in November, he ought to win his maiden before being aimed at the decent six furlongs three year old handicaps. He could be one for the valuable three year old handicap at York (11th June).

MUTAWAALY (IRE) b c Cape Cross (IRE) – Sana Abel (IRE)
His work at home has always been good and he is a horse I like. An easy winner of his only start at Wolverhampton at the end of last year, the form of the race hasn't worked out but we feel he is a nice horse. He will resume in a handicap but he could be better than that. From the family of Oaks winners Eswarah and Midway Lady, he is bred to stay a mile and a half.

MYTIMEHASCOME b f Montjeu (IRE) – Vital Statistics
I love her and, even though she remains a maiden, I think she is very good. Fifth on her debut at Newmarket, the trip was too sharp and then she was drawn low at Kempton. Only beaten a length, they went no gallop early on and she finished strongly and was unlucky not to win. Her work has always been good and I will be disappointed if she isn't a stakes filly. We will look for another maiden and, then all being well, she will line up in an Oaks trial.

NADA b f Teofilo (IRE) – Zomaradah
A beautifully bred filly, she is a half-sister to Dubawi and certainly has the pedigree to be good. She moves well at home but we haven't really tested the engine yet.

NEW WORLD POWER (JPN) b c Deep Impact (JPN) – Listen (IRE)
Another exciting unraced horse who we like a lot. By Deep Impact, who has been a superstar, he is an athlete who endured a long journey from Japan. We will start him off over ten furlongs and I hope he is good.

NEZWAAH b f Dubawi (IRE) – Ferdoos
Quite a decent filly out of a Listed winner we used to train, we haven't been surprised by either of her two wins so far. A straightforward filly with a good attitude, she won nicely on her debut at Chelmsford in January and then she followed up in a handicap at Wolverhampton less than a month later. Despite a ten pounds rise, I feel she will remain competitive off her mark (83) and we have even entered her in the French Oaks. We will wait for the turf now and there is a possibility she will run in a ten furlongs three year old handicap at Salisbury (71-85) on the 1st May. A mile and a quarter with some dig in the ground will be ideal because I don't think she will want it too quick. She isn't certain to stay a mile and a half either.

NOTARY b f Lawman (FR) – Purity
Third on her debut at Newmarket in July, she didn't really handle the track at Goodwood next time but still managed to win. She is a filly I like and her mark looks OK. I don't think she will be running beyond a mile.

OWASEYF (USA) b f Medaglia D'Oro (USA) – Nasmatt
Unraced, she looks a middle distance filly in the making. I like her and she will probably start off in a ten furlongs maiden in the spring. She could make her debut on the all-weather.

PENNY LANE FOREVER b f Pivotal – Ventura Highway
An unraced half-sister to Lingfield Derby Trial winner Alessandro Volta, she is likely to make her debut over seven furlongs but will stay a mile. She is quite a nice filly who I like.

POINT OF VIEW (IRE) b c New Approach (IRE) – Artisti
An expensive yearling, he is a promising unraced colt who we like a lot. All being well, he will make his debut in a ten furlongs maiden in April.

SHABEEB (USA) b c Smart Strike (CAN) – Sortita (GER)
He is a half-brother to Mutashaded, who was placed in the King Edward VII Stakes at Royal Ascot for us a few years ago. Still a frame last year, he has done well physically during the winter and he is a colt I really like. Sixth on his only start at Newbury, he is from a very good family and will come into his own over ten and twelve furlongs.

SHARJA QUEEN b f Pivotal – Dubai Queen (USA)
From the family of Dubawi, she is a likeable filly who chased home Lumiere at Newmarket on her debut before winning next time at Ffos Las. Depending on her work during the spring, she could reappear in a Guineas trial. I expect her to stay a mile this year.

SPANISH CITY ch c Exceed And Excel (AUS) – Annabelle's Charm (IRE)
Well bred being a half-brother to Middle Park Stakes winner Charming Thought, he is a lovely horse who was placed in both his races last year. The ground was against him on each occasion at Haydock and Newcastle and I think he will develop into a very good sprinter on fast ground this year. He will hopefully win his maiden and we will go from there.

SUN LOVER b c Oasis Dream – Come Touch The Sun (IRE)
A promising colt who raced twice last year finishing third at Newmarket on his second start. He won't be reappearing until the summer though, due to a minor setback, but he should win races.

TAILWIND b c Dubawi (IRE) – Time Saved
A well bred son of Dubawi, he is another promising young horse who won his maiden at the second time of asking. Runner-up over seven furlongs at Wolverhampton, he was suited by the drop back in trip at Kempton next time. He, too, has suffered a small injury and therefore won't be in action until the second half of the season. Despite being a half-brother to a King Edward VII Stakes winner (Plea Bargain), he looks a sprinter.

TANEEN (USA) b or br c Speightstown (USA) – Moon And Sun (USA)
Ran an encouraging race on his debut at Salisbury finishing third and confirmed the promise when winning well at Newmarket next time. We were going to run him again but he had a minor niggle so we decided to put him away for the winter. He is 100% and the plan is to start him off in the six furlongs handicap for three year olds at Newmarket's Craven meeting (14th April). He is a promising colt.

TIERCEL b c Olden Times – Sharp Mode (USA)
A half-brother to Amralah, he is another promising colt who ran well on his debut at Sandown finishing a close third. We shouldn't have run him in the Group 3 Autumn Stakes at Newmarket next time. His work has always been very good and, although he may not want any further than ten furlongs, he is a nice prospect.

TOUMAR ch f Sea The Stars (IRE) – Tingling (USA)
A three lengths winner on her debut at Wolverhampton during the winter, the form is nothing to write home about and she only finished third on her handicap debut at Chelmsford next time but we like her and I hope she will progress.

UAE PRINCE (IRE) b c Sea The Stars (IRE) – By Request
Unraced, he was an expensive purchase as a yearling and is a colt full of potential. His work has been good and we will see how he gets on in a ten furlongs maiden in the spring.

WEST DRIVE (IRE) ch c Sea The Stars (IRE) – Fair Sailing (IRE)
He is slowly getting the hang of things finishing second at Nottingham on his final start. Qualified for handicaps, he shouldn't have any problem staying a mile and a half.

ZABEEL PRINCE (IRE) ch c Lope De Vega (IRE) – Princess Serena (USA)
A well bred unraced colt, he looks a nice type. I would imagine he will start off over a mile in April or May.

ZABEEL PRINCESS b f Dubawi (IRE) – Mundana (IRE)
Similar to Zabeel Prince, she has a nice pedigree and, all being well, she will make her debut in the spring. Her physique suggests six or seven furlongs may be her trip.

TRAINER'S HORSE TO FOLLOW: MYTIMEHASCOME

HANDICAP SNIPS?

Last year's feature included the likes of **MARGARET'S MISSION (25/1, 3/1, 4/1), MULTELLIE (7/2 & 5/2), NIGHT GENERATION (3 wins), ROYAL ALTITUDE (5/2)** and **SIR CHAUVELIN (6/1)**.

ARABIAN ILLUSION (FR)

4 ch g Makfi – Arabian Spell (IRE) (Desert Prince (IRE))
Trainer: A.M.BALDING. Kingsclere, Berkshire.

Andrew Balding had another very good season in 2015 with 95 domestic winners and prize-money of £1,539,900. While things didn't go to plan with one time Derby hope Elm Park, stablemate Tullius won the Group 2 Skybet York Stakes in July. The yard appear to have a well handicapped four year old in the shape of Arabian Illusion. Third behind subsequent Group 2 winner Balios as a juvenile, he was placed in maidens at Haydock and Kempton over a mile last summer. However, the Makfi gelding improved markedly when stepped up to ten furlongs at Goodwood (Soft) in September. A three and a quarter lengths winner from the 79 rated Tidal Moon, his rider Jim Crowley said afterwards: **"He is an improving horse who has been crying out for this trip. He tolerated the testing ground and prefers it good."** Despite running well behind the fast improving Arthenus at York the following month, he wasn't suited by the drop back to nine furlongs. Only beaten four lengths receiving eight pounds from James Fanshawe's winner, he is unbeaten over ten furlongs and may stay further. His half-brother Blissful Moment was runner-up in the Duke of Edinburgh Stakes at Royal Ascot in 2011. I will be surprised if Andrew Balding can't win a good ten or twelve furlongs handicap with Arabian Illusion this year.

FIDRA BAY (IRE)

3 b f Roderic O'Connor (IRE) – Halicardia (Halling (USA))
Trainer: G.A.SWINBANK. Melsonsby, North Yorkshire.

The lightly raced daughter of Roderic O'Connor, who cost €23,000, caught the eye in no uncertain terms on her second start at Carlisle (7f : Good/Firm) in September, whilst I was working for *Racing UK*. Slowly away, she kept on in really taking fashion to finish sixth behind the likes of Thesis (runner-up in the Group 2 Rockfel Stakes next time), Golden Stunner (rated 80) and Invermere (won since) under Neil Farley. Only beaten around six lengths, I would be inclined to forget her third run at Redcar on easier ground a fortnight later because it may have been a case of getting her handicapped and job done. The other point to make is the fact Fidra Bay made her debut over an inadequate five furlongs on Northumberland Plate day at Newcastle – trainers tend to run some of their nicer horses on a decent day's racing and provide their owners with a good day out. She wasn't disgraced at Gosforth Park either running on to finish sixth behind Plagiarism (rated 88), Paddy Power (90) and Wolowitz (97 – won 4 out of 4 since). Alan Swinbank's filly will come into her own over a mile and ten furlongs and it will be disappointing if she doesn't improve considerably on her current mark of 68.

Keep an eye on the stable's dual and unbeaten bumper winner **HAPPY HOLLOW** if he switches to the Flat this spring/summer. A four year old gelded son of Beat Hollow, he has looked a smart horse winning at Southwell and Wetherby this year and can only improve with experience. Alan has done extremely well with his former bumper horses going down the Flat route, including Pattern winners Alfie Flits, Collier Hill and Turbo Linn.

HAROLD LLOYD

4 b g Cape Cross (IRE) – Silent Act (USA) (Theatrical (USA))

Trainer: H.CANDY. Wantage, Oxon.

A big imposing gelding by Cape Cross, Henry Candy's four year old has only raced four times and looks attractively weighted off a rating of 79. Third in maidens over a mile and ten furlongs at Nottingham and Sandown, he wasn't disgraced behind Grand Inquisitor (rated 96) and Master of Speed respectively, before winning at the latter venue in July (1m 2f : Good). A half length scorer from Zamperini (now rated 85), he made all the running and battled on well to repel the challenge of Mike Murphy's runner-up. His rider Fergus Sweeney said afterwards: **"Last time Harold Lloyd hung on ground that was too quick for him. He should progress, he's a lovely stamp of horse and there are better things to come."** Absent since, his trainer appeared pleased with him when we spoke in February. Bearing in mind his dam won over a mile and a half, Harry Lloyd can improve again when tackling a longer trip.

MEDIATION

4 b f Azamour (IRE) – Macleya (GER) (Winged Love (IRE))

Trainer: R.VARIAN. Newmarket, Suffolk.

Cheveley Park Stud owned fillies invariably improve with age and Mediation is certainly from a family who got better with time. Her dam progressed from handicaps to winning a Group 2 in France (1m 4f) between 2005 and 2007. Speaking to Roger Varian in February one got the distinct impression he felt the Azamour filly was favourably treated off 82 and, long-term, her main goal is to win some black type. A late maturing filly, she was runner-up behind the progressive Carnachy (rated 95) in a ten furlongs maiden at Newbury (Soft) in August before finishing third to Movie Set at Ascot the following month. Mediation got off the mark at the third attempt in no uncertain fashion at Chelmsford in November when powering to a four lengths success under Jack Mitchell. Yet to race beyond ten furlongs, her dam was narrowly beaten in the Prix Royal Oak at Longchamp for Andre Fabre. Therefore, Mediation is open to plenty of improvement when stepping up in distance this year.

SAINTED

3 ch f Dutch Art – Blithe (Pivotal)

Trainer: W.J.HAGGAS. Newmarket, Suffolk.

This once raced filly is from a family William Haggas knows particularly well having trained her mother and full-brother Telmeyd (rated 106). She made her debut on the final day of the turf season in a six furlongs maiden at Doncaster (Heavy). The Dutch Art filly displayed a good attitude in blustery conditions to get the better of Richard Guest's well regarded Udontdodou by three parts of a length with the pair clear of the remainder. The majority of the family, which also includes proven mudlark Penitent, tended to prefer ease in the ground and she ought to be a filly to follow over trips around seven furlongs this year. Her trainer feels she is attractively treated off a mark of 76.

THE CASHEL MAN (IRE)

4 b g High Chaparral (IRE) – Hadarama (IRE) (Sinndar (IRE))

Trainer: D.SIMCOCK. Newmarket, Suffolk.

Even though the Sir Robert Ogden owned The Cashel Man improved by twenty five pounds (63 – 88) last season, there is every reason to believe he has got even more to offer as a four year old. Indeed, he looks tailormade for races such as the Chester Cup (4th May), Ascot Stakes (14th June) and Northumberland Plate (25th June – although he has yet to race on the all-weather). Campaigned over eight and ten furlongs as a juvenile, the High Chaparral gelding progressed markedly once tackling distances over a mile and six plus. Successful at Redcar, Nottingham and Newmarket, he appreciates fast ground and reportedly found conditions too slow when only sixth on his final start at Ascot behind Burmese. Unexposed over marathon trips, David Simcock's charge can win a big handicap at least during 2016.

UDONTDODOU

3 b g Fastnet Rock (AUS) – Forever Times (So Factual (USA))
Trainer: R.GUEST. Ingmanthorpe, Wetherby, West Yorkshire.

Grand National winning jockey Richard Guest did a terrific job with Udododontu last season winning twice at Redcar and York before finishing a neck second in the Britannia Stakes at Royal Ascot. Later sold to Godolphin, he has already won in Meydan during the winter and is now rated 102. It is a tough act to follow but it will be interesting to see what he can achieve with the similarly named Udontdodou, who was first brought to my attention when the gelded son of Fastnet Rock made his debut at York in October, whilst I was working for *Racing UK*. I was told beforehand that the half-brother to Group 3 winner and Cheveley Park Stakes runner-up Sunday Times was highly regarded but he spoilt his chance by being slowly away. Improved efforts followed though at Redcar and Doncaster, where he finished third and second respectively. Only beaten three quarters of a length at the latter track behind the aforementioned Sainted, he has yet to race beyond six furlongs but will be suited by further this year. All three races have been on a soft or heavy surface but his dam (Forever Times) appreciated rattling fast ground and Sunday Times was much better on a quick terrain, too. Therefore Udontdodou may improve considerably on better ground and over a longer trip. Officially rated 79, don't be surprised if he heads back to York for the same seven furlongs three year old handicap (76 - 95) his former stablemate won last year at the Dante meeting (11th May).

VON BLUCHER (IRE)

3 ch c Zoffany (IRE) – Tropical Lady (IRE) (Sri Pekan (USA))
Trainer: J.H.M.GOSDEN. Newmarket, Suffolk.

Zoffany was crowned top first season sire in 2015 having been responsible for a host of high quality juveniles, including Foundation (Royal Lodge Stakes), Illuminate (Albany), Washington DC (Windsor Castle) and Waterloo Bridge (Norfolk). The son of Dansili also produced the John Gosden trained Von Blucher who looks the type to win a good three year old handicap at least this year. Named after Prussian General Gebhard Von Blucher, who helped defeat Napoleon at Waterloo, he was placed in two of his first three maidens at Sandown (Good/Firm) and Epsom (Heavy) over seven furlongs but then appeared suited by a step up to a mile for the first time at Lingfield in October. Partnered by Ryan Moore, he was well supported beforehand and readily saw off the challenge of subsequent dual winner Ennaadd (now rated 98) by a length and a half. It was another eight lengths back to the third. Considering what Roger Varian's runner-up has achieved since, Von Blucher doesn't look badly handicapped off a mark of 86. Clearly effective over eight furlongs, his dam was a dual Group winner over ten furlongs for Jim Bolger, so he may stay further. Regardless of his optimum trip, he can win a good prize this summer.

There will doubtless be a few **Sir Mark Prescott** trained three year olds who will improve dramatically from their juvenile performances when tackling longer distances this year. A couple of likely types include **ABBEYLEIX**. Yet to be given an official rating, he is a gelded son of Sir Percy and is a half-brother to middle distance/stayers Alcaeus (a six times winner over 1m 2f - 1m 6f in 2013) and Albert Bridge (won over 1m 5f for Ralph Beckett) amongst others. Bought for €55,000, he had three runs within 22 days in late October/November. Third at Kempton (1m) on his second run, he wasn't knocked about when a running on sixth behind the potentially smart Predilection over the same course and distance on his final outing. He is likely to be a different proposition over middle distances this term. Stablemate **CARTWRIGHT** entered the notebook when a running on fifth on his racecourse bow at Redcar (7f : Soft) in early November. Well held on his next two outings on the all-weather at Wolverhampton and Southwell (3 races within 23 days), he was allocated a mark of 57, which looks workable, judged on his initial run. A well bred son of High Chaparral, he has been gelded during the winter. Bought for 160,000gns as a yearling, he is out of One So Marvellous and is a half-brother to Hughie Morrison's dual Listed winner Coquet. Entered in the Derby at one stage last year, he could be thrown in off his rating and is the sort to rack up a mid summer sequence.

MAIDENS in WAITING

The following 10 three year olds caught the eye in juvenile events last season and will hopefully be losing their maiden tag shortly.

ACROSS THE STARS (IRE)

3 b c Sea The Stars (IRE) – Victoria Cross (IRE) (Mark of Esteem (IRE))
Trainer: Sir M.R.STOUTE. Newmarket, Suffolk.
Career Form Figures: 22

Bought for 600,000gns, the son of Sea The Stars is a half-brother to dual Group 2 winner Bronze Cannon. Runner-up in both his races as a juvenile, he chased home two potentially smart colts at Nottingham (1m : Soft) and Wolverhampton (1m), namely Mengli Khan and Daily Bulletin. Beaten around three and a half lengths on each occasion, he left the impression middle distances will bring out the best in him as a three year old. Entered in the Derby, he has progressed well during the winter and could develop into a candidate for something like the London Gold Cup at Newbury (14th May) – the same connections won the race with Cannock Chase in 2014 – or the King George V Stakes at Royal Ascot (16th June).

DUFAY (IRE)

3 b f Dubawi (IRE) – White Moonstone (USA) (Dynaformer (USA))
Trainer: C.APPLEBY. Newmarket, Suffolk.
Career Form Figures: 3

Charlie Appleby trained 41 juvenile winners in 2015 and, while the beautifully bred Dufay failed to make a contribution, it will be a surprise if she doesn't as a three year old. A daughter of Dubawi out of White Moonstone, her dam was unbeaten in four races as a two year old, including the May Hill and Fillies Mile Stakes. Dufay made her belated racecourse debut in a seven furlongs maiden on the polytrack at Lingfield in mid December and certainly wasn't subjected to a forceful ride. Drawn wide in stall 10, Adam Kirby dropped his mount out early on and, having been pulled wide once straightening for home, she stayed on well under an educational ride. That kindness looks sure to be rewarded this year. Beaten three lengths by John Gosden's Auntinet, she is from the family of Albasharah who was a Listed winner over ten furlongs. She looks a smashing middle distance prospect for Godolphin.

FASTNET TEMPEST

3 b g Fastnet Rock (AUS) – Dame Blanche (IRE) (Be My Guest (USA))
Trainer: W.J.HAGGAS. Newmarket, Suffolk.
Career Form Figures: 5

The gelded son of Fastnet Rock produced one of the most eyecatching performances by a juvenile all season when a strong finishing fifth in a hotly contested seven furlongs maiden on the Rowley Mile (Good/Soft) in October. The race was won by Charlie Hills' Mootaharer (half-brother to Muhaarar), who Paul Hanagan believes will be a very nice colt over ten furlongs this year. Joe Fanning partnered William Haggas' horse and, having been very slowly away and appearing to be going nowhere at halfway, the penny suddenly dropped and he thundered home before meeting interference late on. Five and a half lengths behind the winner, Fastnet Tempest's half-sister Excellent Girl won over ten furlongs in France and he is going to relish an extra furlong or two as a three year old. A reproduction of his Newmarket performance alone will see him win plenty of races this season.

HIGH HOPES

3 b f Zamindar (USA) – Dixielake (IRE) (Lake Coniston (IRE))
Trainer: D.SIMCOCK. Newmarket, Suffolk.
Career Form Figures: 2

David Simcock has a strong team for this season, including a number of promising three year old maidens. High Hopes is a lovely big scopey filly by Zamindar who entered plenty of notebooks when a fast finishing second on her only start at Newbury (1m : Good/Soft) in the Autumn. Jamie Spencer's mount came under pressure with a couple of furlongs to run but she responded to pressure and was beaten less than two lengths by Hughie Morrison's potentially smart filly Last Tango Inparis. The stable's juveniles invariably improve a lot for their initial experience and one can imagine High Hopes coming into her own over trips around ten furlongs as a three year old.

IN THE CITY

3 ch c Exceed And Excel (AUS) – Soft Morning (Pivotal)
Trainer: W.J.HAGGAS. Newmarket, Suffolk.
Career Form Figures: 4

Owners Simon Munir and Isaac Souede tasted Grade 1 glory during the winter courtesy of Bristol De Mai and Footpad under National Hunt rules but they are also responsible for a highly promising three year old on the Flat in the once raced In The City. A colt by Exceed And Excel who cost 100,000gns, he finished a most encouraging fourth on his debut at Newmarket (7f : Good/Firm) in August. Only beaten four and three quarters of a length by subsequent Group 2 Champagne Stakes winner Emotionless, the race also contained Perkunas (2nd – now rated 99), Tidal Wave (3rd – won since and rated 85) and Venturous (won twice since and rated 97). William Haggas' charge stayed on well at the finish suggesting he will be suited by a mile plus this year. He didn't run again, due to problems with his feet, but he is reportedly going well again now and shouldn't have too much trouble winning his maiden before hopefully going on to bigger and better things.

MUTARAJJIL (IRE)

3 b c Acclamation – Rouge Noir (USA) (Saint Ballado (CAN))
Trainer: R.VARIAN. Newmarket, Suffolk.
Career Form Figures: 92

Roger Varian has already earmarked the valuable three year old Charity Sprint at York (11th June) as a possible target for the twice raced Mutarajjil. A colt by Acclamation who was acquired for 105,000gns, he is a half-brother to Brian Meehan's Listed five furlongs Listed winner Light The Fire. Fancied to go close on his debut in a six and a half furlongs maiden at Newbury in late October (Good/Soft), he appeared to be unsuited by the slow conditions and trailed in a well beaten last of nine. Switched to the polytrack for his next run at Kempton less than three weeks later, he looked a different horse and was unfortunate not to lose his maiden tag at the second time of asking. A nose in arrears of Martyn Meade's Consulting, Paul Hanagan's mount only just failed to get up. Six furlongs on fast ground on turf is expected to bring out the best in Mutarajjil this year and he can win his maiden before being aimed at the good sprint handicaps for his age group. Provided he has run beforehand, there is one at Newmarket's Guineas meeting (81-100) on Saturday 30th April – Twilight Son won the race last year with Magical Memory in third – and another one over the same course and distance (0-105) on Saturday 14th May. They are both options en route to a trip to the Knavesmire in June.

SEPTEMBER STARS (IRE)

3 ch f Sea The Stars (IRE) – Altesse Imperiale (IRE) (Rock of Gibraltar (IRE))
Trainer: R.BECKETT. Kimpton Down, Hampshire.
Career Form Figures: 3

Ralph Beckett has already won the Epsom Oaks twice with Look Here (2008) and Talent (2013) and he appears to have a decent team of three year old fillies for this year, too. It would therefore be no surprise to see one of them develop into a live contender for the 2016 version in June. That squad has been strengthened still further with the arrival of the former Brian Meehan trained September Stars. A daughter of Sea The Stars who cost 260,000gns as a yearling, she was introduced in what is traditionally a strong one mile fillies' maiden at Doncaster in late October – the likes of Gertrude Bell, Izzi Top, Speedy Boarding and Star of Seville have all competed in it in recent years. The race went the way of the highly regarded Zest with September Stars only a length behind in third. Sent off 10/1, she finished with a flourish and is bred to appreciate at least ten furlongs this year. Ralph Beckett has another potentially very useful filly on his hands. New stable jockey Fran Berry has a lot to look forward to.

I suggest her new stablemate **ANASTRA** is another name to bear in mind when considering possible Oaks candidates. A €190,000 purchase, she is a daughter of Kamsin and was an effortless three lengths winner of her only start in Division One of the extended eight furlongs Oh So Sharp Fillies' Maiden at Nottingham in late September (the time was quicker than the other division). From a good German middle distance family, Graham Gibbons rode her at Colwick Park and said afterwards: **"She is a smart filly for next year."**

SPANISH CITY

3 ch c Exceed And Excel (AUS) – Annabelle's Charm (IRE) (Indian Ridge)
Trainer: R.VARIAN. Newmarket, Suffolk.
Career Form Figures: 32

Charming Thought was a top-class juvenile for Godolphin and Charlie Appleby in 2014 winning the Group 1 Middle Park Stakes. Unfortunately, an injury prevented him from racing the following year. His half-brother Spanish City is a three year old who is held in high esteem by Roger Varian and, despite being out an eight (Listed) and ten furlongs winner, he is expected to be at his best over sprint trips. Owned and bred by Craig Bennett's Merry Fox Stud, the son of Exceed And Excel was placed in both his races last year but his trainer believes he will improve markedly once tackling faster ground. A close third on his debut at Haydock (6f : Good) in August behind Richard Fahey's Firedanser, he was sent off 8/13 favourite at Newcastle (6f : Good/Soft) next time. Having travelled strongly for much of the race, he looked like winning entering the final quarter of a mile but couldn't quicken in the rain softened ground late on and was comfortably held by World His Oyster (third won since). His trainer spoke enthusiastically about Spanish City when we chatted in February and he is expected to develop into a useful sprint handicapper, at least, granted a sound surface.

SWISS RANGE

3 b f Zamindar (USA) – Spanish Sun (USA) (El Prado (IRE))
Trainer: J.H.M.GOSDEN. Newmarket, Suffolk.
Career Form Figures: 2

Spanish Sun won the Ribblesdale Stakes at Royal Ascot for Khalid Abdullah and Sir Michael Stoute in 2003 and Swiss Range appears to have inherited some of her mother's ability, judged on her encouraging career debut at Newmarket (7f : Soft) last backend. Significantly, the daughter of Zamindar made her racecourse bow in the same fillies' maiden John Gosden introduced subsequent Group 1 winners Dar Re Mi (runner-up in 2007) and The Fugue (won in 2011). Nicky Mackay's mount attempted to make all and she had all her rivals, bar one, in trouble entering the dip on the Rowley Mile. Worn down by Luca Cumani's more experienced and highly regarded winner Tiptree, she was beaten a length and a half but had pulled eight lengths clear of the third. Sent off 5/4 favourite, Swiss Range was clearly expected to run well. Entered in the French Oaks at Chantilly in June, she will hopefully win her maiden in the spring before making an impact in black type races over ten furlongs plus this year. She looks a smart filly in the making.

TAQDEER (IRE)

3 ch c Fast Company (IRE) – Brigantia (Pivotal)
Trainer: J.H.M.GOSDEN. Newmarket, Suffolk.
Career Form Figures: 2

Still entered in the 2000 Guineas, the son of Fast Company is a big, scopey individual who ought to develop into a useful three year old. Bought for 140,000gns as a yearling, he made his first public appearance in a seven furlongs maiden at Wolverhampton in early December and, while he failed to justify short odds, he still ran well on a track which clearly didn't bring out the best in him. Slowly away and green throughout, John Gosden's colt was making up ground hand over fist but found the winning post coming too soon. Denied by half a length by Brian Meehan's Take The Helm (1 from 5 since and rated 93), he is highly regarded and will be a different proposition with the experience under his belt and when encountering a more conventional track. He will also appreciate at least a mile this year.

STABLE GOSSIP

As in previous years, I obtained the lowdown on a number of Sir Michael Stoute's horses during my annual visit to Newmarket in February. In addition, I have received news from other yards throughout the country with some other horses to keep an eye on this season.

Sir Michael STOUTE
Freemason Lodge, Newmarket

OLDER HORSES

DARTMOUTH was a progressive handicapper last year winning three times, including at Glorious Goodwood. Third in a Listed event at Kempton on his final run, he is rated 102. There could be another big middle distance handicap in him, perhaps the Duke of Edinburgh Stakes (17th June), before he switches back to Pattern races. There is a feeling the son of Dubawi has more to offer. **EXOSPHERE** is another lightly raced four year old with Listed/Group race pretensions this season. He, too, won on three occasions last year finishing third in the Listed Doonside Cup at Ayr in September. Yet to race beyond ten furlongs, the yard feel there is a big prize in him when stepping up to twelve furlongs for the first time.

THREE YEAR OLDS

ABDON is a half-brother to high-class juvenile Berkshire and the Cacique colt won his only start at Newbury in August. Even though he hasn't grown much from two to three, he is described as a nice horse who still holds a Derby entry. He has been pleasing in his work. That comment also applies to **ABINGDON**. Owned and bred by Ballymacoll Stud, she stayed on well to finish fourth in what appeared a decent maiden at Kempton in late November. From the family of Greek Dance and Islington, she is a fine, big filly who is going particularly well. The Street Cry filly should have no trouble winning her maiden before her sights are raised. It took **ARAB POET** four races to get off the mark but the Poet's Voice colt is expected to develop into a useful handicapper this year. Rated 83, he won over six furlongs at Lingfield in the Autumn. Despite being described as 'hot headed,' he has plenty of talent and can win more races. **FIDAAWY** finished eighth on his only start in a seven furlongs maiden at Newmarket won by Crazy Horse (subsequently won the Group 3 Horris Hill Stakes). By New Approach, he has begun to settle down since being gelded during the winter. He is beginning to go the right way and could have a bright future. **MIDTERM** is the big hope amongst the three year old colts following his victory at Newbury last October. A son of Galileo out of Midday, he is impeccably bred and has reportedly thrived during the winter. Training well, he is entered in the Derby and is likely to reappear in a trial during the spring. He is a potentially exciting prospect and most definitely one to follow. **POET'S WORLD** is a half-brother to dual Group 3 winner Malabar and he finished an encouraging fourth on his only start at Newmarket last backend. The son of Poet's Voice will appreciate a step up to a mile and ten furlongs and it will be disappointing if he can't win a maiden. He is a nice prospect. There is a belief that **QUEEN'S TRUST** is one of the yard's best three year olds. An impressive winner on her debut at Kempton, the Dansili filly then finished fifth in the Group 3 Oh So Sharp Stakes at HQ. Sent off favourite that day, she has done particularly well from two to three and is considered a Pattern filly in the making. **SCOTTISH SUMMIT** is another who belongs to Ballymacoll Stud. A son of Shamardal, he was fourth at Wolverhampton in November and, while he is described as lazy who doesn't do a stroke at home, he will win his maiden and should be a decent middle distance three year old. **THETIS** won her maiden at Carlisle before finishing second in the Group 2 Rockfel Stakes at Newmarket. The Invincible Spirit filly has done well physically during the winter and will make her return in a Guineas trial. **ULYSSES** is out of the Oaks winner Light Shift and he shaped with distinct promise on his only run at Newbury in late October. The Galileo colt finished sixth but has endured his share of problems during the winter. However, he is a nice type who is coming along steadily now.

Another ex-Olly Stevens inmate who was sent to the sales by Qatar Racing last Autumn was the lightly raced **HEISMAN**, who has won 2 of his 8 races. The Teofilo gelding was bought by **George Baker** for **42,000gns** and it is hoped the five year old will finally fulfil his undoubted potential. A big, strapping horse, he won twice on the all-weather as a three year old but was without a win last term. A decent fourth behind You're Fired at York in October off a mark of 88, he has reportedly had a wind operation since joining his new yard. By all accounts, he won't be running until the summer but he strikes me as the sort to develop into a Cambridgeshire horse. I think he is better than he has shown so far.

NORTHERN NOTES

Middleham based **Karl Burke** had another very good season with 57 domestic winners in 2016. The Ontawinner owned Quiet Reflection developed into a high-class juvenile filly winning the Listed Harry Rosebery Stakes at Ayr and the Group 3 Cornwallis Stakes at HQ, while Odeliz was a Group 1 winner in Italy in October. I received news during the winter regarding a few of the Spigot Lodge inmates.

The stable appears to have a decent squad of three year olds and I suggest keeping an eye on the following. **BIODYNAMIC** was very green on his sole start at Nottingham last backend but stayed on well to finish fifth. A colt by New Approach and a half-brother to six times winner Sunraider, he looks capable of winning a maiden before going on to better things.

TIMELESS ART is a horse I have got a lot of time for having seen his performance at York in October. A colt by Medicean who cost €40,000, he is a well bred individual who travelled strongly on the Knavesmire having been squeezed up at the start. Third behind the well thought of Garcia that day, he had previously been sent off favourite on his debut at Ascot when finishing only seventh. Entered in the German and Irish 2000 Guineas, he will benefit from a longer trip this year and is expected to develop into a smart three year old handicapper, at least, this season before making an even better four year old.

WHOLESOME is held in very high regard hence her entry in the 1000 Guineas at Newmarket. A daughter of Lemon Drop Kid, she raced twice in seven furlongs maidens at HQ, including when only beaten half a length by Godolphin's subsequent Group 3 winner First Victory in late September. A step up to a mile will be very much in her favour and she looks a black type filly in the making. She has reportedly thrived during the winter and is most definitely one to follow.

Of the older horses, **MOTHERS FINEST** is a filly who featured in this section last year. A winner at Haydock during the spring, she ran well in Listed company at the likes of York, Longchamp and Newmarket. Officially rated 95, the four year old is expected to contest the top handicaps and black type events and, being from the family of the stable's Dante winner and Epsom Derby runner-up Libertarian, she is likely to benefit from a step up to ten furlongs this year.

Richard Fahey had a memorable 2015 with three Group 2 victories courtesy of juveniles Birchwood (Superlative Stakes), Donjuan Triumphant (Criterium de Maisons-Laffitte) and Ribchester (Mill Reef) and a domestic tally of 235 winners, which left him runner-up in the trainers' title behind runaway winner John Gosden.

A couple of the Musley Bank older horses to keep a sharp eye on this year include the progressive **HIGH BAROQUE**. The four year old improved with every start last year winning his maiden over ten furlongs at Pontefract in August following two runs on the all-weather. He then finished a close second on his handicap debut at Redcar over the same trip in early October off a mark of 85. A two pounds rise is unlikely to halt his progress and, bearing in mind he is related to the likes of Quarter Moon and Thomas Chippendale (plus his dam was runner-up in the Oaks and Prix Vermeille), he ought to relish a step up to twelve furlongs for the first time this year. There is a good middle distance handicap to be won with the Lookin At Lucky gelding, especially when considering he has only raced four times.

PERRAULT was bought out of Ralph Beckett's yard for 32,000gns in October and he, too, is low mileage having only raced a handful of times. A half-brother to the former William Jarvis trained Qushchi (triple winner over 1m 4f), he was a six lengths winner of a ten furlongs maiden at Chepstow last May before finishing third in a decent handicap at Sandown behind Muqtaser. Sent off 11/4 favourite, he stayed on well behind Roger Varian's winner. Disappointing in two subsequent outings over a mile and a half at Newbury and Newmarket (wore blinkers), he has been dropped three pounds since his latest start to a mark of 84. A change of scenery and a gelding operation could bring about a return to form and there is every possibility we still haven't seen the best of him.

Amongst the three year olds, **CONSTANTINO** looks the sort who will only improve with another winter behind him. Considered a baby last year, the Sir Robert Ogden owned half-brother to dual Group 1 winner Amazing Maria (David O'Meara) was ninth on his debut in the Convivial Maiden at York's Ebor Festival. The son of Danehill Dancer looked much more streetwise next time when making all to win a seven furlongs maiden at Ayr's Western meeting in September by a neck. Granted an official rating of 80, he ought to take advantage of such a mark in eight and ten furlongs three year old handicaps.

One mile handicaps will also be on **GARCIA**'s agenda at some stage this year. A big, tall gelded son of Paco Boy, who has reportedly done well during the winter, he built on his initial outing at Newcastle over six furlongs when winning at York (7f : Good/Soft) next time. A length scorer, he is certainly not devoid of speed but will be suited by a mile eventually. In the meantime, he could contest the 76-95 three year old handicap over seven furlongs on the opening day of York's Dante Festival (11th May). The stable won it with Baccarat in 2012. Rated 83, Garcia looks favourably treated. The Silver Bowl at Haydock Park (21st May) is a race Richard Fahey has won twice (Anna Pavlova (2006) & Gabrial (2012) and it would be no surprise to see either Constantino or Garcia develop into serious contenders for the valuable eight furlongs event.

North Yorkshire trainer **Paul Midgley** is a man to be feared when it comes to sprinters and the former jump jockey won the Epsom Dash with Desert Law (bought for 32,000gns) and Listed events in Ireland last year with Line of Reason and Monsieur Joe. He was active at the Newmarket Horses in Training Sale last Autumn and, along with the ex-Richard Hannon trained **NINJAGO** (32,000gns), he bought two very interesting recruits, including **GAMESOME**. A five year old gelded son of Rock of Gibraltar, he has only won 1 of his 11 races and is officially rated 99. A juvenile winner at Nottingham in 2013, he ran some good races in defeat last year. A running on fifth behind Eastern Impact in a competitive six furlongs handicap at Newmarket's Guineas meeting, he was then sixth in the Wokingham Stakes at Royal Ascot and only beaten a length behind Huntman's Close when third at Windsor a week later. Previously trained by the now retired Olly Stevens, he was acquired for **75,000gns** and it would be no surprise to see Midgley win a heritage handicap with him.

RELATED has also joined the Sandfield Farm operation having been purchased for **65,000gns**. A half-brother to Group 1 winning juvenile Wootton Bassett, the six year old was bought out of David Simcock's yard and has 4 wins on his CV. Effective over six and seven furlongs, he won at Kempton in March last year before finishing fourth in the Wokingham and Bunbury Cup at Royal Ascot and Newmarket respectively. Officially rated 97, he finished fourth on his first run for his new trainer at Kempton on Easter Saturday. A strongly run race on fast ground brings out the best in him and his two main targets this summer are reportedly the Bunbury Cup (9th July), once again, and the Stewards' Cup (30th July). There could be a big prize in him, too.

TOM'S TOP 8 for 2016
By Tom O'RYAN

For the FOURTH consecutive year, my *Racing UK* colleague **Tom O'Ryan** has kindly put together a list of horses to follow for the new season. Given the former Journalist of the Year's close association with the **Richard Fahey** stable (his brother Robin is assistant), he has elected to concentrate on the Musley Bank operation this year and nominated eight horses to watch out for, four of which are juveniles. Last year's feature included **DANCING YEARS (8/1), MECCA'S ANGEL** (Group 1 Nunthorpe Stakes winner), **PACNGO (4/1 & 5/1)**, **SPRING OFFENSIVE (2/1)** and **TWILIGHT SON** (Group 1 Betfred Sprint Cup @ **10/1**, plus **11/10, 5/1**).

DON'T TOUCH 4 b g Dutch Art – Expressive

Achieved the extraordinary feat last season of being unbeaten in five outings and winning the Ayr Gold Cup within four months of first stepping on to a racecourse, having being unraced the previous year as a juvenile. He has done very well over the winter and looks an even stronger more mature horse this year. He has the most wonderful temperament and, although he has yet to race beyond six furlongs, there is every chance he could stay seven furlongs and even a mile, if required, at some stage of his career. In the meantime, he is likely to start back in the Greenlands Stakes at the Curragh on May 21st as he sets out on his second campaign off a mark of 106 with every chance of making an impression in Pattern race company.

GIDDY 3 b f Kyllachy – Light Hearted

Owned by Cheveley Park, she won a five furlong maiden race at Beverley last August on her debut, justifying favouritism and fulfilling the promise she had shown at home. She then went to Ayr for a red-hot 18-runner nursery over the same distance at the Gold Cup meeting the following month. She was all the rage on the course and was sent off the 5/2 favourite, but she failed to perform to her best and finished down the field in a race won by stablemate Donjuan Triumphant, who went on to win at Listed and Group 2 level before the season was over. Giddy never ran again as a two-year-old and begins her second season off a mark of 77, which looks attractive. A daughter of Kyllachy out of a Green Desert mare, sprinting will obviously be her game.

ONE BOY (IRE) 5 ch g Captain Gerrard (IRE) – Paris Song (IRE)

A newcomer to the yard having been bought at Newmarket's Tattersalls Horses-in-Training Sales last October for 19,000gns out of Michael Dods' Darlington stable for whom he won three times. He's a grand little horse with a good outlook and he's settled-in well at Musley Bank. Now a five-year-old, he'll be seen out in sprint handicaps on northern tracks and, having gone through last season without a win, he has dropped to a nice mark of 75, which is a full ten pounds lower than he was in the spring of 2014 after winning at Newcastle. It'll be disappointing if he doesn't find opportunity knocking.

RIBCHESTER (IRE) 3 b c Iffraaj – Mujarah (IRE)

A horse who stood out from the crowd last season, even before he ran, he finished second at Doncaster on his debut and then filled the runner-up slot in the Gimcrack as a once-raced maiden, which was a fine effort and one which attracted Godolphin to buy him. He quickly showed himself to to be a useful purchase as he won the Group 2 Mill Reef Stakes at Newbury on his third and final start as a juvenile. He has strengthened up and matured mentally since and is doing his work in more relaxed fashion this season. He is clearly a smart horse and might well line-up in either the English or French 2,000 Guineas with one run beforehand to provide an extra clue as to whether he is up to Classic standard. He's a really likeable horse who gives the impression he'll improve as the season goes on.

TWO-YEAR-OLDS

CHAMPION HARBOUR (IRE) b c Harbour Watch (IRE) – Drastic Measure (Pivotal)
A colt by Harbour Watch out of Drastic Measure, he cost 45,000gns at Tattersalls last October. He possesses plenty of size, strength and scope and is also fairly precocious. He's doing everything right at home and looks a likely winner.

SIX STRINGS b c Requinto (IRE) – Island Music (IRE) (Mujahid (USA))
A son of first-season sire Requinto out of Island Strings, who cost €50,000 at Goffs in September. He is a grand type of colt, who moves well, looks nicely balanced and goes about his work with enthusiasm. No questions have been asked of him yet, but he gives the impression that he's got an engine.

Unnamed b c Dream Ahead (USA) – Expectation (IRE) (Night Shift (USA))
A well-grown, strong and scopey colt, who takes everything in his stride at home and is a great mover. He cost €145,000 at Goff's last September and looks promising for David Armstrong, who has had so many good horses in the yard previously.

Unnamed b c Mayson – Pious (Bishop of Cashel)
A Cheveley Park homebred colt who was bought for 150,000gns and a son of the first crop of top-notch sprinter Mayson, who was such a popular horse at Musley Bank. There are several youngsters by him in the yard now and the signs are encouraging that he will make a useful stallion. This colt has a lovely way about him, plus he's a half-brother to Supplicant, a former stablemate, who won the Group 2 Mill Reef Stakes in 2013.

Apprentice to watch
ADAM McNAMARA spent last season in his native Ireland with Johnny Murtagh and had nine rides without success. He crossed to Richard Fahey last autumn and goes into the turf season with three all-weather winners to his credit. Good value for his seven pounds allowance, he is likely to attract plenty of opportunities and enjoy a good year.

UNRACED THREE YEAR OLDS

The following section nominates a select number of three year olds who were unable to race as juveniles for whatever reason. However, they are reportedly well regarded and ought to be making up for lost time in 2016.

BLUES SISTER b f Compton Place – Persario
Trainer: J.R.FANSHAWE. Newmarket, Suffolk.
Deacon Blues developed into a top-class sprinter who improved with age. He enjoyed a fantastic season in 2011 winning the Wokingham off a mark of 98 before capturing four Pattern races and ending his career with an official rating of 120. This filly is a full-sister to him and therefore a half-sister to stablemate The Tin Man, who was thoroughly progressive for the Fanshawe yard last year. Held up by one or two minor niggles last year, she is reportedly a strong filly who has shown her fair share of ability at home. Like her other family members, expect her to improve with every run.

FRONTIERSMAN br c Dubawi (IRE) – Ouija Board (Cape Cross (IRE))
Trainer: C.APPLEBY. Newmarket, Suffolk.
Possibly one for later in the year, he is out of the brilliant dual Classic winner and 7 times winning Group 1 scorer Ouija Board. The son of Dubawi is therefore a half-brother to Ballydoyle's triple Classic winner Australia. Owned by Godolphin, Charlie Appleby has entered him in the Irish Derby and Group 1 Grand Prix de Paris at Saint-Cloud in July.

HUGE FUTURE b c Shamardal (USA) – Time Honoured (Sadler's Wells (USA))
Trainer: S.BIN SUROOR. Newmarket, Suffolk.
A well bred son of Shamardal, he comes from the family of Time Charter and holds an entry in the Derby. Considered above average, he cost €260,000 and, all being well, will be making his debut at one of the bigger tracks during the spring.

ISTIQLAAL b c Oasis Dream – Independence (Selkirk (USA))
Trainer: C.APPLEBY. Newmarket, Suffolk.
A 250,000gns purchase at the Breeze-Ups last spring, the Godolphin owned colt has a superb pedigree being a full-brother to Great Voltigeur winner and St Leger third Monitor Closely and a half-brother to Eclipse winner Mount Nelson. Entered in the Irish 2000 Guineas and Irish Derby, it would be no surprise to see him make his debut in something like the Wood Ditton Stakes at Newmarket (13th April). He is one to catch on his first racecourse appearance.

LORD NAPIER (IRE) b c Galileo (IRE) – Jacqueline (IND) (King Charlemagne (USA))
Trainer: J.H.M.GOSDEN. Newmarket, Suffolk.
Entered in the Derby, he is a half-brother to David O'Meara's dual winner Primogeniture and is bred to come into his own over middle distances. Owned by the Coolmore operation, he has taken time but is another to watch out for in a ten furlongs maiden in the spring.

LUSORY b c Shamardal (USA) – Playful Act (IRE) (Sadler's Wells (USA))
Trainer: C.APPLEBY. Newmarket, Suffolk.
A colt by Shamardal, his dam won the Group 1 Fillies Mile and Group 2 Lancashire Oaks for Robert Sangster and John Gosden in 2004 and 2005 respectively. From the family of Group 1 winners Nathaniel and Great Heavens, he holds entries in the English, French and Irish Derbys, plus the Grand Prix de Paris at Saint-Cloud (14th July). He is bred to be very good and his homework has reportedly pleased connections.

MUNTAHAA (IRE) gr c Dansili – Qertaas (IRE) (Linamix (FR))
Trainer: J.H.M.GOSDEN. Newmarket, Suffolk.
Another Epsom Derby entrant for the champion trainer, he is a homebred son of Dansili whose family members include Virginia Waters and Chachamaidee. His dam was a Listed winner over thirteen furlongs and he has reportedly improved from two to three and is much more the finished article now.

SKIFFLE b f Dubawi (IRE) – Princesse Dansante (IRE) (King's Best (USA))
Trainer: C.APPLEBY. Newmarket, Suffolk.
A half-sister to the former Godolphin owned Golden Town, who won the Convivial Maiden Stakes at York in 2013, she is reportedly useful and has been given some smart entries as a result. The Charlie Appleby trained filly is in the Group 1 Prix Saint-Alary at Deauville (16th May) and both the French and Irish Oaks. She is another one to watch out for on her debut.

APPENDIX

As in previous years, I have attempted to highlight a number of horses, in various categories, who are expected to contest the major prizes this season. With a few exceptions, I have tended to concentrate on horses which aren't featured in the various other sections of *Ahead On The Flat*.

SPRINTERS

Michael Dods resisted the temptation to run **MECCA'S ANGEL** on fast ground at Royal Ascot in June and campaigned her sparingly in 2015. However, he was rewarded when the daughter of Dark Angel won the Group 1 Nunthorpe Stakes at York by a couple of lengths. Conceding twenty four pounds to the US trained Acapulco, she stayed on strongly down the centre of the track under Paul Mulrennan, who said afterwards: **"She proved today she's the real deal and that when she gets her toe in, she's awesome. When the ground comes for her, she's very special."** She has won 8 of her 14 races and there is no reason why she won't continue to be a real force in the top five furlongs events. A return to York in August is likely to be her ultimate goal, although her connections will be tempted by a tilt at the Prix de L'Abbaye in October, granted suitable conditions. She is already a course and distance winner at Longchamp.

TWILIGHT SON progressed through the handicap ranks last year before developing into a top-class sprinter. Henry Candy's colt began his three year old career off a mark of 83 and, having won three of his four races last term, the son of Kyllachy is now rated 117. A short head winner of the Group 1 Betfred Sprint Cup at Haydock, his trainer said afterwards: **"He's a natural and an incredibly tough horse. He just took time – he's twice the size he was last year and keeps improving."** The only defeat in his career thus far came in the Qipco British Champions Sprint Stakes at Ascot. Beaten a couple of lengths by champion sprinter Muhaarar, his wide draw in stall 20 didn't help but he found Charlie Hills' colt too strong in any case. **"His dad, Kyllachy, did much better at four and I think he'll be better as well,"** believes Candy. It is also worth noting his trainer's comments following Twilight Son's victory in the Charity Sprint at York in June when rated 94: **"He's going to be a serious beast next year. He's changing by the week. He's getting bigger and stronger all the time."** Ideally suited by some ease in the ground, he is already a Group 1 winner and is likely to reappear in the Group 2 Duke of York Stakes (11th May). Cheveley Park Stud bought a majority share in him in early July which means Ryan Moore (rode him at Ascot on his final run) will presumably partner the four year old this year when available.

John Gosden trained Oasis Dream to win the Middle Park, July Cup and Nunthorpe Stakes in 2002 and 2003 and the son of Green Desert is one of the finest sprinters we have seen this century. However, the champion trainer believes **SHALAA** is even quicker than his former stablemate. The son of Invincible Spirit, who cost 170,000gns, won five of his six races, including the Group 1 Middle Park Stakes at HQ on his final outing. **"He's gone very, very fast and Ryan Moore (rode Rouleau) said he had never been so fast over four furlongs up the Rowley Mile. He's the fastest two year old I've trained. He's incredibly fast."** Prior to that, the Al Shaqab owned colt had won the Group 1 Prix Morny at Deauville on unsuitably slow ground by a length and three quarters from the now retired Gutaifan. Frankie Dettori enthused afterwards: **"He's the best two year old I've ridden. It was heavy ground, but his class got him through. He doesn't mind horses upsides him and I'd love to find one to get in behind, but I haven't found one fast enough yet."** His connections are resisting the temptation of training him for the 2000 Guineas with sprinting very much on his agenda once again this year. The Commonwealth Cup at Royal Ascot (17th June) is his first big target, although he is likely to tackle the Group 3 Pavilion Stakes (27th April) over the same course and distance en route. Reported to have thrived during the winter, Dettori remarked towards the end of March: **"He's built like a mini Ben Johnson. He's got muscles on top of muscles."** He is a hugely exciting prospect.

Another juvenile from last year who left a lasting impression was **ACAPULCO**'s display in the Queen Mary Stakes at Royal Ascot. A length and a half winner from Easton Angel, she powered clear under Ryan Moore, who said afterwards: **"Acapulco is very special. Wesley said she's like a four year old and she rides like one. I just cruised up and she had far too many gears for them. I'd say she's all speed."** The Scat Daddy filly then attempted to become the first juvenile to win the Nunthorpe Stakes at York since

Kingsgate Native in 2007 before she found the aforementioned Mecca's Angel two lengths too strong. The easy ground didn't play to her strengths with her trainer Wesley Ward remarking: **"She'd really prefer firm ground. She's got a big future. She's very sound and has got a world of speed. I think she's got some big days coming."** Reappearing in a six furlongs claimer at Turfway Park in February, she won by a length and a half. The King's Stand Stakes at Royal Ascot (14th June) will presumably be on her agenda. Her trainer has had 6 winners at the Royal meeting since 2009. Such a big imposing filly last year, it may be a case of whether her opposition have caught her up physically this season.

Charlie Hills may no longer have champion sprinter Muhaarar to call upon but he still has a strong looking team of speedsters. **COTAI GLORY** was a high-class juvenile in 2014 winning the Group 3 Molecomb Stakes at Goodwood and was desperately unlucky not to follow up in the Flying Childers at Doncaster when swerving across the track and unshipping George Baker (6121U1). While he found it tougher last year, the Exceed And Excel colt won the Listed Scarborough Stakes at Doncaster in September with Baker saying: **"He is a very smart horse on his day and I think the ground is as soft as he wants. In the Nunthorpe, he didn't really show much but it was loose, tacky ground and he is a fast ground horse."** Hills added: **"I said before the Nunthorpe, if he didn't win it this year, he could next year and that's definitely the case. A lot of sprinters can miss their three year old season and there's plenty to look forward to next year on fast ground. I think he is really special. He's very fast – probably one of the fastest horses I'll ever train."** Granted quick ground, there could be a big prize in him this year.

Stablemate **MAGICAL MEMORY** became the first three year old to win the Stewards' Cup since Danetime (1997) when beating Toofi by three parts of a length at Goodwood in August off a mark of 102 under Frankie Dettori (2 from 2). Rated 87 at the end of his juvenile career, he had a small chip in a joint and was gelded before he turned three but never looked back last season. A three times winner, the son of Zebedee was supplemented for the Betfred Sprint at Haydock on his final start, and was only denied by three parts of a length. It was the third time he chased home Twilight Son in 2015. **"He's got a great attitude and he's getting better. We haven't seen the best of him. He hasn't got any penalties and he could run in the Palace House Stakes at Newmarket (30th April) or the Temple Stakes at Haydock (21st May),"** revealed Hills at the end of last season.

The Lambourn trainer's other star sprinter **STRATH BURN** came within a short head of winning the Group 1 Betfred Sprint at Haydock. Drawn widest of all in stall 16, the Equiano colt did extremely well to finish so close having had nothing to race with. His handler was understandably proud of his effort saying: **"He has a lot of class and can only get better as he's a big, imposing horse."** He had previously won the Group 3 Hackwood Stakes at Newbury by a length. Ideally suited by good or slower conditions, he disappointed on his final run at Ascot on Champions Day and has had a chip removed from his knee and also had a couple of quarter cracks since. Provided he returns to full fitness in 2016, the Qatar Racing owned four year old looks another powerful string to Charlie Hills' bow.

THE TIN MAN is a half-brother to Deacon Blues, who improved with age, and James Fanshawe's gelding is another who progressed through the ranks last year. Unraced as a juvenile, the son of Equiano won three times, including handicaps at Doncaster and Ascot off 79 and 91. A four and a half lengths winner on the latter occasion, the trainer's wife Jacko said afterwards: **"Deacon Blues improved with age and we hope this one will continue in the same fashion. The Tin Man has always looked a nice horse. He disappointed last time as did Ribbons at Deauville and both had been on antibiotics. He was gelded after his first run as he ran so badly and was hollering before, during and after the race."** Supplemented for £40,000 for the Group 1 Qipco British Champions Sprint Stakes at Ascot (Deacon Blues won the race in 2011), having been taken out of the race following his disappointing run at York in September, Tom Queally's (3 from 5) mount ran a cracker to finish fourth. Beaten less than four lengths, it was his first run outside handicap company. Officially rated 112, The Tin Man could easily win at the highest level as a four year old.

Cheshire based Tom Dascombe has a couple of very useful sprinters to keep an eye on this year. **KACHY** is out of a dam who won over twelve furlongs but the son of Kyllachy looked all speed as a juvenile winning both his starts. A decisive winner of a novice event at Chester on his debut in June, he then beat King of Rooks by three parts of a length in the Group 3 Molecomb Stakes at Glorious Goodwood. **"We knew he was good. I thought he would win. He's a very exciting horse,"** commented his trainer afterwards. He was due to contest the Gimcrack Stakes over six furlongs but wasn't seen again last year. Unexposed, he could be anything.

Stablemate **DAWN'S EARLY LIGHT** has yet to race outside handicap company and it remains to be seen whether the gelded son of Starspangledbanner will progress into Pattern company. However, given his form figures at Ascot (152) and an official rating of 98, it is possible he will develop into a live contender for the Wokingham Stakes at the Royal meeting (18th June). Unraced as a juvenile, the grey won twice in handicaps last term at Pontefract and Ascot off 77 and 84 before chasing home The Tin Man at the latter track on his final start. The four year old has only raced eight times.

Finally, two Irish trained horses to consider in this division. Dermot Weld has taken charge of the 2014 Breeders' Cup Turf Sprint winner **BOBBY'S KITTEN**. The five year old son of Kitten's Joy only raced three times last season but is a five times winner in the US and, having plied his trade over a mile or even ten furlongs earlier in his career, he is very much at home over sprint trips nowadays. An eight and a half lengths winner of a Listed race at Cork (6f : Heavy) on Easter Monday on his first run for Weld, he is a fascinating recruit to the European scene. His record at Grade 1 level is 3083194.

ROUND TWO is something of a forgotten horse having not been seen since finishing seventh in the Coventry Stakes at Royal Ascot. The Teofilo colt was sent off 9/4 favourite having won his first two starts for Jim Bolger. A two lengths winner of the Listed Marble Hill Stakes at the Curragh from subsequent Royal Ascot scorer Washington DC, his trainer said afterwards: **"He's everything you would like in a racehorse. I've never had a horse as straightforward as he is and the trip doesn't seem to matter. Nothing matters. I think he will go on any ground. If you couldn't get excited by him, you just wouldn't be alive. I'd say he is the quickest I've had since Polonia (won the 1987 Prix de L'Abbaye)."**

MILERS

SOLOW has been a revelation since dropping back in trip in August 2014. Freddy Head's six year old has won his last ten races over eight and nine furlongs, including five times at Group 1 level. Unbeaten in six races last year, including the Queen Anne, Sussex and QEII Stakes in the UK, he also won on his return in a conditions event at Chantilly (Standard) in early March. **"He's a brilliant horse, a tough miler who can stay. He has a lot of stamina. We are going to try to come back and win the same races. The programme will be the same,"** stated his trainer at Ascot in October. Maxime Guyon (7 from 7) also added: **"Solow is the best horse I have ridden. I don't know if I can ride another one like him. He is amazing, the best."** He will be very hard to beat in the Queen Anne Stakes (14th June) once again on the opening day of the Royal meeting.

Aidan O'Brien has enjoyed a lot of success with those horses he has received from Australia. Haradasun (Queen Anne), So You Think (Prince of Wales's Stakes) and Starspangledbanner (Golden Jubilee) all won at Royal Ascot and the Ballydoyle outfit will be hoping to repeat the trick with Champion two year old **VANCOUVER**. The son of Medaglia d'Oro has won three of his four starts, including the Grade 1 Golden Slipper Stakes over six furlongs at Rosehill in March last year. His previous trainer Gai Waterhouse commented in January: **"As an unbeaten champion two year-old and winner of the Golden Slipper, he has nothing more to prove in Australia; I have no doubt that he is world-class and this plan gives him the best opportunity of proving himself on the international stage, with a view to possible dual-hemisphere stud duties. We'll obviously be sad to see him go and I'm sure Aidan will have a lot of fun with him – Coolmore has followed this route very successfully in the past with** So You Think, Starspangledbanner**, Haradasun and others and I wish Aidan every success with a horse I consider as talented as any."** His new trainer added: **"We were very impressed with the class and speed he showed in the Golden Slipper. He's a champion 2yo and it's very exciting to be getting a horse of his quality. All the big races in Europe up to a mile will be considered for him with Royal Ascot being one of the main targets."** It will be interesting to see if he is steered towards the Queen Anne or Diamond Jubilee Stakes in June. Either way, he is another exciting addition to the European scene.

KODI BEAR had a frustrating start and end to his three year old career. Forced to miss the 2000 Guineas, due to an infection in his lymph drainage canal, he could only finish eighth in the QEII at Ascot on Champions Day in October. However, in between, Clive Cox's star stable looked very smart winning three times with his trainer saying in June: **"He's one of the best we've ever had, of that there's no doubt."** A four and a half lengths winner of the Group 3 Sovereign Stakes at Salisbury (1m : Good), he was equally emphatic in victory in the Group 2 Celebration Mile at Goodwood (Soft) in August. His record in Group 1 company is 248 but he remains open to further improvement having only had nine races during his career. Gerald Mosse (2 from 3) is expected to maintain the partnership. Races such as the Bet365 Mile at Sandown (22nd April) and Lockinge Stakes at Newbury (14th May) are obvious spring targets.

The Lockinge Stakes is very much on Henry Candy's mind as far as **LIMATO** is concerned. Unbeaten as a juvenile in 2014, the Tagula gelding won twice last season, including a brilliant performance in the Group 2 Park Stakes (7f : Good) at Doncaster's St Leger meeting. Following his three and three quarters of a length win, his trainer said: **"That was very exciting. Andrea (Atzeni) could not believe the gears the horse has got. It was amazing. It was a major risk running him on the ground but now he's older and stronger, I think he can handle at least good to soft. I'll be happier running him over seven furlongs now than in sprints, and I wouldn't rule out a mile."** Runner-up on his final start in the Group 1 Prix de la Foret at Longchamp only three weeks later, Candy remarked: **"I personally thought it was one race too many. I know he finished very well at the end, but I think he wants a long rest and freshening up. He's been on the go a heck of a long time. Ryan (Moore) was a little bit undecided about going a mile, but I feel it will suit him ideally. He's bred to get it and he's not as quick as he was."** If he stays eight furlongs, there must be every chance he will gain his first win at the highest level (Group 1 form figures: 22).

David Simcock has taken charge of **LIGHTNING SPEAR** following the retirement of Olly Stevens. The five year old has won half of his eight career starts and is officially rated 115. Having won handicaps at Lingfield and Salisbury off marks of 91 and 96 during the first half of the season, the son of Pivotal produced a career best effort when a length and a half second behind Arod in the Group 2 Summer Mile at Ascot (Good/Firm). Fourth next time in the Group 1 Prix Jacques Le Marois, he was below par on his final two runs, including over ten furlongs in the Champions Stakes at Ascot last time. There are Pattern races to be won with Simcock's new recruit.

Aidan O'Brien has already won the 2000 Guineas seven times and he is responsible for the warm ante-post favourite in **AIR FORCE BLUE**. The War Front colt won 4 of his 5 races last year, including three at Group 1 level. A two lengths winner of the Phoenix Stakes (stable won the race for the 14th time) at the Curragh, he then won the National Stakes by three lengths and, in doing so, supplied O'Brien with his 11th win in the Group 1 event. Joseph O'Brien said afterwards: **"He has a huge engine. He travelled very good throughout the race and with a furlong and a half to go, he was still cantering. I haven't ridden many as good as him. He travels, relaxes and has a lot of speed. He's very exciting."** He then rounded off his juvenile career with an even more striking display in the Dewhurst Stakes at Newmarket. A three and a quarter lengths winner, his trainer enthused: **"We were very happy after yesterday as Ryan (Moore) came in from winning on the filly (Minding) and said he'd never ridden anything like her. I said to him, 'wait until you ride this one tomorrow.' The reality is that the filly would lead AFB to about halfway and then he would blow her away – that's how good he is. He's something we haven't had before. I'd say there's no doubt he's the best two year old we've had."** His only defeat came in the Coventry Stakes at Royal Ascot but he hasn't looked back since and will take all the beating in the colt's first Classic on the Rowley Mile (30th April).

Talking of **MINDING**, she still looks the stable chief hope for the 1000 Guineas the following day even though she may not want rattling fast ground. A filly by Galileo out of dual Group 1 winner Lillie Langtry, she won the Moyglare Stud Stakes (7f : Yielding) at the Curragh before producing a devastating display in the Group 1 Fillies Mile at HQ. A four and a half lengths scorer, Ryan Moore rode her for the first time and remarked afterwards: **"I don't think Minding could have been more impressive on the day. She travelled beautifully throughout, just cantering the whole way, and as soon as I pulled her out, the race was over and she just powered up the hill. She handled everything beautifully."** It remains to be seen whether she will stay a mile and a half in time because her dam never raced beyond a mile.

At a lesser level, I was very taken by the performances of **ARTHENUS** during the Autumn. James Fanshawe's gelding won his final three races at Nottingham, Ascot and York progressing from a mark of 87 to 100. On the brink of Pattern races, James Fanshawe commented at Ascot in early September: **"Arthenus was showing promise as a colt but he's really impressed for being gelded. He loves this ground and has some talent."** A head winner at York the following month over nine furlongs, his breeder and part owner Andrew Coombs stated: **"We will put Arthenus away now and there is more to come, he was very slow to develop. We have had to be patient but trainer and jockey think he is going to be a good horse and he will win decent races."** Suited by some ease in the ground, he can win a big handicap before plying his trade at a higher level later in the season.

MIDDLE DISTANCE

JACK HOBBS progressed from winning a maiden at Wolverhampton to becoming the first British trained winner of the Irish Derby since 1993 in 182 days last season. A five lengths winner at the Curragh, having finished second behind stablemate Golden Horn in the Dante and Epsom Derby, John Ferguson said afterwards: **"When Sheikh Mohammed bought Jack Hobbs, who is by Halling out of a Swain mare, we really felt his future was as a four and five year old. The fact he's been second in the Derby at Epsom and the winner of an Irish Derby is just an unbelievable bonus."** Following his easy win in the Group 3 September Stakes at Kempton, John Gosden stated: **"I think Jack Hobbs is an improving horse, like his father. His father got better at four and five. There is no reason a horse of his scope, frame and pedigree is not going to improve with age."** A length and three quarters third in the Qipco Champion Stakes at Ascot in October, the champion trainer said: **"Jack Hobbs is next year's horse. He's a big, overgrown kid and I couldn't be more thrilled with him. I said he is still such an immature horse."** Expected to reappear in the Jockey Club Stakes at Newmarket (30th April), the Coronation Cup at Epsom (4th June) has been mentioned as his first main target.

Another Classic winner **SIMPLE VERSE** also achieved a lot in a short space of time for Ralph Beckett in 2015. Unraced as a juvenile, she won five times last year and, having finished second in a twelve furlongs handicap off 77 at Goodwood in May, she never looked back thereafter. The Duke of Marmalade filly won her next four races, including the St Leger (on appeal having passed the post in front) at Doncaster and the Qipco British Champions Fillies & Mares Stakes at Ascot. Following her three parts of a length win, one of her owners Sheikh Fahad Al Thani said: **"I think she showed today she's one of the best mile and a half horses around. We're looking forward to next year and hopefully she'll be competitive in all the big races like the King George."** With Andrea Atzeni parting company with Qatar Racing, Oisin Murphy (1 from 1) will be riding Simple Verse for the first time since she won the Bibury Cup at Salisbury in June.

NEW BAY had a terrific season last year winning four times, including the Prix du Jockey Club at Chantilly and Group 2 Prix Niel. Two and a quarter lengths third in the Prix de L'Arc de Triomphe behind Golden Horn, he reportedly had one or two issues with his feet last season. Provided those problems are behind him, **he could be one of the stars of the summer**. Andre Fabre is master with his older middle distance horses and he could be a major contender for races such as the Coronation Cup (4th June - Fabre won it six times), Prince of Wales's Stakes and, ultimately, the Arc once again. The extended ten furlongs Prix Ganay at Saint-Cloud (1st May) looks a logical starting point, a race the stable have won four times (Creator (1990), Subotica (1992), Indian Danehill (2000) & Cutlass Bay (2010)).

FOUND may not have contested any of the Classics last year but she rounded off her three year old career with victory in the Breeders' Cup Turf at Keeneland. A half length winner from Golden Horn, she was tackling twelve furlongs for only the second time having encountered traffic problems in the Prix de L'Arc de Triomphe behind the same rival. Beaten five lengths in ninth at Longchamp in October, she will reportedly be targeted at the race again this year. In the meantime, the Galileo filly may reappear in the Mooresbridge Stakes at the Curragh (2nd May) before returning to the same track for the Group 1 Tattersalls Gold Cup (22nd May).

RACING HISTORY is a full-brother to the top-class Farhh and the son of Pivotal has inherited a fair share of his sibling's ability. Successful in three of his four races last term, he won a ten furlongs handicap at Chester in July before following up in the Group 3 Winter Hill Stakes at Windsor (1m 2f : Good/Soft) by a length from subsequent Grade 1 Canadian International Stakes winner Cannock Chase. His trainer Saeed Bin Suroor remarked: **"He needs soft ground, but I've always liked him and he reminds me of his brother. It's similar the way they improved. He's a better horse this year than last and will be better again next year."** William Buick (2 from 2) did the steering at the Thames track and added: **"He's very exciting. He's only going to keep progressing. He goes very well on soft ground."** He finished the year with a creditable fourth in the Champions Stakes at Ascot behind Fascinating Rock. Rated 117, Racing History has only raced a handful of times and can win a Group 1 over ten furlongs on easy ground this year.

I am a big fan of **DARTMOUTH** who looks capable of winning another big handicap before going down the Pattern route once again. The Duke of Edinburgh Stakes (17th June) at Royal Ascot looks an obvious target off his rating of 102. Sir Michael Stoute has won the twelve furlongs event six times since 1998 and the Dubawi colt is already a course and distance winner. Successful three times last term, he won handicaps off 78, 83 and 89. The four year old was particularly impressive at Glorious Goodwood in early August when beating Antiquarium by two lengths. His trainer stated afterwards: **"This fella is really good. His last two**

victories have been very smooth and I'm impressed with him. He has a lot of potential, a good mind, is very sound and is going the right way." Third in a Listed race at Kempton on his final run in November, he is the sort Stoute excels with and he can develop into a Listed/Group horse later in the season.

David Simcock has a couple of lightly raced four year olds to keep tabs on this season. **BATEEL** is an unbeaten daughter of Dubawi who is rated 97. Successful at Salisbury over ten furlongs in May, she has followed up in handicaps over a mile and a half at Goodwood and Newmarket off marks of 81 and 89. All three of her starts have been on good to soft or slower ground and she looks at least Listed class in such conditions. It would be no surprise to see her develop into a Pinnacle (28th May) or Lancashire Oaks Stakes (2nd July) filly (both at Haydock Park).

Stablemate **CARNACHY** was similarly progressive during the second half of last season. Like Bateel, the Mastercraftsman filly didn't race as a juvenile and she finished second on her first two outings at Carlisle and Chepstow over nine and eight furlongs respectively. A combination of slower ground and a longer trip clearly suited her in her next two starts though winning at Newbury (1m 2f : Soft) and Goodwood (1m 4f : Good/Soft). She was particularly impressive on her handicap debut at the latter venue when beating Revision by four lengths off a rating of 84. A rise of eleven pounds may not be enough to prevent her from winning another handicap before she dips her toe in a black type event. Both Simcock fillies seemingly relish easy ground and, when conditions are in their favour, they can win a good prize or two this year.

ARGUS is only rated 92 at present but Ralph Beckett's lightly raced four year old may also be competing in Pattern races by the second half of the season. A colt by Rip Van Winkle, he is a half-brother to the 2011 Canadian International winner Sarah Lynx and was successful in three of his five races last year. A half length scorer from Mistiroc at Doncaster (1m 4f : Good/Soft) in late October, his trainer said: **"Argus has had a lot of problems with his feet, but he's a lovely horse with a good attitude, who could develop into a stakes horse next season."** Possibly at his best on good or slower ground, he could be one for the 0-105 twelve furlongs handicap at Newmarket's Guineas meeting (1st May) en route to something like the Duke of Edinburgh or Old Newton Cup at Haydock (2nd July).

Dermot Weld has a couple of older horses who should be making an impact in Pattern races this season. **ALMELA** is a half-sister to John Oxx's 2009 Irish St Leger and Prix du Cadran winner Alandi. Officially rated 100, the Sea The Stars filly has only raced three times winning a twelve furlongs maiden at Galway (Soft) by nineteen lengths in August. **"She was a late developer, both mentally and physically, who should improve. She's bred to want an ease**," commented the trainer's son Kris. Her rider Pat Smullen added: **"She's still raw."** Runner-up in two Listed races at the same track and Naas, she is open to plenty of improvement.

RADANPOUR hasn't been spotted since finishing a tailed off last in the Irish Derby behind Jack Hobbs. However, the Sea The Stars colt remains in training and we have seen how Dermot Weld brought Fascinating Rock back to the highest level following a curtailed three year old career. He won his first three races at Tipperary (1m 1f), Gowran (1m 4f) and Leopardstown (1m 4f). Already a Listed winner, his trainer said at Gowran in May: **"He's a very progressive colt. He coped well with the ground (Heavy). He is still a big, immature horse."** Rated 99, he has winning form on heavy and good to firm ground.

Finally, three German trained horses who could make an impact in European Group 1 races in 2016. **KARPINO** is unbeaten in three starts and is officially rated 116. Trained by Andreas Wohler and owned by Qatar Racing, he won a Group 3 at Krefeld (1m : Good/Soft) in April before winning the German 2000 Guineas by four and a half lengths at Cologne (Good) the following month. A setback ruled him out of the German Derby and he hasn't been seen since. However, the owner's racing manager David Redvers said in August: **"I think it's more likely he will be an Arc horse for next year."** Provided he regains full fitness, the Cape Cross could be a very exciting prospect. His stablemate **QUASILLO** is another unbeaten four year old who hasn't raced since the spring. Unraced as a juvenile, the Sea The Stars colt won by two lengths on his debut at Munich (1m 3f : Good) in April before following up in a Group 3 at Hanover (1m 2f) by two and a half lengths. He, too, was forced to miss the German Derby due to injury. **NUTAN** provided Peter Schiergen with his fifth win in the German Derby and his rider Andrasch Starke his seventh when beating Palace Prince by a handful of lengths at Hamburg in July. One and a half lengths third behind Luca Cumani's Second Step in Group 1 company at Hoppegarten in August, he missed the rest of the season but remains unexposed. The Duke of Marmalade colt has only raced five times (each run on good ground) and is officially rated 118.

STAYERS

Aidan O'Brien has won the Ascot Gold Cup on no less than six occasions since 2006 and Ballydoyle may have a couple of prime candidates for the 2016 renewal. **BONDI BEACH** was a Group 3 winner last year before finishing half a length second in the Great Voltigeur Stakes at York and then denied by a head in the St Leger behind Simple Verse. Awarded the race in the stewards' room afterwards, the Galileo colt then lost it following an appeal by the 'winning' connections. Colm O'Donoghue was on board at Town Moor and he said: **"Bondi Beach is a lovely big colt. It's only the fifth start of his life. He can only improve and the winter will stand him well."** Beaten six and a quarter lengths in the Melbourne Cup, the lightly raced colt is still unexposed and could be a real force in staying events this summer.

Stablemate **ORDER OF ST GEORGE** finished a short head behind Bondi Beach in the Group 3 Curragh Cup in late June but never looked back thereafter. He won his next three starts, culminating in an eleven lengths victory in the Irish St Leger at the Curragh (1m 6f : Good). He was providing his trainer with his third win in the race and his son Joseph stated: **"He is a lovely colt. He handles easy ground well, so conditions suited and he stays very well. He can also quicken."** The son of Galileo had previously won Her Majesty's Plate at Down Royal (1m 5f : Good/Firm) by five and a half lengths and the Group 3 Irish St Leger Trial (Soft) by seven and a half lengths. Officially rated 124, he is a most exciting staying prospect who has improved markedly since stepping up in distance.

Owners Rich and Susannah Ricci have a couple of very good prospects for this division. Willie Mullins has won the Ascot Stakes (14th June) twice in recent years (Simenon (2012) and Clondaw Warrior (2015)) and the ex-French trained **LIMINI** has been provisionally earmarked for the two and a half miles event. A three times winner for Nicolas Clement, she beat subsequent dual Group 2 winner Manatee at Chateaubriant (1m 5f : Soft) in September 2014. Bought soon afterwards by Ireland's champion jumps trainer, the Peintre Celebre mare has won all three of her starts over hurdles, including the Grade 2 Dawn Run Mares' Novices' Hurdle at the Cheltenham Festival in March by four and a half lengths. Rated 145 over timber, she looks well treated off a mark in the high 80s on the level. By all accounts, Ryan Moore, who partnered Mullins' previous two winners, is already being lined up for the ride in June.

Stablemate **MAX DYNAMITE** is rated 141 over hurdles but he ran three tremendous races on the Flat last term. Runner-up in the Northumberland Plate off 104 from a wide draw, the Great Journey gelding was an impressive four and a half lengths winner of the Lonsdale Cup at York in August under Frankie Dettori. He then looked most unfortunate not to follow up in the Melbourne Cup having met trouble in running. Only denied by half a length, he is still low mileage under both codes. The Ascot Gold Cup is his main summer target followed by the Galway Hurdle (28th July), a race in which he finished second in 2015. Max Dynamite has already accumulated £676,159 in prize-money even though he has only won three races throughout his career. Even if doesn't win at the Royal meeting in June, he will take some stopping off his mark at Galway.

VAZIRABAD provided Alain de Royer-Dupre with his second win in the Prix Royal Oak (Tiraaz (1998) at Saint-Cloud (1m 7f : Soft) in October when beating Siljan's Saga by a length. **"His acceleration is what marks him out. He switches off very well and then when you ask him, he really comes alive. I was a bit worried about the soft ground, but he's now proved he goes on anything. Everything is possible and he could run well at a mile and a half, but he's a gelding and stays so well, so we may as well make use of that,"** commented the grey's trainer afterwards. The son of Manduro won five of his seven races last year collecting Group 2 and 3 victories at Longchamp en route to Saint-Cloud. Christophe Soumillon (5 from 5) gets on particularly well with him and Vazirabad started his four year old career in the best possible way when winning the Group 2 Dubai Gold Cup at Meydan on Easter Saturday. A neck winner from Big Orange, he has the option of dropping in trip or tackling two and a half miles for the first time and attempting to provide France with their first win in the Ascot Gold Cup (16th June) since 2005.

MR SINGH was being prepared for the St Leger but scoped dirty and therefore missed some work, which ruled him out of the final Classic. Absent since, he remains a four year old of considerable potential. Runner-up in the Group 2 King Edward VII Stakes at Royal Ascot behind Balios, the High Chaparral colt appreciated the drop in grade and step up in trip when providing John Gosden with his fifth win (4 times in the last 5 years) in the Group 3 Bahrain Trophy at Newmarket in July. **"Mr Singh is strengthening up all the time and has a nice gear change,"** commented Frankie Dettori afterwards. A two and a half lengths winner, he enjoys a sound surface and it remains to be seen whether he returns to twelve furlongs or continues over longer distances. Races like the Group 3 John Porter Stakes at Newbury (16th April) or Group 2 Jockey Club Stakes at HQ (30th April) appeal as possible starting points.

One of the most profitable betting angles last year was following **Hughie Morrison trained runners at Chelmsford City**. The East Ilsley based handler sent out 16 winners from 34 runners (47%) at the Essex track in 2015 returning a £1 level stakes profit of £35.64. The relatively lightly raced **ATALAN** contributed two of those wins and he looks a potentially well treated young stayer with more to offer. A half-brother to stablemate Vent De Force, who won the Melrose Stakes in 2014 before winning the Group 3 Henry II Stakes at Sandown last year, he needs to translate his all-weather form (121) to the turf (6,10,10,7,8,7) this term. Gelded during the winter, he was considered both mentally and physically backward last season but it didn't prevent him from registering a couple of victories over staying trips at the track formerly known as Great Leighs. Successful off marks of 55 and 65, he was a head scorer from Goldan Jess in August with part owner Terry Bird saying: **"He will make a lovely four year old."** Only seventh on his final run at Redcar when dropped back in trip, Atalan appears at home over two miles and could be one for those two and a quarter mile staying events at Pontefract during the course of the season. Otherwise, keep a close eye on him when he returns to Chelmsford City, along with anything else Hughie Morrison decides to run at the track. "**He is a real child at the moment, both physically and mentally, and has a lot of growing up to do. Next year is when I would expect him to really blossom,"** commented Atalan's trainer in May last year.

Marcus Tregoning trained Askar Tau to win three Pattern races, including the Doncaster Cup in 2009, and the Derby winning trainer has another nice staying prospect on his hands in **BURMESE**. Unraced as a juvenile, the Sir Percy gelding finished runner-up on his first three starts before winning his next three. Victories at Bath, Kempton and Ascot (2m : Good) saw his rating climb from 80 to 96. A two and a quarter lengths winner from Deauville Dancer on the latter occasion, his trainer said: **"Burmese is going the right way as we hoped and William (Buick) likes him a lot. I hope he can make the next step next year. Hopefully he will be back for Royal Ascot next year – it's just a question of whether it will be for the Queen Alexandra or the Gold Cup."** The other option though is the 0-100 Ascot Stakes – effective on fast ground and with William Buick (2 from 2) on board, he would have leading claims. Tregoning hasn't trained a Royal winner since 2003 and this unexposed four year old could be the one to end his barren run.

Sir Mark Prescott is without a winner at Royal Ascot since 1996 when Pivotal won the King's Stand Stakes. However, one wonders whether he may also have the Ascot Stakes on **SEA PRIDE**'s agenda, even though she is unproven on fast ground. A well bred five year old mare by Sea The Stars, she started her career by running in four bumpers, winning at Southwell and being Listed placed at Aintree last spring. Switched to the Flat in September, she won by six lengths at Kempton (1m 4f) from Pecking Order (won by nine lengths since). Her rider Luke Morris believes: **"Sea Pride is a big girl and has taken a lot of time to come to herself. She has done it well but is still raw and could go on to better things."** Beaten a short head by Cheltenham Festival winner Ted Veale at Listowel (1m 6f : Yielding/Soft) ten days later, she then finished a length and a quarter third behind Digeanta in the Irish Cesarewitch at the Curragh (2m : Good) off a mark of 92. Only raised two pounds, she has a lot more to offer and could even develop into an English Cesarewitch horse. There is a good staying prize to be won with her.

The two miles two event could be the long-term goal for **MAGIC CIRCLE**, too. Unplaced in three races as juvenile, the gelded son of Makfi improved immeasurably once stepped up in distance last term. Rated 60 when winning at Doncaster in May over twelve furlongs, Ralph Beckett's charge won three more races off marks of 66, 72, and 78 and is now rated 86. All four wins were gained on easy ground and he stays two miles thoroughly. Following his two and a half lengths victory at Doncaster (1m 6f : Good/Soft) in late October, his jockey Harry Bentley (3 from 3) said: **"He did it well and loves soft ground. He is a proper stayer to look forward to next year."** Unfortunately for Bentley, who has signed up to ride for Roger Varian this year, newly appointed stable jockey Fran Berry is set to ride the progressive four year old for the first time.

INDEX

SELECTED HORSE = BOLD *Talking Trainers = Italics*

EMAIL ONLY SERVICE

Similar to the last couple of years, I am running an **EMAIL ONLY SERVICE** from October to December exclusively. To give new clients an idea of what is on offer, I have included some examples from last year's service.

What The Clients Said:

"Awesome result the magicman strikes again. Won with plenty in hand and not a moments worry great write up spot on again and results speak for themselves best service I've tried, keep up the fantastic work sir. Very happy customer!" **C.R.**

"Superb information again Mark, I managed to get some 11/4, will certainly pay for Xmas. Different class." **S.R.**

"The email service as usual has been brilliant and this season's OJA seems to continue to unearth amazing insight if you have the time to trust and follow it in detail over a period. Thanks as always for your outstanding value for money publications." **S.L.**

"Thanks very much for the fantastic service you have supplied, I have been involved with racing tipsters for over 30 years and never had as good a strike rate as yourself, out of this world." **A.H.**

"Thank you for an excellent tipping service throughout the three months. It has been a pleasure and profitable to be a member of your service. Your indepth knowledge and analysis of the race has been excellent. I honestly rate your service as one of the best and most profitable." **D.K.**

"Thanks for your email Mark would just like to say your selections and insight has been awesome. Keep up the good work sir your service is the best." **C.R.**

"Just want to say thanks for running the service again this year, I have ended up with a nice £756 profit from it so I'm obviously very happy with that so thanks a lot!" **D.M.**

"Thank you for a very successful and profitable email service. My personal highlight was the win of Aloomomo whose romp round Uttoxeter was a joy. Keep up the good work with all your services, the books and updates, they are simply the best by a very long way." **C.B.**

2015: 6 Winners from 11 selections 55%
October 4 winners from 4 selections

WINNERS: CULTURATI (Advised @ 2/1 WON at 15/8), PRESENTING LISA (Advised @ 5/2 WON at 13/8), SYKES (5/2), ALOOMOMO (Advised @ 100/30 WON at 5/4), MOSSIES WELL (Advised @ 4/1 WON at 6/4), VIRGILIO (Advised @ 3/1 WON at 5/2)

Quote: *"Charlie Appleby must be looking forward to running the exciting Emotionless in the Dewhurst Stakes at Newmarket on Saturday. His juveniles have been in good form with the stable sending out 33 two year old winners during 2015. That tally looks set to be added to in the opening nursery at York tomorrow (**1.45**). Godolphin two year olds are invariably well handicapped on their nursery debuts with Start Time being a prime example at Windsor on Monday. That very much looks the case as far as **CULTURATI** is concerned with an opening mark of 89. A well bred son of Dubawi, who has raced three times (twice on soft ground), he was only beaten a neck by subsequent Group 3 Acomb Stakes winner Recorder (rated 105) on his debut at Newmarket in July. Back in fifth that day was Muntazah, who was since won at Leicester and finished third in the Group 2 Royal Lodge Stakes and is officially rated 103. A mile may well have stretched Culturati next time at the same track when chasing home Ventura Storm (won again since and now rated 98) but he made no mistake on his third outing. Sent off 6/5 favourite in a seven furlongs maiden at Ascot on slow ground, he cruised to the front over two furlongs out before getting tired late on. Adam Kirby's mount still prevailed by a short head. Both the runner-up and third have won since. In other words, the form of his three races is particularly solid. With that in mind, Culturati looks potentially thrown in off 89. The drop back to six furlongs is a minor concern but he showed a lot of speed at Ascot. His dam won a Listed race on good to soft ground and he has already proved he relishes easy conditions. In terms of the opposition, Tidal Wave looks a threat. He, too, is dropping in trip having raced too keenly over seven furlongs last time. Richard Hannon's Canford Cliffs colt has only raced on good or faster ground but his dam won twice on heavy so there is every chance he will cope with the conditions on the Knavesmire. Richard Fahey runs three and Mark Johnston is always a threat with his juveniles. However, I am hoping Culturati will outclass his rivals and develop into a Pattern performer himself."*

SELECTION: CULTURATI (2/1 Paddy Power, 15/8 Coral, William Hill, 7/4 Bet365 & Ladbrokes) 1.45 York. WON @ 15/8

Quote: *"Alan King has his string in good form with Grumeti winning the Cesarewitch last weekend, while both Oceane and Duke of Sonning have won juvenile hurdles during the last fortnight. Whilst interviewing the head of Barbury Castle for One Jump Ahead during the summer, it was clear he felt former Irish pointer **PRESENTING LISA** had more to offer. Bought for 40,000gns at the Cheltenham November sale having won one of her three Irish points (won on good ground by twelve lengths), the Presenting mare won on her Rules debut for King in a bumper last December. Only fourth on her two runs over hurdles at Huntingdon and Towcester, her trainer explained in OJA: **"A winning Irish point-to-pointer, she is a decent mare who I like. She was an easy winner at Towcester in a bumper on her first run for us before Christmas but wasn't quite right thereafter. She had a couple of runs but didn't scope great so we gave her a good break. She is another who will be going mares' novice hurdling and will be suited by two and a half miles plus."** In other words, there were excuses for her below par runs over hurdles. With those comments in mind, it is interesting to note she goes down the handicap route at Market Rasen (4.25) tomorrow and contests the two and a half mile mares' handicap hurdle off a lenient looking mark of 105. Good ground suits, she goes well fresh and is unexposed. It will be disappointing if she can't go very close."*

SELECTION: PRESENTING LISA (5/2 BetVictor, Ladbrokes, Skybet, 9/4 Bet365, Betfred, Boylesports, Coral & William Hill) 4.25 Market Rasen. WON @ 13/8

Quote: *"In all likelihood, the ground at Aintree tomorrow will be good to soft following rain on Saturday morning/afternoon. That won't be a problem for the Philip Hobbs trained* **SYKES** *in the staying conditional jockeys' handicap hurdle at 1.55. The Mountain High gelding won an English point-to-point on good to soft and I think he will appreciate the step up to three miles. A nine lengths winner at Worcester a year ago, his trainer explained in One Jump Ahead:* ***"A winning English pointer, he raced twice for us last season winning over hurdles at Worcester in October. He then suffered with a minor pelvic problem hence he hasn't raced since. Allocated a mark of 114, it looks fair and I will be disappointed if he can't be competitive off such a rating. He will stay three miles."*** *Absent for eleven months, the six year old made an encouraging return to action at Newton Abbot in late September when a length second in an extended two miles five handicap hurdle off a mark of 114. Admittedly, the winner has disappointed since and Sykes has been raised four pounds. However, he travelled strongly through the race and possibly paid for racing too keenly early (fresh having been off for so long). With the run under his belt, he will hopefully settle better and relish the longer trip. Already a winner over two miles seven, he is set to be partnered by the promising Ciaran Gethings (rode stablemate War Sound to win the Swinton Hurdle in the spring) and I can't believe a mark of 118 is the sealing of his ability. Every year, Philip only includes horses in his interview in OJA which he feels will win races and is rarely wrong with assessments. Sykes has been given sufficient time to recover since his last race (27 days), so I don't think the bounce factor will be an issue. The fact he can race keenly is a minor concern, especially stepping up in trip, but he settled well enough when winning at Worcester last year and the likes of Benefit of Youth and Come To The Party ought to provide a decent early tempo. In terms of opposition, Gone Forever is respected but Brian Ellison feels he is at his best over two and a half miles on soft ground and this may be a prep before he goes chasing. Tantamount rates a danger because he is a course winner, his trainer is in fine form (3 winners at Kelso on Saturday) and he sports a tongue tie for the first time. The fact the six year old hasn't won for nearly two years slightly tempers enthusiasm though. The Jonjo O'Neill trained Optimistic Bias is another live threat. A former Irish pointer, he is unexposed and was a winner at Southwell last spring. He probably has more to offer off his mark of 119, he runs well fresh and is set to be ridden for the first time by Patrick Cowley (ridden 3 winners from only 13 rides for Jonjo this season). I like stablemate Box Office on the same card at 3.00 (stepping up in trip, fitted with a tongue tie for the first and was given a very sympathetic ride at Chepstow on his reappearance, plus Barry Geraghty stays in the UK to ride him rather than heading back to Ireland) but trying to second guess Jonjo O'Neill is an impossible task. Sykes has the benefit of a run this season though and the Hobbs team continue in excellent form. Proved on sharp tracks, I am anticipating plenty of improvement over this longer trip."*

SELECTION: SYKES 1.55 Aintree DEAD-HEATED @ 5/2

Quote: *"The ground is currently described as good to soft, good in places on the chase course at* **Uttoxeter** *but a significant amount of rain is forecast overnight. Therefore the likelihood is that the two and a half miles handicap chase, which rounds off the card at* **4.10***, will be run in testing conditions. That is good news for the ex-French trained gelding* **ALOOMOMO***, who carries plenty of stable confidence. Previously handled by Yannick Fouin, he won a bumper in France in October 2013 and was bought for €80,000 soon afterwards by Raymond Anderson Green and The Large G & T Partnership syndicate. Without a win in his subsequent eight starts, he reportedly suffered with ulcers before being transferred to Warren Greatrex last season. The five year old raced twice for the head of Uplands, producing a very encouraging effort at Carlisle over three miles two in March. Only beaten five lengths in fourth, the race was a 0-130 handicap chase (compared to tomorrow's 0-120) which contained the likes of Russe Blanc and Fill The*

Power. Switched back to hurdles at Ayr in April for his only other run for Greatrex, he almost certainly found the ground too lively (good) and his future lies over fences. Whilst interviewing Warren for One Jump Ahead during the summer, he recommended I included Aloomomo, saying the following: ***"Previously trained in France, he raced twice for us during the spring. Fourth at Carlisle, the trip stretched him, but James Reveley, who rode him in France, was impressed with him. He then had a run over hurdles at the Scottish National meeting at Ayr because his owner Ray Green was keen for him to go there. We gave him a break afterwards and he has come back in looking a million dollars. I think trips around three miles will suit him and I hope he is on a fair mark."*** *I spoke to Ray (Green) at lunchtime today and he is expecting a big run. He feels Aloomomo's optimum conditions will prove to be three miles on soft/heavy ground. The gelding will therefore be ridden handily tomorrow by Gavin Sheehan (Gold Ingot is the other possible front runner). He said Warren feels he is a completely different horse this season and, in his own mind, wouldn't be surprised if he is rated around 130 by the end of the season. If that proves the case, he is thrown in here off 108. A sound jumper, the more rain the better and his stable are in decent form – Greatrex trained runners since the 22nd October have finished 11132."*

SELECTION: ALOOMOMO (100/30 Betfred, 3/1 Bet365, BetVictor, Ladbrokes) 4.10 Uttoxeter. WON @ 5/4 by 12 lengths

Quote: *"All eyes will be on the first day of the Paddy Power Festival at Cheltenham tomorrow but there is also jumping action at Hexham, where conditions will be bottomless. Indeed, they won't be jumping the fence at the top of the hill in the novices' handicap chase at* ***1.15****. Borders' trainer Sandy Thomson has his small team in decent form at present with Blue Kascade winning at Wetherby last month and the likes of Oscar Lateen, Neptune Equester and stable star Seeyouatmidnight have all finished in the money during the last fortnight. While two miles is undoubtedly on the sharp side for* ***MOSSIES WELL*** *a bold showing is anticipated on his chasing debut at the Northumberland track nevertheless. A former Irish pointer, he was fourth behind the high-class Free Expression before finishing second in his only other point when handled by Eugene O'Sullivan. Bought soon afterwards for 24,000gns, he raced a handful of times for his new handler last winter. An unlucky third behind Sir Vinski at Ayr (badly hampered before finishing strongly) in January, he was an easy eleven lengths winner at the same track a couple of months later. The Morozov gelding handles soft/heavy ground and is reunited with James Reveley (rode him at Ayr in January). Indeed, I contacted James's agent yesterday and he stated that the rider is keen to come over from France to partner Mossies Well before he heads back to Paris to ride at the weekend (has only got two rides on the Hexham card and the other is an ex-Flat racer rated 45). Therefore, I can't imagine the gelding is having a run out. Bred to improve as a chaser, I am hoping Mossies Well will be too good for the opposition. The Sue Smith trained Forward Flight currently heads the market but he has already had three runs over fences and he, too, may want further. I suspect he will set the pace, which will suit Sandy Thomson's charge. The one I fear most, especially with a fence missed out, is Peter Niven's Engrossing. The six year old had some decent form with the likes of Glingerburn and Days of Heaven and will be speedier than Mossies Well. However, he isn't bred to excel as a chaser and I am hoping the combination of fences in bottomless conditions will prove his undoing."*

SELECTION: MOSSIES WELL E/W @ 4/1 (Bet365, BetVictor) & 7/2 (Ladbrokes, Coral, Betfred, Skybet, Boylesports). WON @ 6/4

Quote: *"Dan Skelton won the two and a half miles handicap at Aintree (**2.45**) tomorrow a couple of years ago with Like Minded. Paul Nicholls' former assistant appears to have an outstanding chance of winning the 2015 renewal with the ex-French trained **VIRGILIO**. It is worth recalling Skelton's comments in One Jump Ahead: **"A very tough horse, he won twice in the space of six days at Warwick and Aintree in May, having previously been trained in France. An easy winner at the former, he was entitled to win at the latter under his penalty but it was a quick turnaround and he beat a good horse (Sea Lord). His two wins were gained on contrasting ground and I think he is open to plenty of improvement. He is likely to go to Aintree (7th November) for a conditions race, where he won't have to carry a penalty. If that went to plan, we could consider something like the Ascot Hurdle (21st November)."** The fact Skelton was even considering a race like the Grade 2 Ascot Hurdle, he must feel the six year old is well treated tomorrow off 138. A winner over hurdles in France, he was absent from December 2013 until May this year. As discussed, he then won twice at Warwick and Aintree off marks of 118 and 125 on his first two runs for his new handler. A six lengths winner on the latter occasion, he beat subsequent winner Sea Lord. Effective on testing ground (already soft at Aintree and more rain forecast overnight), he goes well fresh (204 days) and I was told by a contact in the yard this afternoon that Virgilio has had an 'away day' and worked on the grass at home a handful of times. In other words, fitness shouldn't be an issue. He looked a strong stayer when winning over course and distance during the spring and there is every likelihood Bowdler's Magic will provide a generous early gallop. The stable have sent out six winners since the 24th November. In terms of the opposition, I feel Un Ace, Karinga Dancer and Fort Worth would prefer better ground. Cheltenham Festival winner Qualando is feared because he could improve over the longer trip but Paul Nicholls' four year old (his age group have won 3 of the last 8 renewals) was beaten over twenty lengths on his reappearance. I will be disappointed if Virgilio doesn't go close."*

SELECTION: VIRGILIO (3/1 Ladbrokes, 11/4 Bet365, Betfred, BetVictor, Coral, Skybet, William Hill) 2.45 Aintree. WON @ 5/2 by 8 lengths.

EMAIL ONLY
AHEAD ON THE FLAT UPDATES 2016

Once again, I shall be producing **3 *Ahead On The Flat Updates***. The first *Update* will be a preview of the prestigious **Royal Ascot** meeting in June, the second will be a preview of the historic four day **York Ebor** meeting in August and the third will concentrate on the **major Autumn races**. There will be an in-depth analysis of races such as the Cambridgeshire and the Prix de L'Arc de Triomphe. **Please note, the *Updates* are ONLY AVAILABLE VIA EMAIL (Not Post).**

It is £8 for the Royal Ascot *Update* and £6 for the York & Autumn *Updates* (or £17 for ALL 3) via **EMAIL**.

Summary of last year's 3 *Ahead On The Flat Updates*:

What The Clients Said:

"Thanks very much Mark for such a quick response. It is a remarkable analysis; I certainly did not expect anything so detailed and extensive." **G.S.**

"Just a quick note to say thank you for the heads up regarding Night Generation in your Royal Ascot guide. Safe to say it's paid for itself before it's even started!" **J.S.**

"Just a quick note to say a huge thank you and well done with the Ascot guide (and those coming out of AOTF) what a superb day 2 & 3 we've had. Hoping 4 & 5 are half as good. I've been a subscriber to AOTF & OJA and the email updates for a few years and while we've had some good days I can't remember an update being so prophetic and rewarding as this one. The paragraph on Space Age could have been written after the race! BTW whilst the money from winning bets is very welcome the real reward for me is the solving of the puzzle, which with your notes and my own study was brilliant for day 2/3." **H.J.**

"I have previously only ever bought your publication One Jump Ahead as flat racing had never previously inspired me. I bought it this year for the first time and have been following your Top 40 plus other titbits published and have enjoyed watching your selections as well as getting a nice little profit at the same time. I also purchased the Ascot update and what a find that has been. You're guidance is to put it mildly "genius". I had a good first day following your selections, but had a spectacular second day. These included Acapulco at 11/2, Amazing Maria at 40/1, 33/1 and 25/1 & Free Eagle 3/1. However the Crème de la crème came in the Royal Hunt Cup where you nominated 3 horses to follow, in a massive field. I backed all 3 separately and had them in a combination Tricast. As you know they finished 1st,2nd and 3rd !!!! I also had other accumulative bets again producing a healthy profit. Yesterday was my most profitable day of punting ever and all for the price of £6 for your update. What an absolute bargain." **M.H.**

"Well done Mark - you nearly went thru the card day two of Ascot. 1 2 3 in the Hunt Cup marvellous." **S.C.**

"Just wanted to congratulate you on an amazing day 2 of Royal Ascot, four winners on the day, the standout selection being Amazing Maria - simply amazing, Mark!" **J.D.**

"Unbelievable tipping today Amazing Maria was genius but to pick the first three home in the Royal Hunt Cup was something else. Thanks a lot." **A.P.**

"Well done today - a fantastic result for you including the 1/2/3 in the Royal Hunt Cup - just a shame I did not do a trifecta! Still I took your confidence on Acapulco as my big bet of the day so thank you!" ***E.L.***

"More like Amazing Mark! Brilliant tipping Mark, just brilliant. Thank You again!" **J.S.**

"You have no idea how happy you have just made me. Four winners in a row, 5/1,25/1,3/1,12/1 Tricast in the 30 runner Hunt Cup. My best day in racing ever! No need to prove it because your clients know it, but you are the best. Thanks so much." **M.F.**

"Hope you put your 3 selections in a combination tricast in the Royal Hunt cup!!! I didn't but I did have them all e/w & a reverse forecast on the 1st 2! Top Quality Mark, you're having a memorable day!!" **G.C.**

"The day gets better & better!.. GM Hopkins 12/1 £20 win.. Temptress 10/1 £10e/w and Chill the Kite £10e/w... 1st 2nd 3rd!!!.. Amazing. Thank you...." **D.W.**

"What a day Mark, you're a genius..4 winners..first 3 in Hunt Cup..unlucky in first with Sir Isaac Newton. Thanks once again." **A.M.**

"Unbelievable Update Mark 28/1. 5/1 and 3/1 today well done." **D.J.**

"Great analysis and information amazing tipping Acapulco and Amazing Maria. Sir Isaac Newton looked to have no luck could have been three top tips. Thanks so much." **R.J.**

"Brilliant tipping mark took 40/1 Amazing Maria...thank you very much." **A.M.**

"You are a legend backed Acapulco, Amazing Maria and Free Eagle today so far, many thanks." **C.M**

"I guess your inbox will be overwhelmed with congratulatory messages, but I just felt I had to write to add my own. I've lost count of the number of winners you have put up this week, a remarkable achievement by anyone's standards, and it's a huge thank you and well done from me, and probably from many others." **W.S.**

"Well done again Mark the Ascot update has offered so much top class information and analysis, another great day and, although I can only bet small, you have made my Ascot so much more enjoyable despite me being a National Hunt fan , so thanks again for enhancing my enjoyment." **R.J.**

"I have never been in touch before but I am a long term subscriber and fan. I must say that the latest update is just sensational. I have won over 12k on the week but more than that it has been great fun betting with confidence. I love reading your analysis and then placing my bets using your advice as a benchmark." **R.L.**

"Done it again with still one day to go, I'd like to thank you again for an unbelievable few days." **D.J.**

"Although I have had your books for several years this is the first time I have subscribed to your Updates. I just wanted to say what a great decision that was. I only place small bets but it has been a very good week. Your race analyses were often spot on, and some really inspired, e.g. Amazing Maria, but more than that I really enjoyed reading them. There was so much information which I am sure will be useful in the months ahead; I can't wait for the York Update. Thanks very much for such an excellent insight into the week's racing." **G.S.**

"In a deep and competitive field, that's got to rate as your finest tipping day ever. Fantastic work – many congratulations." **S.P.**

"I don't know if you are home yet, but wherever you are, you must be swimming in champagne and compliments. What a week. Many congratulations." **I.C.**

"Thanks the Update service was brilliant. Makes buying you're book and updates a no brainer. Well done and you have set the bar high." **C.B.**

"Thank you Mark for your tremendous work. I didn't manage to catch all the winners but it has been a brilliant week's betting at Royal Ascot. You are the only one I trust and follow and have been for many years and will continue to do so. Keep up the good work." **T.N.**

"I have utilised this book on the last two jump seasons to great success. But this year brought the flat edition along with updates and with a day to go I've had 8 winners plus I'm the best part of £400 to the good. Keep up the good work." **G.W.**

"Ryan Moore - Top Jockey at Royal Ascot with 9 winners but "eclipsed" by Mark Howard Top Tipster with a fabulous 11 winners. Thank you Mark for a remarkable achievement and for providing your Clients with such a rewarding Royal Ascot - simply superb and justly deserved for all the hard work you put into your research and in advising the value bets. A healthy profit achieved from backing your advices - will enjoy our summer holiday even more as a result. Quite simply "the best" Client Service around." **I.G.**

"What an exhilarating 5 days of top quality racing at Royal Ascot. Until last week, I was not really a great fan of Flat racing, as I love the National Hunt season. However, thanks to your update I have completely changed my mind. Yes the £1,000 winnings has certainly been a primary factor, but I now have a much deeper appreciation of the very fine margins that can make the difference between a horse winning and losing a flat race. Sir Isaac Newton being a prime example. Among the many winners, I had multiple seconds. If Temptress had finished first instead of a neck second, my Yankee would have paid out £1800 instead of £200. In addition to your marvellous winning tips, I also backed Trip to Paris Ante post at 25/1 (before he was supplemented!) and I won on Curvy. Given my strong financial betting bank by mid-week. It was a tremendous spectacle and my enjoyment, enthusiasm and final profit was largely down to your knowledge, expertise and judgement. I have long been a subscriber to your NH books and updates. I am now a convert to your Flat service too. Many thanks for sharing your knowledge and experience with the general public. It gives those of us who are wise enough to make a small investment in your guides, a much greater chance of competing with the Bookmakers." **J.S.**

"As always your publications are quite remarkable value for money and you have an unbeatable eye for winners, many congratulations. Pity I didn't follow you in with Amazing Maria but I'm sure everyone who did will be forever grateful. Looking forward to the Ebor meeting update already but you have set the bar so high now it will be difficult to follow last week. Many thanks." **S.L.**

"And I thought you were better with jumpers LOL! Probably the best performance by any pundit at Royal Ascot over the last twenty years." **D.R.**

"Thank you so much for the excellent advice you gave in your Royal Ascot Update. Following it enabled me to have more winners at this meeting than ever before. I also congratulate you on the quality of your writing - the Update was a really good read!" **M.C.**

"I tend to have my picks sorted out before your info comes through. When we both agreed on Amazing Maria and Space Age, was green light to treble the bet. Can't wait for York. Loving your work!" **A.C.**

"A belated thank you for an absolutely astonishing Ascot Update. I returned from holiday yesterday to some very healthy looking betting accounts! Not being able to access my accounts from South Africa I got a mate to place the bets for me, he'd like to pass on his thanks too. He followed me (you!) in on all the bets and thought I was a genius until I confessed that the info was coming from an ACTUAL GENIUS! I think my wife would also like to pass on her thanks as you are largely responsible for the diamond ring that I bought her in Cape Town!" **T.D.**

ROYAL ASCOT 2015

11 WINNERS: **SOLOW (11/8), GLENEAGLES (8/15), ACAPULCO (Advised @ 6/1), AMAZING MARIA (Advised @ 33/1), FREE EAGLE (Advised @ 3/1), GM HOPKINS (Advised @ 12/1), TIME TEST (15/8), SPACE AGE (9/1), ILLUMINATE (4/1), ARAB DAWN (6/1), MAHSOOB (7/4)**

Plus: **ROYAL HUNT CUP**: 3 selections: **GM HOPKINS (Advised @ 12/1 – WON), TEMPTRESS (Advised @ 14/1 – 2nd), CHIL THE KITE (Advised @ 25/1 – 3rd).** TRICAST: **£1189.72**

PAUL HANAGAN's NAP of the week: MAHSOOB (WON the Wolferton Handicap @ 7/4)

Quote: *"**AMAZING MARIA** was a high-class two year old for Ed Dunlop winning the Prestige Stakes at Goodwood. Disappointing last term, including when finishing last in the Oaks, she joined David O'Meara at the start of this year. While held in handicap company over C&D in May behind Temptress, she looked back to her best last time when two and a half lengths third behind the unbeaten Brooch in the Group 2 Landwades Stud Stakes. The daughter of Mastercraftsman likes fast ground and handles the track well. Officially rated 105, she could go well at big prices and couldn't be in better hands."* **ADVISED @ 33/1 WON the Duke of Cambridge Stakes at 25/1**

Quote: *"**FREE EAGLE** is arguably one of the best horses Dermot Weld has trained but injuries have restricted the son of High Chaparral to four outings. Rated 120, he suffered a stress fracture of his tibia during the spring last year and therefore he didn't reappear until September. However, he produced a stunning display in the Group 3 Enterprise Stakes at Leopardstown when beating his rivals by upwards of seven lengths. A length and a half third behind Noble Mission and Al Kazeem on heavy ground in the Champions Stakes over C&D in October, it was an excellent run considering his lack of experience. He was due to contest the Tattersalls Gold Cup last month but a head cold ruled him out and he comes here for his reappearance. His first time out record though is 11 and being a half-brother to Custom Cut and Sapphire, he is bred to get even better with age."* **Advised @ 3/1 WON the Prince of Wales's Stakes at 5/2**

Quotes: **Royal Hunt Cup**: *"**GM HOPKINS** is rated 103 having won 3 of his 9 races. A three times winner in 2014, including the Silver Cambridgeshire by two and three parts of a length off 91, he could only finish tenth in the Lincoln on his seasonal reappearance. However, the four year old was back to form at Newbury last month when a running on second behind Spark Plug off 99. Ryan Moore partners him for the first time."*

*"Granted a favourable draw and luck in running, I am keen on the chances of **TEMPTRESS (14/1)**. Unbeaten at the track, she is unexposed and the form of her latest win has worked out well. I also suggest saving on **CHIL THE KITE (25/1)** and **GM HOPKINS (12/1)**."* **1st 3 home in the Royal Hunt Cup – Advised @ 12/1, 14/1 & 25/1**.

Quote: *"**TIME TEST** has always been held in high esteem by Roger Charlton and he never finished out of the first two in three races last year. A well bred son of Dubawi out of the high-class Passage of Time, he won the London Gold Cup at Newbury, the same ten furlong event Cannock Chase won en route to success here last season. Held up by Ryan Moore, he showed a good attitude to go through a gap before quickening away to win by a length and a quarter from Dissolution. He won off a mark of 93 and now finds himself on 103. Reportedly working well with Al Kazeem prior to his Newbury win, he is rapidly on the upgrade. This is likely to be the fastest ground he has encountered but I am expecting him to go very close."* **WON the Tercentenary Stakes by three and a quarter lengths @ 15/8**

Quote: *"The one I like is the Godolphin owned **SPACE AGE**. A colt by New Approach, he will be tackling a mile and a half for the first time but the manner in which he finished in the London Gold Cup at Newbury behind Time Test last month over ten furlongs suggests he will have no trouble staying. Beaten five and a half lengths on that occasion, he won next time at Newmarket from Suffused.*

Raised three pounds to a mark of 88, the Charlie Appleby trained colt remains fairly treated and, granted luck in running, he should go close." **WON the King George V Stakes @ 9/1**

Quote: *"**ILLUMINATE** bids to provide the Hannon stable with their sixth win in the race and the daughter of Zoffany looked a high-class prospect when beating stablemate Great Page (won a Listed race at Naas by three lengths since) by two and three parts of a length in a conditions event at Salisbury in May. Queen Mary runner-up Tiggy Wiggy had won the same race twelve months earlier. Bought for 95,000gns, her form looks strong and six furlongs on quick ground looks ideal. Her profile is faultless."* **WON the Albany Stakes @ 4/1**

Quote: *"**ARAB DAWN** has evidently been trained with this in mind. Five lengths fifth in the King George V Handicap over C&D twelve months ago off a mark of 90, he was an encouraging third on his return to action at Newmarket's Guineas meeting behind Astronereus off 93. The gelded son of Dalakhani's record over twelve furlongs is 523 and he gets on particularly well with Richard Hughes (1123). Hughie Morrison has won this with Waverley (2003) and Cill Rialaig (2010) and the four year old has leading claims."* **WON the Duke of Edinburgh Stakes @ 6/1**

Plus: **ARTHENUS (10/11, 3/1, 100/30), BESS OF HARDWICK (4/6), NIGHT GENERATION (9/4, 10/11, 1/2)**

Quote: *"James Fanshawe has endured a quiet first half of the season thus far with only four winners. However, the head of Pegasus Stables appears to have a surefire winner in **ARTHENUS**. A twice raced son of Dutch Art, he showed a glimpse of promise on his sole outing as a juvenile last year at Kempton in November. However, he looked much more streetwise on his reappearance at Doncaster in May when only beaten a length in a mile maiden on easy ground. Partnered by Graham Lee, he stayed on strongly to finish third behind Mustaaqeem. The winner is now rated 88 having finished a neck second in the Wood Ditton Stakes at Newmarket on his debut for Sir Michael Stoute. Arthenus is capable of winning a maiden but I suspect he will show his very best form once handicapped. He could be progressive."* **WON 3 times @ 10/11, 3/1 & 100/30**

Quote: *"**NIGHT GENERATION**, featured on page 115, may have only finished fifth on his handicap debut at Lingfield this month, but he is a horse to follow when stepped up further in trip. A big strapping son of Sholokhov, he looked ill at ease on the track and will be much more at home over twelve furlongs plus on a galloping course. It shouldn't be long before he loses his maiden tag off a mark of 55. Indeed, I will be disappointed if he doesn't win over a mile and a half at Carlisle on Monday (5.15)."* **WON at Carlisle @ 9/4**

YORK EBOR FESTIVAL 2015

3 WINNERS: **TASLEET (2/1), BESHARAH (Advised @ 6/1), MISTRUSTING (5/2), plus TOE THE LINE (Advised @ 40/1 – 4th at 25/1)**

Quote: *"**TASLEET** bids to provide William Haggas with his third successive victory in the race and he sets the standard with an official rating of 109. The Showcasing colt, who was acquired for 52,000gns, has improved with every start. An easy maiden winner at Chepstow, he then won the Listed Rose Bowl Stakes at Newbury before running well in the Richmond Stakes at Goodwood. Beaten less than three lengths by the high-class Shalaa, he was the choice of Paul Hanagan that day (the same owner also had July Stakes third Elronaq in there). A reproduction of that display will make him very hard to beat even allowing for the fact he is forced to concede upwards of five pounds to the majority of his rivals."* **WON the DBS Premier Yearling Stakes @ 2/1**

Quote: *"**BESHARAH** is battle hardened and has developed into a smart juvenile filly. Bought for 85,000gns, she is a three times winner and has improved since finishing four lengths third in the Queen Mary Stakes at Royal Ascot behind Acapulco. Denied by a nose in the Duchess of Cambridge Stakes at Newmarket behind Illuminate, she then outclassed her rivals in the Princess Margaret*

Stakes at Ascot last month. A three lengths winner, she handles any ground and her record over the trip is 21. William Haggas won this three years ago with Rosdhu Queen and he has another major player for the 2015 renewal. The Kodiac filly is thriving at present." **Advised @ 6/1 won the Lowther Stakes at 11/4**

Quote: *"**MISTRUSTING** is making a quick return to action having won at Newmarket on Friday evening. The Godolphin owned filly will carry a six pound penalty following her two and a half lengths victory from the same connections' Wordcraft. It was the daughter of Shamardal's first run since finishing a length and a quarter second behind subsequent Stewards' Cup winner Magical Memory (rated 87 at the time and now 108) at Leicester in May. Indeed, she was conceding three pounds to Charlie Hills' winner. Effective on good and fast ground, she has a leading chance."* **WON at 5/2**

Quote: *"**TOE THE LINE** had a productive campaign in 2014 winning three times, including a Listed race at the Curragh (2 miles) in September. John Kiely's mare hasn't managed a win this year but there were signs of her hitting form at Roscommon last time when third in another Listed contest. Beaten three lengths by Panama Hat, the winner has subsequently finished three parts of a length second in the American St Leger at Arlington Park, and the runner-up, Altesse, has finished second again in Group 3 company. In other words, the form looks solid and she invariably produces her best performances around this time of year (3 wins in September). She handles any ground and, despite the fact she is six year old, she has only had fifteen races in her career. Jamie Spencer rides."* **Advised @ 40/1 finished fourth in the Ebor at 25/1**

Plus: **MARKABAH**: *"Roger Varian's filly showed more last time though at Thirsk when finishing second in a one mile maiden. Dropping back in trip, she was slowly into stride once again but came within a length of Charlie Hills' Calima Breeze (third since off 80) with the pair pulling clear of the remainder. I contacted Paul Hanagan the same evening and he said she works very well at home but has failed to reproduce it on the track. Sheikh Hamdan's number one rider also said she was crying out for further and will come into her own over at least ten furlongs. Don't be surprised if she leaves her previous form behind in future."* **WON at Chelmsford (23/11/15) by five lengths @ 6/1**

THE TIN MAN: *"Deacon Blues was a high-class sprinter for **James Fanshawe** winning the Wokingham Stakes at Royal Ascot in 2011 and four Pattern races during the same season. His half-brother **THE TIN MAN** has some way to go before matching those achievements but the three year old has won two of his first three races and looks a most progressive sprinter in his own right. All three of his races have been over six furlongs at Doncaster and, having won a maiden on his second outing in late June, he created a favourable impression when winning on his handicap debut at Town Moor off a mark of 79. Always travelling powerfully for Tom Queally, he only had to be kept up to his work to beat Kassbaan by two and a half lengths. The gelded son of Equiano has been raised ten pounds, as a result, but I will be surprised if he can't defy it. Interestingly, James Fanshawe has given him an entry in the Group 1 British Champions Sprint Stakes at Ascot in mid October, a race his brother won four years ago. There is a big sprint prize in The Tin Man between now and the end of the season and, given the fact Deacon Blues improved with age, he is likely to make an even better four year old."* **WON at Ascot (2/10/15) by four and a half lengths @ 4/1**

AUTUMN 2015

CAMBRIDGESHIRE HANDICAP: *"**MAN OF HARLECH** is related to the likes of Eisteddford, Border Patrol and Boston Lodge (placed over nine furlongs) and is at his best on slow ground. An emphatic winner at Ffos Las in such conditions in August off a mark of 85, he then chased home Bronze Angel at Doncaster last time. Beaten a length and a half, he remains fairly treated off 92 and his rider David Probert expects him to stay the trip (won over an extended one mile at Windsor as a three year old). The key to his chance though is likely to be the ground with his record on good to soft or softer reading 131."* **Advised e/w @ 28/1 – 4th at 20/1**

Quote: *"**DIGEANTA** was one of my selections in the race (Cesarewitch) last year and Willie Mullins'* *gelding ran well from a poor draw (stall 25) in fifth. Only beaten two and a quarter lengths on good ground off 87, he is four pounds higher this time. Seventh in the Ascot Stakes in June, he won comprehensively over two miles at the Curragh the following month. A remote thirteenth at Leopardstown in his prep, it is hoped Pat Smullen (1 from 4) takes the ride. Landing Light (2003) and Aaim To Prosper (2012) won the race this century as eight year olds. Granted a better draw, I am expecting him to go close once again. He has won 4 of his 14 races on the Flat."* **WON the Irish Cesarewitch @ 16/1**

Quote: *"Roger Charlton has sent out a handful of juvenile winners this year and a couple of two year olds from Beckhampton to watch out for between now and the end of the season include the once raced* ***CHESTER STREET****. A colt by Invincible Spirit, he is a half-brother to Great St Wilfred and Ayr Gold Cup winner Don't Touch and was bought for 70,000gns as a yearling. He made a pleasing start to his career when a running on seventh at Leicester (7f : Good). Reportedly in need of the run, his finishing effort was eyecatching and he could be one for those backend maidens at Newbury next month. Charlton invariably does well at those meetings (Lady Tyne & McCreery both won at the Berkshire track in October as juveniles)."* **WON next time at Kempton @ 8/11**

Quote: *"It will be fascinating to see what David O'Meara can achieve with the seemingly well handicapped* ***USTINOV****. A half-brother to Pattern winners Lustrous and Melody In Love, the gelded son of Exceed And Excel has only raced once for the Helmsley handler having previously been in the care of Brian Meehan. A juvenile winner at Nottingham last year, he showed very little in his next five races for his former trainer. Switched to O'Meara in August, he showed an immediate sign of returning to form when third in a six furlongs handicap at Redcar behind Buccaneers Vault off a mark of 74. Once rated 88 last year, it will be a surprise if he doesn't win races for his new yard either this season or next. Don't forget when Smoothtalkinrascal joined David O'Meara from Brian Meehan at the end of 2012, he was rated 92 – by the end of the 2013 season, the Kodiac gelding had reached a mark of 105. Lightning may well strike twice. He holds an entry at Ayr next Tuesday (29th September)."* **WON next two starts, including at Ayr, at 100/30 & 5/4**

The price remains the same at £6.00 each (£8.00 Royal Ascot) or £17 for ALL THREE.

AHEAD ON THE FLAT UPDATES ORDER FORM (EMAIL ONLY)

AVAILABLE AT £6.00 EACH (£8 ROYAL ASCOT) OR £17.00 FOR ALL 3

☐ **ROYAL ASCOT PREVIEW 2016**
(Will be emailed on Sunday 12th JUNE)

☐ **YORK EBOR PREVIEW 2016**
(Will be emailed on Monday 15th AUGUST)

☐ **AUTUMN UPDATE 2016**
(Will be emailed on Thursday 22nd SEPTEMBER)

☐ **OR £17.00 FOR ALL 3**

Total Cheque / Postal Order value £............... made payable to Mark Howard Publications Ltd. Please send to Mark Howard Publications Ltd. 69 Fairgarth Drive, Kirkby Lonsdale, Carnforth, Lancashire. LA6 2FB.

NAME: ....

ADDRESS: ....

.... POST CODE: ....

Email Address: ....

Alternatively, order via **www.mhpublications.co.uk**

ONE JUMP AHEAD 2016/2017

The 24th edition of *One Jump Ahead*, the Top National Hunt Horses to Follow for 2016/17, will be published in early September. It will be formulated along the same lines as previous years with various categories such as *The Top 40 Prospects* **(2016 Cheltenham Festival winners MINELLA ROCCO (8/1) & YORKHILL (3/1))**, *What's The Craic In Ireland*, *Bromley's Best Buys* etc. There will also be a dozen stable interviews with the leading National Hunt trainers. *One Jump Ahead* will contain 156 pages and costs £9.99.

I shall be producing **FIVE** *One Jump Ahead Updates.* As usual the first *Update* will be geared towards the Paddy Power meeting at Cheltenham in November **(Winners included SAUSALITO SUNRISE (7/1), LEAVE AT DAWN (7/2), UNOWHATIMEANHARRY (7/2)**, plus **BUYWISE (Advised @ 16/1 – 2nd)**). The *Christmas Special* will concentrate on the principle races around the Festive period (**MINELLA FORU (Advised @ 14/1 WON the Paddy Power Chase)**, **TEA FOR TWO (9/4)**). In addition, there will be a February *Update,* a Cheltenham Festival Preview **(9 winners in 2016, including SUPERB STORY (Advised @ 14/1), DIAMOND KING (12/1), DIEGO DU CHARMIL (13/2)** and **CAUSE OF CAUSES (Advised @ 6/1))** and an *Update* for the Aintree Grand National meeting.

Due to rising postal/paper and ink costs, **THE UPDATES WILL ONLY BE AVAILABLE VIA EMAIL. It will NOT be possible to receive them VIA POST.** The price remains the same at £6 per *Update* (except £10 for the Cheltenham Festival version).

ORDER FORM

☐ ONE JUMP AHEAD 2016/17 (BOOK ONLY)	£9.99
UPDATES (EMAIL ONLY):	
☐ CHELTENHAM PADDY POWER MEETING 2016	£6.00
☐ CHRISTMAS SPECIAL 2016	£6.00
☐ FEBRUARY 2017	£6.00
☐ CHELTENHAM FESTIVAL 2017	£10.00
☐ AINTREE GRAND NATIONAL 2017	£6.00
☐ ALL 5 *UPDATES*	£34.00
☐ ONE JUMP AHEAD + ALL 5 UPDATES	£37.99

Total Cheque / Postal Order value £............ made payable to Mark Howard Publications Ltd. Please send to Mark Howard Publications Ltd. 69 Fairgarth Drive, Kirkby Lonsdale, Carnforth, Lancashire. LA6 2FB.